Developing Your Prophetic Gifting

C.G. Cooke

Sovereign World

Sovereign World Ltd
PO Box 777
Tonbridge
Kent TN11 0ZS
England

Scripture quotations are from The American Standard Bible
© The Lockman Foundation, La Habra, California.
Special Bible Study Aids © Thomas Nelson, Inc., Nashville, USA.

ISBN: 1 85240 144 3

This Sovereign World book is distributed in North America by Renew Books, a ministry of Gospel Light, Ventura, California, USA. For a free catalog of resources from Renew Books/ Gospel Light, please contact your Christian supplier or call 1-800-4-GOSPEL.

Typeset by CRB Associates, Norwich.
Printed in England by Clays Ltd, St Ives plc.

Dedication

This book is dedicated to Heather Cooke, my wife. A great and important gift from God who loves me, makes me laugh, amazes me with her honesty and loyalty, and has always supported me, no matter what!

My son Ben, a good man with a tender heart and a true spirit of justice. What a guy!

My son Seth, funny, creative, noisy. A leader of men for sure.

My daughter Sophie, kind, thoughtful, good fun. A lover of the finer things in life like Manchester United and her old man.

Why are all my children like my wife?

Acknowledgements

My thanks and gratitude to all the following:

- My mother Gladys, a remarkably courageous woman who never gives up on life. Stepfather Harry, a good and decent man.
- John and Dorothy Bentliffe, who brought me into the kingdom and have maintained an interest and involvement in this 'son in the faith' ever since.
- Dee and Maggie who gave my family love and support at a critical time. Duncan and Jane Foster who have given amazing support and love for many years.
- Graham Perrins, who gave me a love of scripture and a great grounding in teaching on prophetics. An excellent teacher!
- Kevin Allan, my good friend, and a man I love for his wisdom and faithfulness. A man to trust.
- City Gate Church, Southampton. A good family, noisy, funny, caring, occasionally frustrating, often endearing. It's the place to be!
- The Pioneer Network, full of passionate people with a huge desire to establish the kingdom and build New Testament Church.
- The Pioneer Team of leaders and ministries. For honesty, integrity, truth and fun they have no equal, anywhere in the world.

- Charles and Paula Slagle, good friends, full of grace and kindness.
- All my partners in prayer and those who financially support the ministry Fasten your seat belts, we're in for a great ride!
- Carole Shiers, my PA, who manages me wonderfully well and is a huge asset. Despite my influence, she still does everything properly and on time. Amazing!
- To all the thousands of people trained through School of Prophecy. Keep the faith. Maintain the standard. Never forget to model all that is good in prophetic ministry.
- Finally and most importantly, to a gracious Heavenly Father. The kindest Person I have ever known. My eternal thanks.

Contents

7

Contents

Contents

Contents

Foreword

I first met Graham Cooke over a decade ago, and soon after, he took the difficult decision to uproot his wife Heather and the children to join me and the church here in Southampton. In geographical terms the move was insignificant, a mere 30 miles up the road. In social and economic terms the move was outrageous. Graham had no money, no work and no home to come to. As a church we did what we could, finding property that would temporarily be vacant, or in many cases vacated by church members at personal inconvenience, in order to create temporary space for a family of five. It was the least we could do, and although it may sound noble, compared to the personal cost to Graham and the family, it was insignificant. What's more, we really wanted them to be with us anyway, and if you want something or in this case some people, badly enough you are prepared for a measure of sacrifice.

By the grace of God the following year, although still unemployed, a mortgage was arranged and a house purchased. Many more months were to elapse before Graham could find secular work and get his life on some kind of even keel financially and begin to find a way through hardship and uncertainty. It was an extraordinary period of time, extremely difficult yet greatly blessed, and one on which I still look back with a measure of disbelief, amazement and affection.

The church he came to join was a mere 50 or 60 strong at the time, a typical new church, consisting of ordinary people looking to serve the Lord. Superficially we had nothing to offer, certainly nothing in a material sense, and even a leadership role was not guaranteed. I know at the time there were other routes Graham could have gone, with ministry opportunities beginning to open up, yet easier options were put aside for the sake of friendship, relationship and above all, to be part of local church.

Herein lies the heart of the man and the decision he made. Graham does have an extraordinary prophetic anointing, which in recent years has created a great international demand for his ministry. Yet he has always been prepared to lay it aside, for the sake of local church.

The message he brings on prophecy is both clear and exciting but above all down to earth. For too long the prophet, prophecy and the prophetic has been marginalised and minimised, and ultimately missed out on, because the man and the message has so often failed to work within the constraint of local church. Alternatively terrified church leaderships have held the ministry at arms length through fear and ignorance. Either way the net result has meant that the church has suffered, and prophetic ministry has fallen into disrepute.

The pages of this book unfold a different route, mapping a way through so the heartbeat of God's prophetic word can be released into today's church. It is a message Graham expounds with great skill, and with the benefit of much personal experience. Yet most significantly it is a message Graham has demonstrated through his lifestyle and life decisions.

Some things are worth fighting for!

Kevin Allan
Leader of City Gate Church Southampton

INTRODUCTION:

Understanding Prophecy

Chapter 1

Understanding Prophecy

Prophecy is a gift of the Holy Spirit. It does not belong to people. The Holy Spirit gives gifts to people at his own discretion. Anyone can be used in the gift of prophecy provided they are a born-again believer, filled with the Holy Spirit, and open to moving in the supernatural.

Knowing that all spirit-filled Christians can prophesy does not make everyone who does a prophet. There are various levels and stages of prophetic anointing, beginning with the shallow end of basic prophecy, encouragement, edification and comfort. However, moving through levels of prophetic ministry to the office of a prophet requires considerable training, experience and development over a great many years. On average it takes approximately fifteen to twenty years to make a prophet, depending upon the training, discipling and mentoring one has received in that time.

We serve a wonderful God who delights in expressing his heart toward us and making his thoughts plain. Those thoughts will never countermand Scripture, which is profitable for our teaching, correction, reproof and exhortation. In fact it was the inspired words of prophets, given to them by the Spirit, which enabled them to write Scripture in the beginning. Even the Law began as a prophecy (2 Peter 1:21).

Prophecy and Scripture

When governing Israel on their journey through the wilderness, Moses had to listen to the life issues and difficulties of more than a million people. In each of those cases he had to pray and seek the mind of the Lord. This was wearing him out and was a major cause for concern to his father-in-law, Jethro.

Noticing a pattern amongst the constant stream of questions and answers that Moses endured, Jethro proposed a plan. The problems and previous words were written down. When similar problems arose, Moses would have deputies who could deal with those complaints, using the written word from previous prophetic answers given by the prophet. Moses, meanwhile, would continue with presiding over new situations, listening and providing the word of the Lord.

In this way, the people learned to deal with the written or revealed Word of God and the new word given by Moses through prophetic utterance. This system still preoccupies our attention today, in that we have the revealed word of God in Scripture which allows us to make an instant response of obedience to the word of the Lord. This emphasises the need for us to ground people in the Bible so that they are able to determine the heart and will of God for themselves.

When we encounter situations which don't appear to have a clear answer in Scripture, we may need access to prophetic ministry. This ministry will echo Scripture faithfully, will drive us to the feet of Jesus, whilst not usurping our will or forcing us into unsound judgements or actions.

An important question for prophets is always, 'Is this person's need best served by an increased understanding of Scripture?' ... in which case, let us point them to the teaching ministry; or ... 'do they need a **now** word, allied to Scripture which will personalise God's word in a way that increases faith and confidence, whilst releasing people from hindrances and bondages?'

Scripture makes a distinction between prophecy and teaching. In several places, it mentions both prophets and teachers as ministry gifts, clearly emphasising that the two have separate functions with the common aim to grow people to maturity. There has always been a need for both, and one does not have priority or preference over the other. It is not our preference or prejudice that determines which is used, but rather the demands of the situation that we find ourselves in. Each gift has a different goal, both of which are vital if we are to understand the Lord and his ways.

Put simply, teaching allows us to gain a full understanding of God's **principles** for life, growth and service, etc. Prophecy imparts the express **purpose** of God in our current situation. We can understand it better if we think in terms of mind and heart.

Teaching shows us the mind of God whilst prophecy often reveals his heart. It is always important to remember that we serve a great high priest who can be touched by the same things that affect our lives. God thinks and feels.

Many people are rightly worried that an over-dependence on experience at the expense of the solid grounding of the Word that good teaching provides, may lead to error and abuse. On the other side of the scale is the real concern (equally well founded) that the ministry of the Word without the spirit of revelation, which the prophetic enhances, can lead to a correct, but uninspiring and sterile, formality.

To move even in the simple, basic prophetic gift will require an understanding of the mind and heart of God and how to release it. Prophetic words have different strengths of impact, according to the situation, circumstances, faith level and understanding of the receiver; and also the ability, experience, understanding and relationship of the giver to the Holy Spirit.

A strong, clean, purposeful relationship with God, wedded to a life of prayer, study and meditation of Scripture, will always be more productive than a casual familiarity in those areas.

The gift of prophecy also has that future aspect to it. It has that now, but not yet, feel to it. The book of Revelation is a prime example of this expression of the prophetic. The book is entirely prophetic from cover to cover, dealing with predictive prophecy, forthtelling and foretelling.

The gift of prophecy can be intensely personal as well as uniting people in a corporate oneness before God. Many prophetic words in Scripture were given to individuals. These were words of blessing, encouragement, warning, direction, correction and judgement.

Similar types of prophetic utterance were made to whole groups, tribes, cities and nations.

Strategy and tactics

Prophecy can provide dynamic insight into situations not made clear by Scripture. It provides a distinctive perception of the things of God that may not be gained from the accustomed counsel of Scripture.

The Bible provides the overall picture; the grand design of God and how to approach our life in the Spirit. It does not always give us the means or the method to do that effectively. To put it simply, the Bible gives strategy whilst prophecy reveals tactics.

For example, in the story of Jehoshaphat (2 Chronicles 20), the people came together to seek the Lord. They were doing what they knew to do: assemble and pray in the face of overwhelming circumstances. In a time of immense fear, facing extinction and exile as a race, they stood and recounted the history (literally, the Scripture) of their past dealings with the Almighty God. They had the biblical strategy of prayer and fasting for this eventuality. However, it was the entrance of the prophetic that caused a massive increase of faith and confidence. Prophecy made them tactically aware of God's plan for the situation. It was prophecy that pin-pointed the exact whereabouts of the enemy, showed them how to fight and what to expect next. After the entrance of the prophetic, there arose a confidence and a determination to do the will of God.

We need to live by every word that proceeds from the mouth of God; both to order our lives by Scripture and to be led by the Spirit. To earnestly desire to move in prophecy is a vital part of being sons of God.

Humility is a pre-requisite

Prophecy is not for some people more than others. It is not a reward for faithful years of service; it cannot be earned; it is a gift given freely by the Holy Spirit. There will inevitably be some people to whom he entrusts this gift on a regular basis. Those who are moving in an increase of revelation anointing can be said to be moving into a prophetic ministry, rather than just an extensive use of the gift.

When that ministry begins to impact whole people groups, nations and governments; it will signify the change from prophetic ministry to the office of a prophet.

Prophecy does not make some people better than others; there is no structural hierarchy within the gift. There are no superior or inferior believers. Those Christians who perform exploits in supernatural giftings, or who have immense responsibilities within the Kingdom, will have built that influence on a solid base of humility and dependence on God. This level of anointing carries with it a deep sensitivity to the person of the Holy Spirit.

One of the great problems in the realm of prophecy today, is the lack of humility before God; the absence of sensitivity to the Holy Spirit; and a shortage of compassion for people.

Prophecy and history

Prophecy has always been a rich part of the heritage of God's people throughout the ages. Jesus stands supreme as Prophet, Priest and King. Prophetic dispensationalism is a common error in the church today, preaching as it does a two-thirds Jesus. When we own him as Priest and King to his body, but not as Prophet, we strip the church of all supernatural power. Put simply, dispensationalism decrees that the outpouring of the Holy Spirit with all his gifts and graces, was simply given to get the church kick-started, two thousand years ago. Now that we have Scripture, it is argued, we have no need for these extraneous things of the Spirit; the moving of the Spirit belongs to another time or dispensation. Scripture itself clearly admonishes certain people with the injunction not to despise prophecy, but instead to examine it carefully and hold on to the good part of the word after weighing (1 Thessalonians 5:20–21).

Prophecy has been in use throughout church history, greater in some centuries than others. Prophecy usually goes into decline when church leaders usurp their authority and try to control what is said and done in the body of Christ.

Getting hold of the false

Thankfully now we are seeing a resurgence of the prophetic gift and ministry. Unfortunately with the true comes the counterfeit. Abuse, misuse and deception will abound along with the correct use of prophecy. Clearly we need to know how to handle the gift, the ministry, and its impact within the work of God.

There has always been false prophecy along with false

teaching, right throughout church history. Many more churches have been ruined by false teaching than by false prophecy. For example, teaching on accountability in the 1970s led many leaders into heavy shepherding and accusations of control and domination. Accountability is right and proper, but only if it is God-centred and not man-centred. The truth of proper biblical accountability has been marred by the practice that was encouraged. Do we now abandon this truth for fear of abuse or misuse? Or do we seek to introduce proper use of accountable behaviour as an honour to God?

Where there has been abuse, we must work even harder to reclaim the whole ground. The alternative is to have no-go areas in our church life.

Many people's lives have been damaged by wrong pastoral advice, far more than by the prophetic. There would appear to be very few, if any, checks and balances for the role of pastor. It seems that they can get away with anything. Indeed, there are pastors who will not allow themselves to be challenged without an explosion of some sort occurring. To question the activities of some leaders is an invitation to an excommunication or an execution ... ours!

One of the major problems in the church today is the number of people who are inadequately birthed into the kingdom of God. Salvation is more a process than an instantaneous event. Many people's lives are touched in a mighty way by the Holy Spirit and they are brought into a measure of real and dynamic change. However, if this is not followed up by effective foundations of pastoral and discipling input with good teaching, then people's lives cannot be fully claimed for the Gospel.

Poor evangelism and preaching have created a back-door Christianity in which people have come to Christ on the basis of needs being met, rather than the demand to submit to his lordship.

In spite of this, when people talk about balance and

accountability, it is inevitably connected with prophetic ministry. It is true that a prophet on his own is out of balance ... but then, a pastor, teacher or evangelist on their own is also out of balance.

This factor has caused more widespread damage in the church of Jesus Christ than any loose prophetic cannon.

The only answer to misuse in all areas of church life is not non-use but proper use. Truth is always our best safeguard against deviation.

Overcoming the negatives

Do not discourage gifting on the basis that it could be wrong or dangerous. We must use every opportunity to exercise our people in rightly divining the word of truth. Sadly, many leaders are more concerned with avoiding conflicting situations than prospering from them.

It is far easier to create suspicion and fear in people's minds than to tackle the issues involved. Allowing these things is a source of grief to the Holy Spirit, to which the only response is one of apology, repentance and a change of practice.

There has always been false prophecy since the earliest Bible times; we should not be surprised that it happens today. We should remember that the counterfeit of anything proves the existence of the authentic.

We need to allow a desire for the truth to be uppermost in our hearts. Integrity is created when we are prepared to break through however many barriers, no matter the personal cost, in order to live in and be what is right and proper. We need to be the truth, not just know it. The truth that prophecy is for today must be appropriated by the whole church. Part of that ownership is a determination to work through all the anomalies and dilemmas of releasing the prophetic gift and ministry properly.

The church is pregnant with the prophetic word and ministry. Care is needed to bring the whole prophetic seed to full term. The labour pains are yet to come for the whole ministry; the joy of birthing a new prophetic environment throughout the whole body of Christ will be worth all the suffering we must endure.

The following is offered as a guide-line to achieving that end.

Counter-arguments to release prophecy

1. *The Bible replaces spiritual gifts*

The argument runs that because we have the whole revelation of God in Scripture, then the gifts are no longer necessary. It is interesting that many of the people who hold this view would still pray for a miracle or a gift of healing! They take the view that prophecy is done away with when the perfect (that's Scripture) has come. Prophecy being a partial revelation at a particular point in time, must become redundant now that the whole truth of Scripture is present, (1 Corinthians 13:8–10). Yet this perfect word still encourages the church to

> *'pursue love, desire earnestly spiritual gifts, **especially** that you may prophesy.'* (1 Corinthians 14:1)

This whole notion of dispensationalism has been rightly discredited in a large part of the Christian church. It simply conflicts with a number of things which Jesus said concerning the person and the work of the Holy Spirit in chapters 14–16 of John's Gospel.

Moreover, it is totally at odds with the overview of Christ's death, burial, resurrection and ascension to the Father, and the place and work of the Holy Spirit in the ongoing life of the church.

Dispensationalism as a Christian doctrine clashes with all the ferocity and embarrassment of a gong or cymbal played fiercely out of place in an otherwise well orchestrated and harmonious piece of music. It is a confusing, offensive and disturbing hypothesis which does not and cannot sit within Scripture.

The plain meaning of 1 Corinthians 13:8–10 simply refers to the end of all things and a full revelation of God to each believer. For now (by comparison with the full revelation to come), we see dimly but **then** (that's the time to come), when we are face to face with everything God is ... we will be fully known and we will understand all things.

Clearly this is not talking about this life, but about being face to face with God in a time to come ... **then**! In that context, of knowing all things, obviously we will not need the prophetic which works according to our faith. Absolute perfection will reign. I can hardly wait! I have so many questions! It will be so exciting to be face to face with God and to know everything.

In that context, dispensationalism is an insult to the person of Jesus. In all his teaching on the Holy Spirit, he never once mentioned that the gift of the Spirit was temporary, or that his gifts would not last until his return.

The Holy Spirit and his gifts and graces are a permanent fixture in the church to enable the Bride of Christ to be made ready and presentable. Also to preach the Gospel, with signs following, to the ends of the earth ... then shall the end come. So much work is unfinished; we need the Holy Spirit now more than ever. If the Holy Spirt was given with all his gifts, graces and power only to one generation, how will we accomplish all that God has for us to do in ours?

Just as a matter of interest, when did this dispensational barrier fall? Why is there no mention of it in any early Christian writings? I would have thought the whole of Christendom would have been aware that suddenly 'the heavens were as brass'. How did it happen? Was it that suddenly, at noon on April 20th, AD 85, the dispenational barrier fell? Presumably at 11.55 am we could still get healed of sickness or receive a miracle. However, at 12.01 pm, it's down tools, we don't do that any more, heaven is closed! Forget healing, wholeness and fullness, now we have to struggle through. One moment healing is a sign of God's power and the expression of his heart to the world through Christ ... the next, it is forbidden.

At Pentecost, Peter spoke these words,

> *'you will receive the gift of the Holy Spirit, the promise* (of this gift) *is for you and your children and for all who are far off* (in time and distance from God!)*'.*

The qualifying part of this wonderful statement is the last sentence,

> *'For all whom* (as many as!) *the Lord our God shall call to himself.'* (Acts 2:39)

This word is given, this promise made, in the context of a mighty outpouring of the Spirit. It is made in the context of tongues and interpretation. It is made in the context of the supernatural invading the earth, causing an explosion of understanding and desire for God. It is made in the context of the Holy Spirit turning a community and a major city upside down and inside out. It is made in the context of a revolution in society that would have massive repercussions across the whole earth. Into this context, Peter spoke prophetically to those early and largely unsaved people gathered to witness a miracle. He stood and taught from history, weaving in the truth of Jesus for the present day and speaking prophetically about the future.

2. Pre-occupation with gifts prevents effective evangelism

The argument runs that we must strip ourselves of everything that would divert us from our primary objective of preaching the Gospel. It cannot be denied that many places have become self-indulgent 'bless me' clubs where the gifts are practised endlessly on other believers. Many people are chasing after an experiential relationship with the Holy Spirit for the purpose of excitement and self-gratification. Much of this adolescent spiritual behaviour is due to the fact that many Christians have such a poor understanding of the Kingdom of God.

We are here to preach the gospel of the Kingdom and not to build church only. The church comes out of the Kingdom and not vice versa. When we understand that we must lay aside everything to seek the Kingdom, then we will see a renewal occur that will truly honour the Lord.

When we appreciate the fact that everything we know and have must be channelled into establishing the Kingdom; then we will see church, leadership, lifestyle, pastoring, teaching and the gifts of the Spirit in a wholly different light. When this occurs, revival will be upon us.

I believe in prophetic evangelism; words of knowledge for the unsaved; gifts of healing across the whole community; expressing God's heart prophetically in the earth to all peoples. I have been privileged to see non-Christians respond to a prophetic word and begin their journey into the Kingdom. The supernatural presence of the Holy Spirit through his graces and gifts can impact a hard community in a way that simple preaching cannot. Paul said that his preaching was not in word only, but by demonstration of the Holy Spirit.

The truth is that the spiritual gifts get people's attention, thus making the entrance of the word more vibrant and irresistible. I have prophesied many times to non-believers and seen some spectacular results as they 'came to faith'. One lady had not seen her daughter for four years after a family argument. Deciding one day to go to a church where I happened to be speaking, she was completely bowled over when I prophesied to her that not only was her daughter safe, but that she would see her in four days and their rift would be healed. She was amazed at the time (because no-one knew her), and astounded when the word came to pass within the span of time mentioned. In her own words, 'It was like heaven opened and I realised that God knew me but I didn't know him; the knowledge that he was interested and concerned about my family drove me to want to know him for myself.'

3. Is not the fruit more important than the gift?

The church has many people with supernatural gifting and a difficult, unlovable character. It is also true that there are many nice Christians with no overt manifestation of the power of the Spirit in their lives – we need both.

Whilst it is undoubtedly true that the gifts without the fruit are made worthless (1 Corinthians 13:1, 2), it is also true that the Gospel cannot be preached effectively without power (Romans 1:16). The word must be confirmed with signs following. People were attracted to Jesus because of his personality, as well as the miracles.

On my schools of prophecy, many times I have seen people made perfect in love because of their training in the gift of prophecy. Prophecy is communicating the heart of God to his people. God the Father is the kindest person I have ever known. He is full of a matchless grace, peace and rest. His love is from everlasting to everlasting. His grace, mercy, patience and long suffering are legendary. He is slow to anger and swift to bless, abounding in loving-kindness. These truths cannot be communicated without having an effect upon the giver as well as the recipient.

The fruit is not more important than the gift. We must not let the enemy push us into a choice that the Holy Spirit has not asked us to make. In matters of morality, the fruit of our character must always take precedence. In times of development, fruit and gift grow together. Fruit does not grow well in a vacuum. We want the fullness of

God, that means both gift and fruit together. We must insist upon that in all our discipleship forums.

4. *The gifts of the Spirit are dangerous*

I hope so! Dangerous to the world, threatening to the health of the enemy and hazardous to apathy and indifference.

Prophecy is attacking, stimulating and provoking. It is designed to put a sharp edge onto our relationship with God, in terms of how we live our lives and handle truth.

The truth is dangerous. The Bible says the Word of God is like a two-edged sword. It can cut both ways and needs careful handling. Should we stop using Scripture because we may get cut to the quick?

Can we afford to ignore things because they are dangerous? Apathy is the most dangerous attitude in the church, but I know whole churches who have not managed to avoid its clutches. Unbelief is a dangerous cancer, but millions of people world-wide are affected by it.

Should we cease preaching or teaching in case we come into error? Absolutely not! What we must do is work together in the defence of truth and the proclamation of the Word of God. In prophecy we must teach people how to be in the Spirit when they speak. When we preach or teach, then the same principle applies; there is safety in the anointing of God.

Chapter 2

The Value of Prophecy

Undoubtedly, prophecy is a gift and a ministry that we should encourage to the uttermost in our churches. A lot of the misconceptions on prophecy arise out of a lack of knowledge and understanding about what it is, how it works and the way in which we should release it into the local church.

We always denigrate what we do not understand. This chapter is concerned with giving an overview of the value of prophecy in the local church. Hopefully it will make a contribution to our understanding and appreciation of this important gift.

Prophecy restores people's dignity and self-respect

Many Christians are sitting in our churches with very little idea of their own worth and value to the Lord. The enemy and life in general can conspire to strip people of their identity and self worth. Many people have difficulty in establishing a relationship with God as their Father, due to their own poor personal experience in the family home.

Hurts, wounds, rejections and emotional trauma are a part of our lives, both before and after salvation. The Good News is that we serve a God who is committed to our healing at every level (physical, mental, emotional). The goal of God is wholeness of life and fullness of the Spirit. Prophecy is a wonderful part of that healing and renewing process. Prophecy brings us, by direct verbal communication, into contact with God's real perspective on our lives and current situations.

The goal of prophecy in this context is to open our eyes to God's love and care, specifically to enable us to come to our senses and escape from any snare in which the enemy has tried to entrap us. Prophecy reminds us in blunt, but loving, fashion of all that God has provided in Christ Jesus. Prophecy restores our soul, renews our mind, and revives our spirit.

It cuts through the darkness bringing real light, real faith and real confidence. It counters our poor attitudes and negative concepts about ourselves, and creates an understanding and appreciation of our personal value.

It edifies, encourages and comforts the church

These three elements of prophecy, found in 1 Corinthians 14:3, are often the result or by-product of a prophecy as well as the established content within a revelatory word.

If a prophetic word speaks of the greatness, the majesty and the supremacy of God in the heavens, it can stir up the church to fight, to stand their ground, to enter into prevailing prayer and warfare. It has exhorted people to stand firm.

If a word relates to God's compassion, his wholesale forgiveness and willingness to extend mercy and cleansing, it will cause people to have a desire to approach him and rebuild their life. It has edified their spirit and released the kind of faith that the Holy Spirit can work with and build on.

Prophecy will not leave the church feeling confused, degraded or condemned. It will not make people feel inferior or intimidated. Part of prophecy is to bring a strengthening of ties between God and his people. The word edify (to strengthen and build up) occurs seven times in this chapter of Corinthians alone.

Prophecy releases encouragement too. At the right time, in the right way, and with the proper word, the Lord releases a magnificent blessing through the prophetic utterance. This type of word will give a significant boost to the church; it will reassure, inspire and incite people to thanksgiving. It will stimulate faith and create a sense of well-being in the congregation.

Every church will face tests of character, integrity, and commitment to God and one another; loyalty to the vision and local leadership. These tests are a vital part of our corporate growth and development. Fail those tests and we will lose vital ground in the realm of the Spirit.

The church will face many barriers, hindrances and obstructions; each attack designed to move us away from our corporate identity and vision, reduce the expectancy of the supernatural, and eliminate any active faith from our corporate lifestyle. Discouragement will be at our elbow constantly. As a golden rule, in times of discouragement release the prophetic amongst the congregation or send for the prophet.

Encouragement in prophecy releases God's perspective which brings confidence (what the Bible calls hope!). The western understanding of hope is a devalued term. The real meaning is absolute confidence, the kind of confidence that is at rest in turmoil, laughs at the actions of the enemy and produces enough faith to at least stand still and see God, if not actively march forward in power and expectancy.

Prophecy also releases comfort into people's lives made bitter by hardness, pain and difficult circumstances. God does not always shield us from the difficulties of life, though he does promise to be with us as we go through the fires. People do die for their faith every day. Throughout the world, there were over 200,000 martyrs in 1993 alone. Loved ones die, children become terminally ill, inexplicable tragedy can strike completely out of the blue, people's lives can be reduced to rubble by unfaithfulness and divorce. Many people are losing jobs and careers, having homes repossessed because of debt.

Into the scale of human tragedy, the Holy Spirit can drop a word of consolation. That word can alleviate pain, reduce stress, invigorate people's hearts, soothe tension and provide a wealth of support that will ultimately refresh people and gladden their hearts.

Prophecy can bring correction and warning

Many times in Scripture, people were given warnings through prophecy to turn from their wicked ways and repent. The letters to the seven churches (Revelation 2 and 3) contained warnings and requests for change and repentance.

This type of prophecy needs the prior approval of our church leadership (see Chapter 5, 'Guide-lines for Hand-ling Prophecy').

It is very important that we meet with leaders and responsible people prior to any public utterance of this type of word. This pre-meeting can act as a filter to strain off our own frustrations, hurts and personal negativity. This will enable us to give a pure and clean word.

Prophecy can provide direction and enhance vision

Direction, purpose and vision are vital for individuals and groups. Where there is no vision, we have a lot of perishing people! From within the church, the prophetic word can be released that will provide a focus on which we can hang our goals and plans.

Personal and corporate vision can be released with a greater depth of faith and confidence. It is vital that we come to a point of understanding and confidence regarding the call upon our lives from the Lord.

Where there has been a great deal of internal prophecy bringing direction and envisioning, we may need to apply some caution. All words need to be tested, especially, I would add, those that pertain to the direction of the work, yet come in the main from people within the church. To avoid deception, it may be a good idea to ask an established prophetic ministry not attached to the work, to give some confirmation from outside. This person has no flag to wave, or axe to grind, and can be impartial and objective both in the judging process and in bringing a confirming word.

Words of direction and vision that come into the church from outside can have a transforming effect upon the work. I have lost count of the times when God has used me in this way across the world. Many times I have reported prophetically almost word for word whole ideas, concepts and conversations concerning eldership teams, as they have met to discuss the future of the work.

On one occasion, I prophesied a conversation that two elders had had whilst riding to the very meeting where I was speaking! They had been surprised on their journey to discover they both had the same idea about creating a new pastoral initiative. During that meeting I called them both out and laid hands on them for a new pastoral anointing. God is always on time!

Prophecy provides an agenda for prayer

The most sensible thing we can do in a prayer meeting is to find out what God wants to do and ask him to do it. Most successful prayer initiatives have their roots in the prophetic. Prophecy creates a prayer agenda.

In 1982, the Lord began to show me things to come in the British Church:

(a) I saw that the Charity Commission would be given real teeth to expose financial malpractice and comment on value for money in all voluntary agencies, including the church. We will see many agencies' charitable status revoked. Legislation is now coming on line to enforce this. Many churches will be taken to court by the Inland Revenue and sued for financial mismanagement.

(b) The Government is looking to invest millions of pounds in the community and is currently doing a major value for money survey of all voluntary agencies. Some long-established charities will fold and new ones will be created. Now is the time for the church to sacrifice and put together a social action programme that will restore the church to the heart of the community once more.

   God is opening a window in heaven via central and local government that will release huge amounts of money into the Kingdom. We need credible programmes, serious training mixed with patience and wisdom, to enable us to restore the church to the heart of our communities.

(c) There will be a network of deliverance and intercessory ministries spreading right across the nation. This will provide a strategy for warfare, and inter-church/inter-city prayer links that will criss-cross the nation. These networks will share information, training and equipping programmes, and a common warfare strategy for the nation.

(d) Unity is the great target of the Holy Spirit in the 1990's and beyond. We will see a move of God occur that will cut across all streams. As someone said, 'The day of the streams is over; the day of the river has begun.'

We will see the demise of local, regional, national and cultural barriers as the Lord begins a whole new process of unity and liberty.

There will be a United Kingdom. I used to think the name was a joke. However, in 1983 the Lord showed me it was a prophetic name. The Lord is raising up champions in the Celtic nations who will have a tremendous anointing for unity, who will turn the hearts of the nations towards each other. Lack of unity is a major stranglehold on revival.

We will have conferences and conventions, not just aimed at speaking for unity, but actively promoting reconciliation, apology and restoration. Forgiveness and healing will flow. The North/South divide in England will perish. Inter-county and inter-city rivalry will die. Lancashire will stop fighting the War of the Roses with Yorkshire. Cities will be twinned in heart and spirit. Liverpool will stop hating Manchester. This kind of rivalry is repeated throughout the nation.

In the realm of the Spirit, England must recognise that she needs her Celtic brothers. Repentance must flow, ancient hatreds must be laid down.

These conferences will be devoted to tearing down strongholds of history, bigotry, treachery and betrayal. As these things are finally dealt with, we will see economic and spiritual revival breaking out in these areas.

There is blessing in unity that attracts the Holy Spirit. There is a curse in disunity that attracts the demonic. Disunity begins with one person against another and is multiplied through cities, regions and nations. Unity begins with one person making a stand for love and refusing to take sides. What we need is active personal, individual and corporate promoting of unity in every church, household and city to take the nation.

(e) There is a quickening spirit upon the British Church,
     particularly on established, institutional Christianity.
     Several years ago the Lord showed me to lay aside
     25% of my diary for denominational churches. I have
     been in the new church movement for over 20 years.
     Apart from six months in the Brethren, the new
     churches are all I have ever known. I have no miscon-
     ceptions or hang-ups that I am aware of, having
     spent all my Christian experience in a state of blissful
     ignorance concerning the phenomena of life outside a
     new church setting.

     Happily now, several years later, approximately
     70% of my time is spent in the denominations. I'm
     thoroughly enjoying the relationship, making many
     new friends and seeing a revival break out before my
     eyes.

     There is a quickening spirit abroad in these
     churches, a fascinating mix of growth, change, a pas-
     sion for Jesus and a new radicalism about church
     planting and community involvement. There is such
     a great hunger for reality and the supernatural
     presence of God.

     What we thought might take years, could take
     months. Months may be squeezed into weeks as the
     Lord moves up his timetable.

Each of these prophetic words (a–e), have provided me
with an agenda to pray. In prophecy God's will is
expressed. Where God's will is made known, we have the
basis for an ongoing prayer meeting until his will comes
to pass.

Prophecy opens up the teaching of the Word and confirms preaching

> *'If I have the gift of prophecy and can fathom all mys-
> teries and knowledge.'*   (1 Corinthians 13:2)

In Scripture language, a mystery is a secret, hidden thoughts, plans, etc. which are concealed at times from mankind. Many times the Lord has given me a flash of revelation which has driven me to search the Scriptures and opened up new areas of truth for me personally. Until that revelatory insight, to all intents and purposes those things had been hidden from me. The revelation inspires the search for fresh knowledge via the Scriptures.

The tragedy is that some people get the flash of insight but don't follow it through, so birthing error or a heresy, rather than revelatory truth. The truth will be present in part but not in fullness. Corruption enters in the form of men's ideas and concepts which if not checked, will cause real damage. Continuous revelation leads to study and prayer (and vice versa!).

In recent years I have received several prophecies over my life about a flow of revelation. I am now in the process of relinquishing parts of the ministry to give me time to study and pray as part of my response to those prophetic words.

Prophecy can inspire understanding of mysteries and knowledge. Paul confirms this when he writes about his

> *'insight into the mystery of Christ, hidden for genera-
> tions, but now revealed to apostles and prophets.'*
> (Ephesians 3:4, 5)

This is yet another reason why we must promote and provoke active judging and weighing of all prophetic utterances. Now we could have the danger of false doctrine added to the hazard of false prophecy. I have to say personally, I would rather face the danger of false revelation than live in the poverty of no revelation.

Prophecy will not save us from ignorance by itself, nor will it solve all our problems. The Corinthian church had a well-established prophetic presence but that did not save it from the excesses of sin, immorality or carnality.

As Paul admitted,

> '*We know in part and we prophesy in part.*'
>
> (1 Corinthians 13:9)

There is an incompleteness, sometimes, about our prophesying.

Prophecy can also confirm the preaching of the word, both before and after teaching. In many cases, a prophecy has been released in the worship which has confirmed to the speaker that the text or ministry they were about to deliver was ordained by God. Similarly, I have prophesied into churches the very concepts and ideas previously spoken into that work, during previous times of preaching and teaching.

Prophecy can provide evangelistic breakthroughs

The scenario in 1 Corinthians 14:24, 25 is something to which every church should aspire.

> '*If an unbeliever or someone who does not understand should come in while everybody is prophesying, he will be convinced by all that he is a sinner and will be judged by all. The secrets of his heart will be laid bare. So he will fall down and worship God, exclaiming "God is really among you".*'

Imagine a non-believer walking into a meeting where there are several prophetic utterances in turn. The result of prophecy can be dynamic and dramatic. Prophecy is revelatory. By inspiration, God can reveal all things, even innermost secrets.

I have seen many atheists and agnostics persuaded by God through prophecy. It is the work of the Spirit to convict of sin (John 16:8–11). Prophecy can uncover past history which needs to be amended. It can provide an agenda for repentance, restitution and revival.

Prophetic evangelism is a growing phenomena in the church today. It causes breakthroughs into people's lives of the supernatural presence of God. One of my good friends, Charles Slagle, is a prophetic evangelist. At heart, he is an evangelist with a powerful prophetic anointing. He also has great sensitivity to the Spirit and a real compassion for people. My friends and I hosted Charles and Paula for a six week tour in some of our UK churches, with dramatic results. It was amazing how he would pick non-Christians out in a crowded room and speak to them prophetically.

A number of churches I work with are being encouraged to do door to door work by word of knowledge and prophecy. The Lord knows which homes are ripe for sowing and reaping. He knows what is happening in each house. Gaining God's perspective provides a prayer agenda which will enable us to go to certain homes with something specific to say, rather than just a general visit.

Send out the intercessors, find out which homes God is interested and involved in, release in prayer the prophetic word, and send the evangelist on after the event to clean up.

Prophecy can release the church into new doctrine or practices

Firstly, allow me to qualify that statement. We are not talking about new doctrine/practices never before heard of in the universal church. Rather, we are alluding to new doctrine/practices that may be completely new to a particular church. Allow me to illustrate.

Several years ago, the Lord gave me a series of prophetic words for certain churches concerning the type of people the Lord would give them in five years' time. One church in particular was white, wealthy and middle class in outlook. The word was that the Lord was sending the broken and the used, the downtrodden and the poor, the abused and the abuser, people on drugs, alcoholics, those involved in the occult, single parents, the fatherless, the outcasts of society.

To their eternal credit, the church came back several weeks later, asking for help. They fully understood that the entrance of these people would change the face of the church totally. The repercussions of the word were astounding. They knew they had been given years to make the necessary changes in order to accommodate the type of personnel and growth that God would supply.

What was promised prophetically was a harvest of those whom Satan had bound. This would mean a greater intensity of enemy attack on the church, but also would necessitate the church coming into an understanding and practice of warfare that was not common with them at that point in time. We cannot take ground from the enemy if he has ground in our lives.

We began to teach the church defensive spiritual warfare. How to keep our own homes and lives free from enemy attack, fight off sickness and financial need, etc. This was new ground for many of those people, a new truth and a new practice.

Later on we taught them offensive warfare in life (to tackle the enemy where we found him), in prayer and in our worship. We became more militant in our outlook on the whole supernatural warfare issue. In worship, we praised Jesus as the warrior King, and acted out our supremacy in God. Hopefully, without going overboard into triumphalism, we began to put an edge on the authority of the believer.

Lately we are realising that it is time to move on from those places. God is producing a people, a Joshua generation, who are spoiling for a fight. People who will move in on new territory, expecting to fight and expecting to win!

Taking strongholds, possessing the land, and learning to hold ground, occupy it and keep it until the Lord's return, is where the Holy Spirit is working these days.

After the calling comes the training. That church is ready to move into its inheritance. They have an awareness of warfare and authority now that was not present prior to the prophetic word. For them, prophecy introduced them to new doctrine and practices.

Prophecy provides insight into counselling situations

Counselling is a much needed ministry in the church today. Counselling is a necessary part of working out our salvation before God. The problem today in the church is that a poor quality of Gospel has been preached to people. They have received the gospel of, 'have your needs met in Christ'. This breeds a generation of people who expect God and the church to do everything for them.

The real Gospel preached in Acts was God has made this same Jesus both **Lord and Christ**. The inference was, 'Jesus is Lord, what are you going to do about it!' Currently we have a church full of invalids rather than warriors.

Counselling, especially, should be conducted as part of the introduction to church life and the foundations of a spirit-filled walk with God. To be effective, it needs the co-operation of the evangelist, pastor, teacher and the prophetic, who are all conspiring together to bring about a good birth and a decent upbringing in the things of God.

The prophetic can get to the heart of situations in quite a profound way, laying the axe to the root of a problem. The prophetic will allow us to focus on Jesus and that in itself will create movement and change. Without the supernatural, counselling can focus on problems and processes, rather than on Jesus the deliverer.

In counselling, prophecy can be very time saving. It strips away unhelpful attitudes and layers of deception, which people can hide behind. Prophecy with its attendant associates of word of knowledge and word of wisdom, can save us from endless hours of dialogue by exposing situations and bringing a quick release. It provides a source of insight and power to the counsellor.

The entrance of the supernatural means that we cannot get away with lies, deception or cover up. This will provoke a level of honesty and godly fear which will break any stranglehold of sin in the lives of believers.

Prophecy provides a spirit of thanksgiving and praise

Normally, we continue in persevering prayer until either God tells us to stop, the issue is resolved, or we have an assurance of faith that our prayer has been heard and an answer is on the way.

Prophecy can reveal to people exactly what is on God's heart now, and what we should do next in response to the moving of the Spirit. Speaking at a conference a few years ago, the Lord showed me there was a woman in the auditorium who had been fasting and praying for her wayward daughter. He showed me that this mother was desperately concerned that her rebellious daughter would not get into drug-related problems, or be taken advantage of sexually.

As I laid hands on her, the Lord gave me an assurance in prophecy that he was actively involved in this girl's life and that she would come to no harm. Furthermore, the prophetic word told the mother that God had heard her prayers, and was moving to answer them. In response to that, the prophecy continued, the mother was to cease praying and begin giving thanks and praising God for his involvement. For several months afterwards, the mother gave thanks and praised God. In the early period, very little changed and in fact, at one point, considerably worsened. The mother held on to the prophetic word and continued in praise and gratitude to the Lord. Not only has her daughter been fully restored to the Lord and her mother, but the woman's life has been changed immeasurably. She now has a spirit of thanks-giving and a grateful heart. She is a woman who knows how to be released in praise and worship. As such, she is a catalyst herself in leading others into a spirit of thanksgiving.

Prophecy provides a faith injection

Prophecy changes the atmosphere, it opens the door to miracles and provides an injection of faith.

Several years ago, I led a church weekend. There was great sceptism in the church about supernatural gifts and prophecy in particular. The unbelief, mistrust and suspicion were tangible. I knew that unless God moved in and did something special, the weekend could be very difficult.

At this point, the prophet has to be in rest before the Lord. The temptation is to try and move in the spectacular rather than let the Spirit move in the supernatural.

I put all my energy into being quiet and restful before God, choosing to let my vision be filled up with him rather than eyeballing the circumstances.

The enemy does try and push anointed ministry into the spectacular. We need to fight that by humbling ourselves, decreasing that He might increase. We are not here to prove how powerful we are, merely to serve the Lord.

I knew that I should not react to the unbelief and negative outlook of the people, but be still and very aware of the Lord.

In the first meeting, as I came to teach, the Lord gave

me a vision and a prophetic interpretation for a young man in the meeting. I saw his father driving a yellow truck. The Lord showed me which company he worked for and the depot where he was based. I told the boy he could find his father there and that the Lord was doing a work of reconciliation. The church went wild! Apparently, the young man was recently converted and the church had been praying that the Lord would allow him to meet his father, whom he had not seen since four years of age.

Sometimes the Lord does not want to focus on the negative, like unbelief, for example. He will move in the opposite spirit and do something that will cause faith to grow or explode. That prophetic word blew the whole weekend wide open for the supernatural presence of God to come in and change people. Faith began to rise in people that the Lord was mighty, and powerful, and involved with them. The young man followed up the prophetic word and has since been reconciled to his father, who is also now seeking the Lord himself.

Prophecy is vital to spiritual warfare

Paul instructed Timothy that,

> *'by these prophecies previously made concerning you, fight a good fight.'* (1 Timothy 1:18)

We need to use prophecies to fight the enemy and the circumstances of life.

Jehoshaphat defeated the enemy on the basis of a word of prophecy given to him by Jahaziel (2 Chronicles 20:14–17). In one instant, people were changed from a crying, pitiful rabble, fully expecting to be annihilated, to a strong, purposeful body of people who were so confident in God that they went out singing. Never underestimate the power of the prophetic.

Joshua followed a similar pattern of listening and responding to the prophetic word (Joshua 6:1–5). Receiving prophetic instructions for a battle plan from a prophetic word, he saw Jericho fall exactly as the prophecy dictated.

Neither of these methods would be written into a war manual as standard procedure for winning a battle. There is no record of other armies being destroyed by singing, nor a fortified city falling to marching feet and raised voices!

Prophecy and warfare go together.

PART 1:

The Gift of Prophecy

Chapter 3

First Steps in Prophecy

I can't count the number of times in the past twenty years when people have asked me the question, 'how can I tell if it's me, the Lord or the enemy when I'm moving in prophecy?' This is, of course, a legitimate question. We are human beings, subject to pain, disillusionment, hurts, dreams, aspirations, longings and desires. All of these can conspire against us and colour the prophetic word in a different way than God intended.

It is possible for a frustrated person to speak prophetically their own thoughts and opinions which mix with the words that God is really speaking into the situation. The enemy can either inspire that to happen and people could be moved by a spirit other than the Lord's. This only tends to happen when people have buried their hurts and rejection in real anger, and their lives are therefore fertile ground for enemy activity. Alternatively, the enemy can use our unyielded thoughts and impulses and as we speak out of our own spirit, he moves in behind our words to cause mischief.

So we can come under the influence of the enemy either directly (through bitter unresolved issues in our lives) or indirectly (through bad attitudes and simple lack of good relationships).

This, of course, highlights the problems that all true prophetic people have to face. How do we give a pure word of prophecy that glorifies the Lord, has no mixture from our hearts and has no influence of the enemy attached? We then have to add the element of faith into that equation because sometimes we may not be operating in complete certainty; we have to prophesy as far as our faith allows.

What we need almost as a guarantee that we will not dishonour the Lord Jesus, discredit the ministry, or disrupt the body of Christ, is a large dose of humility.

In this life we either humble ourselves or we get humiliated. Humility is not a natural characteristic for any of us – no one is born with it. Our relationship with God builds more effectively as we submit our lives, thoughts and perspectives to Him. Our aim always is to live our lives in the best way possible so that the Holy Spirit is not grieved but is made welcome.

If we prophesy in humility and we make a mistake, the Lord will give us grace to face the issue and put things right. Mistakes are inevitable as we learn how to move out in the supernatural. That is why Scripture is so clear in 1 Thessalonians 5:19–21.

> *'Do not quench the Spirit; do not despise prophetic utterances. But examine everything carefully; hold fast to that which is good.'*

By implication that means we need to be able to sift and separate the good from the bad; the misguided and the misinterpreted. More of that in another chapter.

What we must do, with the help of the Holy Spirit, is to ensure that we live our lives in the best way possible, so that there are no areas in our life that do not belong to the Lord Jesus.

In this chapter I want to determine some key areas of preparation so that we can exercise our minds and hearts in their understanding and practice. Specifically we will examine the elements of Preparation, Expectation and Operation.

Preparation

Prayer

In terms of preparation, prayer is absolutely vital to us. It's so important for everything but in particular with regard to the prophetic. Prayer and prophecy are inextricably linked in terms of their communication process; both involve listening before talking.

Sometimes I think we don't listen enough when we pray. When I pray something I listen straight away, because you never know, God might say 'fine you can have it!' Sometimes we pray more than we ought to because we never hear God say, 'that's fine, I'm with you on that one'. Wherever we pray, whatever we pray, get into a habit of listening straight away. I'm moving in a season in my life at the moment where God is answering prayer fairly immediately! Before, I used to be praying for maybe several days or weeks about an issue, but I'm beginning to hear God that much more clearly. My expectation in terms of my listening is growing, and I'm hearing God begin to say 'yes', and to feel a greater sense of faith when I pray for something that actually God has met it and answered it. There may be no evidence in the physical realm, but something has changed in my spirit.

Obviously we know that prayer is not just being in request mode before God. The wonderful thing about prayer is that you can talk to God about anything and everything wherever you are, whatever you're thinking, whatever you're feeling, you can talk to God about it. You can open up your spirit and go places with God. I like to specialise in one or two line prayers – 'Lord, help this person,' 'Father remember my friends out there in Africa' – keeping the flow of prayer going, keeping that channel of communication open as much as we possibly can.

Apart from that, prayer is a matter of asking the Holy Spirit continually to break in and speak – 'talk to me Father,' 'Holy Spirit break in upon me now at this time and speak to me.' When was the last time you asked the Lord for some encouragement? Specifically? 'Father, right now at this point in time, I need some encouragement. Please would you do something, please would you say something, please help me out.' And then maybe taking short bursts of time out in the day to pray.

Before the Lord called me out into my current ministry, I was the business development manager for a large training and recruitment company. My life was a hectic round of business deals, management problems, employment research, involvement with Government projects, taking training sessions, organising events and overseeing the ongoing business strategy for the company.

There were times in those busy days when I would indicate to my reception staff that I was taking ten minutes out and did not want to be disturbed. I would retreat into my office, close the door and sit quietly, thanking God and listening, praying, wanting his perspectives. Many right decisions came out of those short bursts of 'time out in prayer'. I can't honestly say I always heard God specifically speak in those moments (though sometimes I did!). However my track record at the company, together with continuous promotion amongst the staff, probably means that the Lord influenced me far more than I actually knew.

Just as important was the fact that these short bursts of prayer kept my heart free from ungodly pressure. Prayer keeps the channel of communication open.

Probably two thirds of the rest of the world would change places with us in the West, no matter how poor our lifestyle. To many, we are rich beyond their wildest dreams.

Count your blessings, there are so many things that we could give thanks for. Being grateful to God is very important. I think sometimes if we are not grateful to God, the chances are we are going to be ungrateful to people and ungracious in how we live our life. It is things like gratitude, and thanksgiving and praise and worship that really do keep the presence of God fresh in our hearts. It enables us to be God conscious, which is what we want to be. One of the things that God had against Israel was that he was not in all their thoughts. A lifestyle of thanksgiving. We have so much to be thankful for. 1 Thessalonians 5:16 ... it's not a bad way to live.

Meditation

Next to prayer, I think meditation is very important. Meditation went through a time when it got to be a little bit of a dirty word because of the Eastern religions. I always maintain that these religions take the best things out of the Bible and then try to present them differently. Meditation has been part of the relationship with God for thousands of years. Scripture constantly mentions it. Particularly the Psalms (e.g. 119). It's full of the need to meditate. Meditation simply means to 'consider deeply, to reflect, to be absorbed in thought'. It doesn't hurt to sit down and think about Jesus and meditate on the person of Jesus – how good he is, how kind he is. For me, Jesus is the kindest person I've ever known. He's also the happiest person and has the sunniest disposition of anyone I know. When we get in contact with heaven, we will hear laughter. When we really come into the presence of God, tremendous joy, well-being and peace floods our lives.

At a church weekend one of the men had been going through a really difficult time and I was aware that so many things in his life were miserable. I felt compelled in the meeting to lay hands on him and pray for him to be refilled with the Holy Spirit. He fell on the floor and he laughed for about half an hour. He really laughed. We couldn't do anything. The meeting was hopeless. Everyone fell about in fits of laughter. One of the best meetings they had. He laughed and laughed because God got hold of him and the joy of the Lord filled him, and through him God began to fill all of us and no-one could sit still. We were all walking around and some people dropped to the floor, and everyone was laughing and this wild joy of God filled the place.

I've seen some disturbing counterfeits of this in recent years with some people charging big fees to bring the joy of the Lord into churches. Waves of so called Holy Ghost laughter are prayed for over congregations repeatedly in a number of meetings.

I believe that the joy of the Lord is not to be called up like some genie out of a bottle; nor is it a spiritual manifestation at the request of man. It is the by product of the indwelling presence of God as he sovereignly and graciously causes rivers of living water to rise up from within our hearts. The joy of the Lord comes from within, it is not poured out like cream into coffee.

Sometimes I've taken several days or weeks on one particular passage of scripture. When God is clearly talking to me about something, there is not much point in reading anything else because God is talking to me through those several verses. I've meditated on the things that God is actually highlighting. I have become absorbed in those truths.

As we think deeply about God's actions, I would imagine all of us have got some stories to tell of how we came into, and how we came to be, actually living, working and worshipping where we are now. Our stories would be quite incredible when you think how God draws people together from across different parts of the world.

Many years ago the Lord spoke to me about working in the Caribbean. Since that time I had enjoyed a private ongoing joke with God about my 'island ministry in the sun'. For years I did the rounds of back street churches with tin roofs, where part of the ministry was to scrape the mould off the hymn books! I continued saying, 'one of these days Lord you will give me my desert island ministry.' It got to be a standing joke as I walked into some cold, draughty churches. 'Lord, remember the desert island!'

Again the Lord spoke to me about the Caribbean. Several people confirmed that word to me in various ways. Months later whilst speaking at a prophetic conference in London, I met a man quite by chance in the conference centre.

I had just completed a seminar and was sitting quietly during the coffee break in the office of the senior pastor. The pastor had just completed an interview with a man and left the office, leaving myself and the visitor alone together. At the time I was exhausted and only really thinking about coffee and rest. The man and I struck up a conversation about the conference I was leading. I gave him one of my promotional leaflets thinking he was a local man who might wish to attend the event for the next few days.

He expressed an interest in staging a conference himself. It was at this point that I discovered Dr Noel Woodroffe was from Port of Spain in Trinidad, where he led a church. He asked me if I would like to come and speak at this event. To be honest I thought he was being polite. However, a few months later Noel sent me the air tickets and my long standing joke with the Lord was over. In my spirit I could hear laughter. Noel was only in that place for a few moments ... but long enough for the Lord to bring us together and create a friendship which will endure for many years. Amazing!

We can think about those things. All of us have situations like that, where completely unforeseen things have happened that have set the course of our life in different areas, and it's good sometimes to sit down and actually think back on what God has done in our lives in the last few years. I think it's a real aid to being thankful because there are so many things, so many little 'coincidences' where things happen. It's good to meditate on your own life. To remember and give thanks.

Prophets of old were always recounting their history with God. They used to hand it down to people, 'remember when God did this...' and you find that several hundred years later they are still talking about the Red Sea and what happened there.

Waiting on God

Waiting on God is very important, but with a sense of purpose. I take a notebook everywhere with me because God speaks in the most peculiar places. I haven't yet found a showerproof notebook, but I'm working on it! Sometimes waiting on God means letting God know that you actually love him, that he's important to you, that you take pleasure in who he is. Sometimes when we wait on God nothing may come to us, but that's fine, we're just putting the time in. If God doesn't speak initially, he always speaks eventually. We need to be ready when he does.

Waiting on God means we need to come to a place of quietness and stillness. Not that we merely find a quiet place only, but more importantly that we learn to still the clamouring from within our own minds and hearts.

Meditation (thinking deeply, being absorbed in thought, reflection) and waiting upon God often go together, or one can lead to the other. The eastern religions declare that meditation is the blanking of the mind. Some will even give you a mantra which in many cases is simply the name of a Hindu god. So the endless repetition of the name is actually a form of worship.

Meditation and waiting on God in the Christian faith is the filling of your mind with thoughts of God: becoming God-conscious. Into this quiet, still activity God drops his words like the morning dew, bringing a clear refreshing to our soul and spirit.

Speaking in tongues

Speaking in tongues, for those of us who have the gift, is a very important part of our devotional life and our relationship with God, because it edifies our spirit, and it renews our mind. I love the gift because I can pour out my heart to God in whatever situation I'm in, whether I'm in pain, or tired. I have an expectation when I speak in tongues that somehow God is going to break in and do something. I don't want to use the gift without a sense of expectation because I've learnt that the two things go together.

There are times when I want to have ten minutes adoration of Jesus, where I can sit quietly and pour out my heart about how much he means to me, how much I love him and the whole giving of thanks. When we get into that mode, whenever we hit challenging circumstances, the first thing out of our heart is a spiritual reaction. The first thing out of our mouth is a godly reaction, something that reveres Jesus. It is very important that we learn to move in the opposite spirit to what the rest of the world is using. That's what Jesus meant when he said *'pray for those who use you, bless those who persecute you.'* We are moving in the opposite spirit. The first thing out of us is something that is going to honour God. That's the only way to live.

How do we know that we're being led by the Spirit? The only effective way we can know that we're being led by the Spirit now is, what is our reaction to situations that are happening? If something difficult or bad happens, if our reaction is one of peace, joy, thankfulness, gentleness, humility, we are being led by the Spirit. If what comes out of our mouth is something altogether different and quite opposite, the chances are we are being led by the flesh. We know we are being led by the Spirit, by the kind of character that we are manifesting in given situations. So moving in the opposite spirit is very, very important to us and it's certainly very important to God.

Speaking in tongues builds up a reservoir inside of us, helping us to top up the well within. It keeps us unblocked and in communion with God.

Desire to prophesy

In particular with prophecy, it would help very much if we had a desire to prophesy, because that's half the battle (1 Corinthians 14:1). I've found that there are times when I'm in a situation, I'm tired and hungry and God is saying, 'I want you to stir up your spirit.' In my heart I'm saying, 'Father, I'm tired,' and he's saying, 'son, have a desire, because if you have a desire, I can work.' I stand there and say, 'Lord, I want . . .' and suddenly I find myself moving out and forgetting about the tiredness and I'm doing what God wants. Have a desire. Desire earnestly. Look for it. Expect it. Want it.

Expectation

In addition to those things, if we're going to move in anything, whether it's faith, any of the supernatural gifts, whether we're preaching the gospel, whatever it is we're doing for God, we need to have a sense of expectation. I'm expecting something to happen today. I don't want to live a day without expectation. I can't think of anything worse. We look up, it's Friday evening, we've not had a meaningful conversation with Jesus all week and we've just drifted. What a way to live. When I wake up in the morning I want to have an expectation that God is going to do something.

A number of years ago I believe the Lord spoke to me about moving in the gift of prophecy every day and developing a larger expectation in the Holy Spirit. I'm not saying I have achieved that goal consistently; however the aim and the practice have sharpened the gift and broadened the vision for the prophetic considerably.

When I want to move in prophecy, I'm believing that God can speak into this situation. God can speak into this person's life. The next step from that is that we believe God is going to speak through us. Then we're asking God, 'Lord anoint my eyes, ears, mouth.' With our minds, we should believe we have the mind of Christ (1 Corinthians 2:16). If I've got a choice, I want to ditch my way of thinking. I want to think how Jesus thinks, because God's Spirit knows what is in God's mind, and the same spirit dwells in us. Total wisdom. Total knowledge. Total understanding. All those things are available from God to us. I want to tap into that.

Operation

One of the things we need, to move in prophecy, is a burden and a concern. It's helpful if we're looking around ... God may lay a particular person on our hearts. Pray for them. Get a burden for that person. Be concerned before God for that individual. 'Lord, please speak to them and it would be nice if you spoke through me.' I think we need to allow burdens to grow and to flourish. God deliver us from people who prophesy over us who don't feel anything for us.

It's burden that reveals God's heart. When we have a burden for something and we're praying, the Holy Spirit enables us to begin to put that into words and we begin to feel that God wants to say and do something. That brings us to a sense of conviction. It's conviction that produces expression. When we're convinced that God wants to say something, suddenly the means to express it, the will and desire to express it, is with us, and God marries these things together all at once.

Within the operation of the gift of prophecy, sometimes we need to stir up the gift. Burden should cause us to seek the Lord. God gives us a burden about things because he wants to speak and to act. Whenever he gives us a burden, we need expectation because as far as he's concerned, it's a declaration that he wants to be involved and to speak through us and use us in this situation. He's chosen us to work with him. He's got a burden for this particular person. He's passed that burden onto us because it's a declaration of intent. He wants to speak and we're the chosen vessel. So let's be clear about how it works. When we get a burden it's because God's choosing us to do something. We should feel a sense of rare privilege.

We can stir up the gift. That means that we move out in faith with the right motive. We want to see this person blessed, healed, restored, etc. Then we put ourselves in a place where God can use us. We are aware, hopefully, that the gift of prophecy is resident in all of us. All of us can prophesy. We may not be called to be prophets but every one of us can prophesy, and I hope we want to move out in it a lot more. We call up the gift from within.

Sometimes I'm moving in expectation and saying, 'Father, how do you want to do this?' Sometimes I may pick people out in a situation and ask them to stand. Other times God may get me to pick people out and I ask them to come out to the front of the meeting. At this point I may not have received any prophetic words for them. It's where life gets a little interesting. I'm calling them out in expectation and saying, 'Lord, now what do we do?' and he says nothing! In the absence of God saying anything, I think I'll start at one end and work my way along. So I come to the first person and suddenly God begins to speak and the gift flows. We do these things out of a sense of expectation because we are expecting God to do something. We are expecting God to show up, we are expecting God to move. Therefore, when we go into places, expectation means there is a degree of probability that we will move out in the prophetic gift. We need to anticipate what God wants to do. We are realising before-hand that God may want to do something, and we are choosing to work with him. That's why preparation is so important. Be attentive to the Holy Spirit and stir up the gift.

How does prophecy come?

Visions

Sometimes it comes through visions, pictures or even moving pictures. Probably quite a few of us have had pictures before, that have sparked something off in us. There are two types of vision generally. Firstly, unremarkable vision that uses everyday things around us, maybe even uses our own understanding of things to speak prophetically; e.g. Jeremiah 1:11–12.

The Lord asked the prophet, 'What do you see?' Jeremiah looked around and it was a branch of an almond tree which really got his attention. A perfectly common and ordinary sight, totally unremarkable. However, the interpretation together with the timing and the specific need in the people at the time, all combined to produce a positive and significant prophetic contribution.

Sometimes the vision we have, the picture we have, can use our own human knowledge. I was in a meeting of several hundred people and just about to speak, when the Lord directed me to one person in the middle aisle, a girl in her mid-twenties. I asked her to stand up and all I had was the picture of a hazel tree. I know what a hazel tree is because my father and I were landscape gardeners. All I had was this picture, so I asked the Lord, ' what do you want to say?' There was nothing. I started in what I knew ... 'I'm seeing a picture of a hazel tree...' and began to describe the properties from what I could remember from my training.

I began to say, 'it's got beautiful flowers and fruit, it can grow almost anywhere, it's resistant to disease, the bark and the leaves can be used for medicinal purposes, they can be used as a tonic or a sedative that brings comfort from pain, it can grow and succeed almost anywhere, it's very hardy, very resilient . . . ' and as soon as I came to the end of what I knew, suddenly I began to flow in the prophetic and say, 'that's how God sees you; he thinks you're beautiful, you're going to bear good fruit in your life, you musn't be worried that you're no good, you're tough, you're able to resist the enemy, you'll grow in almost any situation . . . ' and I began to move prophetically. She was now in tears and all her friends were hooting with laughter.

I finished prophesying, prayed for her and got on with the seminar I was doing. At the end of the meeting she came up to me and said, 'thanks for what you said. You don't know this but my name is Hazel', and apparently that very afternoon her friends had been having tea together and she'd sat there in a very bad mood. 'Hazel. Stupid name, Hazel. Why have my parents called me Hazel? Why couldn't I have been called by a prettier name? I hate my name. I wish I could change it.' She came along to the meeting and God picked her out and gave me a vision of a hazel tree. God has an incredible sense of humour. What he was saying in all of that was, 'Excuse me, but I chose your name; I gave it to you and I gave it to you for this purpose.' She told me later she was crying because suddenly she was realising that this name was given to her by God. When she was in the womb, God named her Hazel. A powerful word from a perfectly ordinary and common source.

Secondly, vision can be supernatural rather than unremarkable. Acts 10 recounts the story of two men, one a Greek, devout, kind, trustworthy, to whom God chooses to reveal himself in a sovereign way. The other a Jew, loud, impetuous and a racist. The problem is, how can we bring these two men together when they are separated by such a religious, national and cultural divide; especially in the heart of one man who has been taught separatism from birth?

God chose to minister a supernatural vision to Peter in order to unlock what had become a form of prejudice in his heart to other nationalities. He was given a vision of a sheet lowered from heaven containing a full variety of edible species and a voice saying, *'Arise, Peter, kill and eat.'*

His reaction was, 'I can't do that because these things are unholy, unclean, and I've never done that sort of thing in my life.' The word comes to him very powerfully, 'what God has cleansed, don't you consider unholy.' It happened three times and he was totally bewildered. What on earth did this mean? He had no interpretation for it at that point in time, but whilst he was meditating the Holy Spirit said, 'there are three men downstairs looking for you, arise and go without misgivings because I have sent them ... ' He went away to this house and started preaching the gospel, and while he was talking the Holy Spirit fell upon all these people and a completely brand new type of church was born.

Sometimes we can get pictures that have a prophetic interpretation. Sometimes they are diagnostic in the sense that they give us information about things. Sometimes we will receive a vision and the vision itself may lead us to a word of knowledge. A word of knowledge is usually diagnostic. It tells us something that is happening or that has happened. Once we get that, the next step is to say, 'well Father, in the light of that, what is it that you want to say?' Do not just speak out the first thing we receive, because it may be diagnostic, it may be God giving us information about someone and could result, if we are not careful, in us actually prophesying a problem.

If we practise the art of waiting quietly, perhaps just for a few moments before we open our mouth to prophesy, we may glorify God more in the delivery and save ourselves some considerable heartache. Most mistakes in prophecy occur because we rush in with what we believe God is saying, while he may still be speaking!

Sometimes we may get moving pictures – like on a cinema screen. At one time the leaders of a church in Liverpool asked me to pray for a guy because he was having marriage difficulties. The leading elders said to this man, 'why don't you share with Graham a few things that are going on?' He began to share about his wife, how they'd been having difficulties in their relationship for some time. He had to do his own washing and cooking. She would barely speak to him. She was very uncivil. He related how she seemed uninterested in the Lord; refused to pray with him; avoided church meetings; and generally was a discouraging spiritual factor in the household.

While he was speaking I became really uneasy in my spirit. Taking a step back into God I asked, 'Father, why am I feeling like this? I've no reason to feel like this unless you're making me.' I really like asking God questions; it's one of the ways in which I learn the most. If I don't understand, I ask. I suddenly began to get a 'moving picture' of this man who was talking to me in a blue pin-striped suit, red tie with stripes, holding an overnight bag and a briefcase, walking down to a hotel. With him was a very striking red-head with a bottle green business suit, carrying an overnight bag. They went into this hotel – the Connaught Hotel – and into the reception. Behind the reception desk the manager was a small guy, bald head, black moustache, black suit, white shirt, green spotted tie. He registered them in the name of Coleman and gave them a double room, number 213. I saw them going into the lift and pressing the second floor button. The door closed and the vision ended.

I thought, 'what am I seeing all this for, Father?' All I received was the impression to: 'say it how you see it, son.' I related the whole vision to the people present and the guy went absolutely white and began to shake. The leaders said to him, 'your wife's not a red-head, your name's not Coleman. What's going on?' Suddenly we find out this guy's been having an affair for three years with one of the girls in the office. Is it any wonder his marriage is in difficulties? His wife cannot prove anything, but she knows that something is happening, that the life has gone out of the marriage. She knows he's playing around. She doesn't know how she knows, but she knows.

Again, we saw the wonderful kindness of the Lord who enabled us to break into a situation that sin and the enemy had rendered closed and seemingly impossible.

Dreams

Sometimes we may get dreams. I don't sleep much, but I don't seem to dream. At least, I don't remember them on waking. I've only had two dreams in my life I can remember and they were both very significant. Ordinarily I wouldn't know if I'd dreamt. My wife dreams all the time, and many of her dreams are very significant (Numbers 12:6) ... God spoke to Pharaoh in a dream which only Joseph could interpret; the same thing happened with Nebuchadnezzer, which only Daniel could understand. Joseph had a dream about Mary: the angel said, 'marry the girl!' For him, that dream involved a change of mind because he was doubtful before (Matthew 1). The so-called 'three wise men' were warned in a dream not to return to Herod. Very practical, these dreams. Later on, Joseph had another dream that said 'take the child and flee to Egypt.'

Daniel could understand all kinds of visions and dreams (Daniel 1:17). One of my closest friends has a gift of interpreting dreams. If you're a dreamer you do need to write it down and meditate upon it and share it. Open it up for comment and prayer. It may be for us or someone else. It may or may not be relevant and a few weeks down the line, we may want to put it on the shelf. Get in the habit of writing things down. Treat a dream as you would a prophecy. Write it down and share it with responsible people.

Impressions

Prophecy can come by impressions. An inner conviction – strong or faint – about something. That's why we need to be still before God. It's very important. Being quiet in our spirit. Sometimes we get an impression of pain or anguish. A sense of looking back into the past. Learn to read the signs. There's something in this person's background that's caused them pain and anguish. 'Okay, Father, I'm beginning to get an impression; how do I speak into it?'

In one meeting I was praying for a woman and I felt a tremendous peace wash over me and I felt I was looking forward. I stepped back into God and asked him, and I then had an impression that the peace of God was going to come into her life now, and in the future, in a very big way. When we began to prophesy into her life, it opened up so many things that the Lord wanted to do in her life; but it began by an impression.

Many people begin to pray for others and then realise that what they are praying is in fact prophetic. So they switch from prayer to prophecy in mid flow.

Generally speaking, if we can pray, we can probably prophesy. Instead of opening our mouth to pray, which is a natural and right reaction, it may be better to wait a moment. Take a step back into our spirit, ask a few questions of the Lord and move out in the gift of prophecy instead, if that is how the Spirit is leading.

Seeing words

Sometimes we can see words over people. One or two words. I have seen words appear on someone's forehead such as faith or healing. It's there to alert us that God wants to say something. We can then quiet our spirit and take a step back into God and ask him what he wants to say. Into that quietness God can drop a prophetic word.

That vital first word activates our spirit. Usually it triggers a conceptual understanding of what the Holy Spirit wants to say. For example, hearing or seeing the word healing over someone can cause us to ask questions such as:

- Is it healing for themselves?
- Is it healing for a family member, or someone close to them?
- Does it indicate a healing gift will operate in their church?
- Is the Lord moving that individual into a healing gift?
- Is the Lord calling forth a healing ministry?

As we ask the Lord questions in our spirit, the concept of where and how healing will be released will become clear in our spirit. We can then target and aim the word in the right direction.

It is the same principle with less definitive words such as peace. You believe that the Holy Spirit wants to speak a genuine word (as opposed to a general word) of peace into the life of an individual. Where? How? Why? Peace into what area? Where is the area of turmoil that requires peace to be received?

Is it peace about: financial worries, employment difficulties, relational problems, a health issue, etc, etc? Where do we aim a word like that ... to what area does the Lord wish to bring peace? This is where we need to ensure that our heart is on the same wavelength as the Lord. Scripture teaches that we have a High Priest who can be touched by the feeling of our infirmities. He is in tune with our feelings. In prophecy we are seeking to communicate the spirit of the word, not just a concept. A prophecy should impact on a person's spirit, not just on their mind.

Being quiet is important

The voice of the Lord is like a whisper at times (for example in 1 Kings 19). The voice of God is so soft we have to strain to hear it, that's why it's very important to learn to be still. Being still doesn't necessarily mean you have to get a quiet place somewhere. It means you've got to still the clamouring within. To bring everything to a point of quietness in our heart, mind and spirit. To be still within. It is good to learn to be still. To practise being still. We are not blanking our mind and our thoughts out. We are not trying to turn our mind into a vacuum; we are just being still, and in the peace of God, he speaks. Quietness is so important to the prophet.

Use of Scripture

Scripture can be an aid to prophecy. Often I have prophecy from a scripture verse. Scripture pops into our heart or mind and suddenly the prophetic spirit begins to move on it. I prayed for a man in a very responsible job within a very politically motivated council. People hated him because he was a Spirit-filled Christian. The knives were out for him. People were altering his work, hiding memos, and being very obstructive. There was constant pressure every day and he was beginning to think, 'should I be here?' These people were trying to get him suspended because they wanted to fill his job with one of their colleagues. As we were praying, God gave me Psalm 35, and as I read it I got stirred up because it was all about fighting against the enemy; taking hold of the armour; believing that God is your salvation; those who are against you will be ashamed and confounded, dishonoured and humiliated before God; the angels are with you, be strong, rejoice in God, I'll deliver you. That's what it was all about and I began to be stirred up. I put the Bible down and said, 'This is what I believe God is saying to you...' and began to prophesy. A short time later several of his main antagonists were prosecuted for fraud, drug abuse and mismanagement of funds, and they were sacked. What was interesting was that three Spirit-filled Christians took their place. That was a vital word to stand, to fight and see the salvation of God which came from reading scripture.

Prophecy can come into our lives in a whole variety of ways and it is good not to get locked into one way, but in our hearts and spirits to be open to anything that God may want to do.

Chapter 4

The Practice of Prophecy

Prophecy begins by receiving a burden. It's very important that we allow our hearts to be on the same wave length as God's. God, I believe, wants to give each of us a sense of burden.

God deliver us from being in a church where most of the congregation don't feel any sense of responsibility for the work. If we don't feel a sense of taking the weight collectively for the church, it means we are missing out on the heart of God for the community. Every member of the church should be living with a sense of ownership for the work and the community in which they live. It is out of that burden that God will express his heart.

Objective ... the burden of God's heart

In prophecy the first thing we need to receive is a sense of burden. We need to be looking around in our churches initially, saying 'Who, Lord, do you want to speak to in my church, in my street, in the course of my daily life? Lord give me a burden.' I'm currently living with a sense of burden for five people and I'm confident that I'll get some prophetic input to bring to bear into those people's lives.

When we receive a burden we must ask the Lord questions. Who is it for? What is it you want to do? At the end of this prophecy, what is it you want to achieve in this person's life? What is the objective? Questions are very important to church life in general. What are we doing and why? These are the two most important questions we can ask in church. Sometimes it is the failure to ask those questions that forces a stagnation on the work, in terms of what we're doing and the sense of vision we are communicating. Every two years a church should have a radical review and examine everything we are doing. The revelation we had last year may not be good enough for the year ahead.

In relation to the prophetic we need to be asking God questions; getting a sense of objective. To develop an understanding of how God's heart works towards people is very important. Why is he picking this person out to receive prophecy? What does he want to achieve through this word?

It's that sense of objective that helps us to be clear, specific and significant in terms of what we are prophesying. It focuses the heart of God into that person's life. Without that sense of objective we sometimes fudge the words or pad the prophecy out with too many human insights. That is because we don't have a real sharp focus on what God wants to do.

Diagnosis and prognosis

Very often the first thing we receive may well be diagnostic. There is a difference between the diagnosis and prognosis. Sometimes we can see a vision or have an intimation and what we get initially may actually be quite negative. We may see a fault, a wrong. Very often this can be diagnostic simply because prophecy has three elements to it. There's the word of knowledge, the gift of prophecy and the word of wisdom. A word of knowledge opens up the issue; a word of prophecy speaks God's heart into it; and the word of wisdom tells us how to respond to God.

The first thing we get may actually be a word of knowledge, not prophecy. God is giving us information about this person's life, about their situation. What God is doing is saying, 'this is what is happening and I need you to understand it.' He is giving us a context in which to speak.

Most people prophesy the first thing they receive. We can actually prophesy a word of knowledge that God has given to us as information. It is called prophesying the problem, and has probably damaged more people's lives than any other issue in the prophetic sense. Don't give the first thing you receive; don't be in a hurry to prophesy. Many people feel that they have to get a word out of their mouth as soon as possible.

It may be God showing us something about a situation or person's life that he wants us to know. We need to perfect the art of stepping back into our spirit and saying, 'thank you Father, I understand that about this person's life. Now in the light of that, what is it you want to say to them?' What he gives us to say may be completely the opposite of what we had seen first, because the grace of God may need to come into operation.

The word of knowledge in this instance is diagnostic. The Lord reveals the situation to us as it is at the moment. However, the prophetic word we give may relate to what the Lord is going to do both now and in the future. That is prognosis. In simple terms, diagnosis identifies what is, whilst prognosis indicates what is to come!

It is not enough for us to simply point out what is wrong, if we have no heart to lead a recovery. We have to determine the following: 'Is this first word diagnostic? If so, is it for me personally, so that I become familiar with the situation?' If the answer to both those questions is yes, then we have a context (a set of circumstances) into which God wants to speak. Context always determines what the Lord wants to say.

Now we have privileged information about a person or

a situation which we need to use wisely, with great sensitivity to the Holy Spirit and also with real respect to the people concerned.

A great many years ago I was ministering at a church weekend in Wales. During a leaders' meeting I received a picture for one of the elders present. It was a picture of him with a knife in his hand stabbing the main leader in the back. I asked the Lord for an interpretation; he showed me that this man was taking every opportunity to criticise the main leader and to undermine his authority. He made everything sound spiritual and Christian, nevertheless he was trying to build a platform for himself. He was not a servant; he wanted status and he was profoundly jealous of the main leader's popularity. For the sake of the anecdote we will call the main leader David and the other man Stephen.

I have now received something which is diagnostic; a word of knowledge, which tells me what is happening. This is not a prophecy. I must take a step back into my spirit and ask the Lord various questions; e.g. 'Why are you showing me this?' 'What do you want me to do?'

I felt impressed to bring them both out to the front of the meeting and stand them back to back. I put a broom handle in Stephen's hand and asked him to pretend it was a sword. The Lord gave me this prophetic word for Stephen.

'The Lord has brought you two men together. He has stood you back to back which is a fighting position. He is giving a charge into your life, Stephen, to guard David's back; to look after him because the enemy wants to have and destroy his life, to pull him down by any means possible. He is giving you a charge to guard him and keep him prayerfully. Defend him against the enemy. Be aware that the enemy strategy is to ruin him through the hands of men who lust for power. He has given you to him as a friend to watch over his life. To pray for him, bless him and stand with him. He wants you to be his friend and brother.'

At this point Stephen began to cry. Everyone thought it was because of the immense privilege that the Lord was giving him. The reality was that he was suddenly very aware of his sin and the fact that his scheming had put him on the wrong side of God. It is the job of the Holy Spirit to make us feel bad when we are bad. It is called guilt. Guilt is a friend because it convinces us that we are wrong and that we need to repent and ask God to help us. Condemnation also makes us understand that we have done wrong, but convinces us that we cannot possibly approach God on the matter. It persuades us that God will be angry, disillusioned or unreceptive to our prayers.

Stephen was crying for two reasons. Firstly because he knew he had been wrong and needed to repent. Secondly because the grace of God was being poured out into his life. Instead of judgement he was receiving mercy. He was realising that he had been helping the enemy, but was now determined to take the opportunity that the Lord was giving to be on God's side.

All this was happening internally in his heart without me having to say anything publicly to him. It is vital in prophecy that we do what the Lord has shown us to do and leave the Holy Spirit to do the rest. He is very good at what he does and does not need any help from us. Without me mentioning his sin in public, the Holy Spirit brought Stephen to a point of repentance.

This is important. If we do not understand the diagnostic principle we may prophesy a problem and cause major damage. The Gospel is redemptive; a prophet must be good news, even if that news is repent! There are times when the Lord has no other option but to shout something as though from a rooftop; to air something publicly. Generally, we have to be so far down a road of potential no return, that he considers this is the only way to bring redemption.

Normally it is the goodness and the kindness of God that brings us to repentance. After having received the original picture of Stephen with a knife in his hand, I was prompted to ask the Lord a number of questions. One pertinent question was, 'What is your objective, Father? What is it you want to achieve between these two men?' I believe the Lord intimated that he wanted to redeem their relationship; for these men to be absolutely close in heart and spirit. When I asked him how that would be achieved, he gave me the idea of standing them back to back.

We don't have to speak out the negative always. It depends on the objective. If we fix in our minds that the Gospel is redemptive, it will provide a useful guide-line.

Later that same weekend, I took Stephen aside to check that everything was okay with him. He told me, 'You have no idea how God has blessed me this weekend!' I felt impressed (for his sake) to let him know everything I knew. He broke down in tears; a contrite spirit knows the kindness of God. The fact that the Lord knew his sin, redeeming and blessing him publicly without exposing him, really softened his heart.

The grace of God will keep flowing into our lives most of the time. Sometimes it's the goodness and kindness of God that breaks our hearts. There isn't a person in the church to whom God does not want to reveal his incredible kindness. Many Christians have given up on the kindness of God. Some of our experiences of people around us, have been so bad and so poor that they have resulted in equating God with that kind of experience, but God is completely different, he is not human. He is divine; an altogether different character.

1 Corinthians 14:1–5 tells us that the whole point of the prophetic is to edify, encourage and comfort, to build up, stir up and to cheer up. That's prophecy. The whole central aspect of prophecy is to bring those things to bear in our life. God wants to build us up any way that he can. He wants to stir us up and encourage us, but he also

wants us to know that he's in touch with our pain. He wants to bring comfort when we need comfort.

He's like that; 90% of prophecy on that basic level is stating the obvious. God loves us. He cares for us. He wants the best for us. His kindness and faithfulness is with us. His love is never ending. His loving kindness is eternal. He knows everything about our lives. These things we know anyway, but sometimes we get so locked into our circumstances that we lose sight of even those basic attributes of the character of God, and we need to be reminded. We can read Scripture that contains those vital truths, but sometimes we need the 'now' element of prophecy, allied to Scripture, to actually bring the word home to our circumstances in a dynamic way.

We must not apologise if what we have is not new or fresh. If we have received a word that God loves someone, then we have to say that word in the best way possible.

In prophecy, the objective affects the delivery. If the objective of prophecy is to strengthen people, to add resolve and determination to their lives, our prophesying will reflect that aim. We will prophesy in a bold, forthright manner, dwelling on the supremacy of God and taking care to release a confidence into the people concerned.

Similarly if we have received a word from the Lord about his love for an individual, we should want to communicate that in a way which causes God's love to be spread abroad in their heart. Conviction produces expression. If we are convinced of the love of God ourselves when we speak of this wonderful phenomenon we will convey the spirit of the word, not just the content.

Prophecy communicates spirit to spirit as well as speaking to our minds.

The whole essence of prophecy is that we need to let the Holy Spirit fire our spirits. Personally, the fact that God loves me is probably the single most important truth in my life. That God loves Graham Cooke – me! I know that God loves me. I wake up every day convinced of the love of God; convinced that something wonderful is going to happen today between myself and the Lord, because he loves me. Convinced that in the problems I have in my life at the moment, God is going to help me to find a way through. God is going to do something terrific and dynamic and he's going to help me fight off the enemy and fight through the difficulties. Why? Because God loves me. It doesn't matter what's facing me in life at the moment, I know that God is going to walk with me. The worst that can happen in my situation is that it doesn't change at all; but I will know the presence of God. God will walk me through it, but I'll have to go through everything and endure everything, but even in that, God will not leave me. His presence will be with me. He'll be with me even until the end of the age. The absolute best that can happen is that he changes everything and my concerns disappear. The worst that can happen is that I get to walk by faith for a little while longer. His presence is with me as I endure. Even that is wonderful.

As one of my good friends says, prophecy is 80% preparation; 20% inspiration; 100% perspiration and 1000% trepidation!

Negativity and judgementalism

It's very important that we avoid negativity and judgementalism. If we find it easy to give hard words, there's something wrong with our spirit. If we find it easy to give negative words, then we have no understanding of the grace and goodness of God.

There's always a tension between the ideal and the actual. A prophet when he comes in will always see the horizon. He'll see the ideal. This is where God is taking us. This is what God is doing with us. He will paint a picture because his job is to lift the vision and the perspective of the congregation to see where God is taking them.

Local leaders live with the actual of how things really are and the middle ground between the ideal and the actual is called frustration. What happens to a lot of prophetic people is that they get this vision of the ideal and they have no understanding of the actual. A prophet will come into town, give the people this ideal and the local leaders have to work all this scenario out on the ground. I am tired of what we call back home 'seagull prophets'! – people who fly in, make a loud noise, dump on everyone and fly out again! A lot of the time they often have no understanding of how prophecy is actually worked through in the local church.

We need to understand that prophets are part of the five-fold ministry (Ephesians 4:11) which is essentially a building ministry. A lot of prophets want to have a blessing ministry: blow in, throw a few prophecies around and bless a few people, then blow out again. I want to state publicly that I don't believe that is good enough.

A prophet is in a building ministry. If we are going to prophesy into work, the very least we can do is be available for advice and counsel. I only work with a set number of churches in a given year. I'll give some prophetic input into those places but I'll be around during the course of that twelve months to give them any advice or support. I may have two or three visits, not only to set the church up in terms of vision, but actually to work that vision through on the ground. There is the tension between the ideal and the actual, and I want to work with leaders who are in the 'actual' of their problem. Seeing the horizon is one thing, the question is, 'Lord, how do we get there from here?' That is when a prophet is a builder, working with the apostle, the pastor, and the teacher, to create steps that move the church from the actual of where we are now to the ideal of where God is really taking us.

Deal with frustration

Frustration is an enemy to the prophetic ministry. It will always colour our thinking, infect the word we have, and give us a jaundiced perspective on the life of the church. If we are to represent God's heart and be good servants, we must learn to master our frustration. We need the understanding and the grace of God to move our hearts rather than our own irritation and dissatisfaction.

In rejection we must open our hearts so that the love of God can flow in. Most prophetic people feel rejected because they do not have any relationships of worth and value.

Prophets are often accused of being weird, temperamental, emotional and abnormal. In some places where there is a great ignorance of the role of the prophet, that type of behaviour is seen as normal for prophetic people. Prophets have not cornered the market in abnormality; there are many non-prophetic ministries that seem to fluctuate between the odd-ball and the highly entertaining!

A prophet must have a relationship with the Lord of loving kindness on a personal basis.

A prophet must be good news, even if that news is repent. Prophecy is about restoring people's dignity and self-respect. I hate the enemy because he strips that away from people. He takes away our dignity and self-respect, and he creates a sense of disillusionment in our hearts about ourselves. He creates a sense of 'I'm not worthy, I'm no good, I can't do anything.' He strips us of everything possible. That's why I believe that advertising borders on the demonic a lot of the time, because it is geared to making people feel dissatisfied with their life. That's the whole point of it. Advertisers have to make people dissatisfied with an aspect of their life, and if they can achieve that there is a good chance that maybe people will buy their product.

They create a dissatisfaction about our lifestyle, our figure, our looks, the clothes we wear, and possessions we have. Into that vacuum they put their own product, hoping to entice us to purchase it and fill the void that they created in the first place. They trade on our insecurity and our need to be loved and valued.

The whole of the enemy's strategy works on that same principle. He is geared to making us feel dissatisfied with who we are. He wants to separate us from God, the church, our friends and any useful function we may adopt in furthering the Kingdom.

If he can get us to hate ourselves and tell our hearts that we are of no account, therefore it does not matter if we don't go to the meeting, or pray, or worship because who are we anyway, then apathy will follow. If we allow apathy into our lives then it will hold the door open to unbelief, condemnation, self-loathing, bitterness, anxiety, fear, misery and selfishness. All these things spell passivity. A passive acceptance of life and a demoralised outlook on the things of God.

The prophetic is geared to challenging that whole issue. This is why it is so important that we understand the place of negative words in prophecy. There is a place for negative words in prophecy. There is a place for negative words and judgement (we will look at this in Chapter 7 'Judging and Weighing Prophecy'). However we need a solid grounding in the grace of God before we can be trusted with judgement in prophecy. First, the Holy Spirit will want to educate us in the truth of God's love, his grace, his kindness and mercy. Second, he will want us to flow in words of prophecy that will edify, encourage and comfort God's people. In 1 Corinthians 14 the key word 'edify' is used on several occasions. Let everything be done to edify.

Don't be super-spiritual

Very often the main cause of failure in the prophetic is that we are moving under pressure rather than in peace and relaxation in the knowledge of God. I am under enormous pressure everywhere I go, to move in prophecy. I accept that pressure as part of the ministry, but there is no way that I can live under the weight of false expectations.

Many churches see prophetic ministry as a glorious shortcut. Instead of labouring to create vision in the church from the ground up by talking and spending time with people; leaders will get a prophet to come in and prophesy the vision so that it can be imposed from the top down onto the people.

Prophecy will confirm and broaden the vision; it cannot create one if nothing is there. Vision is created through prayer, seeking God and sharing our hearts with people in the work. If these things are absent we need to be restoring people to God, not creating vision for empty hearts.

Every day I have to push away the burden of other people's expectations. To be still, to live in the grace of God, to be aware of his presence and to be at rest are the goals of prophetic ministry. Into that environment the Lord can drop his word, create faith and release the prophetic flow.

Worship is important to a prophet. Being at rest and peace in our relationship with God is vital.

Revelation and information

If we are not moving in peace and rest, we will find ourselves reacting to situations. Reaction rather than rest is anathema to a prophet. People moving under pressure can often indulge in mental gymnastics rather than in hearing a word in their spirit.

Most people think that prophecy comes from 'out there' into our minds. It doesn't at all. We can't receive prophecy in the mind. The mind receives information. Our spirit receives revelation. We only receive the prophetic in our spirit, not in our mind. Prophecy comes from within, through our spirit and the link between our spirit and our mind is faith. Faith is the vehicle that takes the prophetic word from our spirit into our conscious mind. Our mind is very good at putting things in order. Revelation comes in bits and pieces sometimes. You may get part 4, then part 2, then part 3, then part 1. The mind is brilliant at putting it in order so that it comes out correctly. The link between our spirit and our mind is faith. We must always let our faith loose on the prophetic word first, to come to a point of belief that the word we have is truly from the Lord.

Sometimes we can get a word coming into our spirit that makes no sense whatsoever to our mind. That is because our mind cannot understand revelation, it can only process it, put it into order. Revelation sometimes is not logical. It doesn't make sense. If we let our mind loose on it straight away, our mind will tell us that the word doesn't sound logical. It doesn't make sense. If we seek to process revelation with our mind, we will come into uncertainty and fear. Fear of getting it wrong; fear of going out on a limb; fear of embarrassment and fear of looking stupid in front of others. That fear will cause us to cut our losses and say nothing.

We are then reduced to saying something general (dressed up in spiritual language) that our mind can cope with, rather than a word that is supernatural and significant.

In a series of meetings I was taking in London I gave an appeal in one place for people who were experiencing difficulties in relationships, to come forward and receive prayer. As I worked my way along the line I presently came to a man in his late forties. I had no idea about the relationship in his life causing him pain; the man said nothing to me. All I could do was reach out in my spirit to ask the Lord's perspective.

At this point I have a 50/50 chance of being right in deciding whether it is male or female that he has the problem with. After that, the odds are more significantly against whilst I am deciding if it is wife, mother, sister, daughter, employer, pastor's wife ... or all the male counterparts!

As I reached out to God, I said 'the Lord wants to speak to you about your wife.' At this point I receive a picture of a young lady in her mid to late twenties, long blonde hair, quite tall. My mind is screaming at me that this is his daughter. However in my spirit I heard the word 'wife'.

As I waited and rested briefly in my spirit, I let my faith loose on the original word, ignored my mind and spoke prophetically. The main thrust of the word was that he had been married for three years to a woman twenty years his junior. Under his love and care she has blossomed in her personality and has changed considerably, from a mousy introvert to a more confident and outgoing personality. This had obviously changed the dynamic of their relationship to a point where he was becoming less confident of her love, and more convinced she would leave him for a younger man. Into that situation the Lord spoke a beautiful word of comfort and reassurance which lifted his spirit immeasurably.

Very often a real battle is waged within our lives between our mind and our spirit. Basically our mind wants to be in control, whereas God has created our spirit to know him and move with him. That is why peace, quiet and rest on the inside are so important.

Some people are 'feelers' in the prophetic. We feel people's pain or joy, etc. We feel things from the heart of God. Some people are 'seers'. We see pictures and have dreams. Some people are 'hearers'. Sometimes we can move between all three. It is a good thing not to get locked into one methodology. Try to have a variety of ways to deliver prophetic words; God is full of infinite variety.

Don't look for clues!

Do not move out by what you see or understand in the natural. A lot of prophetic people make the mistake of looking for clues from people. Trying to pick something up from how they look (happy or unhappy!); the way they are sitting; the general 'air' about the individual.

This is very soulish and produces prophecy on that level. If we are going to move out in prophecy the one person we have to be looking at and listening to is the Lord. Don't try and pick up clues from people or circumstances. It never works and usually goes wrong. It leads us into the realm of the soul and the mind, where we can give Satan the opportunity to add mixture to what is going on. What we get may sound spiritual but it's information, not revelation. Sometimes we can completely miss the mark.

I was speaking at a celebration meeting and gave an appeal for ministry which drew a rather large response. As I watched people coming forward I saw an elderly man on crutches; a young guy dressed in the punk tradition with green hair, zips and safety pins everywhere; an entire family coming out together; and I also noticed a stunningly attractive woman, as they all made their way to the front of the hall.

Eventually, after an hour of ministry, I found myself in front of the attractive woman that I had noticed earlier. I asked her name and she replied, in a very throaty voice. I stepped back into my spirit to hear the Lord. The Lord spoke to my spirit these words; 'tell him I am not happy.' Now, we cannot mishear God in our spirit. I asked the Lord what he meant, being conscious that my mind was sending out alarm signals of distress (which it usually does when I receive revelation of this kind). The Lord spoke again, 'Son, his name is Richard and I want you to tell him I know his name and that he must change.'

I took a deep breath and looked at this person. There was no way I could tell; all the clues said she was female. Choosing to live in my spirit, I brought a measure of peace to my mind which was almost imploring me not to do anything stupid. I had to overcome fear and embarrassment also in those seconds of quiet. Speaking out of my innermost being, I said to this person, 'Richard, God knows your real name and he is not happy with your lifestyle. You have to change.' Before I could add anything more, this person let out a string of obscenities, hiked up his long skirt and ran from the building closely followed by several other females! No-one knew who they were and to my current knowledge they have not been seen since. Which just leaves me praying periodically that the Lord will complete his work in the life of a transvestite called Sylvia or Richard!

To illustrate this further, when I was conducting a series of meetings in America, whilst moving in prophetic ministry over the assembly the Lord gave me a word for a man at the rear of the meeting. This guy was dressed like a vagrant, an absolute down and out character.

God began to give me a word for him that he was going to have hundreds of thousands of dollars to give away into the church; that in his business he was going to be leading key business people to the Lord; that he would finance various projects in the community and the nation. I looked at him and he looked like he needed a hand out. The problem was, that sitting directly behind him was this guy in a business suit; looking like a million dollars; looking like he was the executive of a multi-national company. So I was looking at the tramp and the guy right behind him and I was thinking, 'first instinct you have to go with, the word is for the tramp,' but I looked behind and thought, 'have I got these two mixed up?'

I couldn't get any peace about it in myself, so I wandered away and did a few words across the congregation and then came back. I looked at him and thought 'it's got to be the guy behind, he looks the part.' I did a few more words elsewhere and then came back and thought, 'I'm going to have to go for it.' I had to go with what was in my spirit.

Sometimes you've just got to be brave enough to launch out. I got this tramp guy to stand up and started prophesying to him. Nobody knew him and I was convinced that the whole place all thought the same thing: 'he's missed it, it's the guy behind him.' This guy wasn't giving me any help whatsoever. He was looking at me stony-faced. Not a movement on his face.

Some people don't give you any help; sometimes it's because they don't know how to behave: they have never had a prophetic word before. They don't quite know what to do with themselves and they're as embarrassed as we are. Sometimes people's faces are very mobile and they give you a lot of help and encouragement and we can feel confident that we are getting through. At other times people are really trying to psyche out the prophet. A word can be absolutely spot on, but you would never know just by looking at the face of the recipient. I have met people who stood and stared at me, sometimes quite insolently; they have a kind of 'Let's see how good you are,' look on their face.

Try not to look at people's faces for confirmation. Our own peace and rest in the Lord should be sufficient encouragement.

I prophesied over this vagrant and then discovered later he was an extremely wealthy individual who liked dressing down; he was just a 'good ol' boy'! He had heard about the conference and decided to check it out. After I had prophesied over him, he promptly sat down and I carried on with the meeting.

Several moments later I received a word for the guy in

the suit sitting just behind the vagrant. The word I heard in my spirit was, 'the job you have just been interviewed for is yours!' I was still struggling a little over the previous word to the vagrant. Now I was completely unsure in my mind ... 'have I missed it? Did I mix up the first prophecy?' On the surface it seemed like the first word is for the guy who looked like an executive and the second word was for the guy who looked like he was out of work, living on handouts.

As you can imagine, the enemy is not exactly silent at this point. Everything on the inside is screaming at me, 'you fool, you idiot, you've got it wrong!' I'm on the platform trying to be cool, but inside I am a mass of nerve ends. In that situation all we can do is humble ourselves before the Lord. I silently prayed, 'Lord, I will face this situation honourably if I have missed it; I will repent and put things right with people; I will publicly apologise and make sure no-one is damaged by any mistake I have made.'

The enemy hates humility. He cannot penetrate it. Humility always opens a door for the Lord to touch our lives. As I quietly humbled myself on the platform I experienced a peace and a rest in the Lord. I still had this word for the guy in the executive suit. I asked him to stand as I gave him the prophecy and then watched with gladness as he and his family punched the air with delight.

When I spoke to him later I discovered he had been unemployed for two years and had been to his first interview in months that very afternoon. A week later he was offered the job.

I have to say that I was so relieved and very grateful to the Lord. Prophetic ministry is never straightforward; it is ridiculously easy to make mistakes even after years in the ministry. People apply impossible standards to the prophetic office that they don't assign to any other ministry. Some people will be offended by those statements. It is my opinion that if we relaxed the standards and allowed for more grace, we would actually have fewer mistakes and a lot more honesty and integrity in the gifting.

Prophetic ministry is put under immense pressure to perform and to be super spiritual. People sensationalise the gifting and create a hype and a mystique around personalities that is frankly immoral and dangerous. We are called to be ourselves in the Lord, within the scope of our function. I do not have to be under pressure to be prophetic. I have to be myself in Jesus and people can either cope with that or not as the case may be. It is almost inevitable that we will thrill some people and disappoint others, depending on what is happening when we go to particular places.

As Jesus said, 'I can only do what my Father is doing and say what my Father in heaven is saying.' A useful guide-line: never move out by what you see; it will get you into trouble every time. Do not lean on your own understanding.

Prophetic ministry is to draw out of people what the Lord has already put into their lives, not necessarily to try and input something new and fresh. Sometimes prophetic ministry stands with one foot in the past and the other in the future, and brings both those extremes into the present to help people make sense of where they are right now.

Consider the person you are ministering to

When we prophesy over people, we must learn to put margins into the word. Do not be anxious to splurge everything you have received; it is easier to add than to retract. Do not be so eager to prophesy that you fail to consider the needs of the recipient. If we prophesy over an individual for even a few brief moments, we may speak several hundred words. What is that person doing whilst we are speaking? They are probably sitting there in memory mode, frantically trying to remember everything we are saying to them. They will not be able to remember every single sentence or word. Mostly their memory will be quite selective, it will select the words that have an immediate application to their current circumstances. They will only retain a small percentage of what has been said. The main part of the word could be about the future, which may have been overlooked. Later on they will be in a panic over what they cannot remember. The enemy will try and convince them that the words they cannot remember are actually the most important part. So they may be living with a sense of disappointment for a long time afterwards.

Even worse, they may remember the bulk of the words but have retained little or nothing of the spirit behind them. Prophecy communicates spirit to spirit as well as speaking to our mind. There is a spirit to prophecy that sets it above all other communications. With prophecy I received many years ago, I can still receive the spirit impact of it on my heart. The spirit is eternal and we can still hear the spirit language of the Lord down through the years. We can read the written transcript of a prophecy, but if the Holy Spirit touched our spirit at the point of delivery, then no matter how many years later we read the transcribed word, our heart still retains the freshness and the power of the original word.

Prophecy is about communicating spirit to spirit, and I think we need to be sensitive to people. If we are going to prophesy into people's lives we should make sure that what we're saying is recorded. I carry a recorder with me wherever I go. If I didn't have it and God gave me something to say to a person, I would make sure there was a third person present with a notebook. I would want them to write down the detail and the content, but would really need the recipient to sit there and relax. What I want to come across to them is the communication from God's spirit into their spirit, because that will stay with them far longer than the actual content and the memory of the words that I said. They can have the words written down later on and look at them and read them and understand them, but it's the actual spirit of what God is saying that will live with them and change their lives.

We need to be sensitive to people. It's important to make sure that people hear, understand and can respond to what God wants to do and say, but they can't do that if I've just splurged all over them. I'm not actually being fair on them; all I'm doing is exercising my prophetic ministry, not for their benefit but for mine. Everyone can say it was a 'brilliant word', but it's actually done very little good.

Recording prophecy

We must get into a good habit of recording prophecy. A large percentage of Scripture is recorded prophecy, written down as it happened. The priesthood had secretaries; the army had recorders who faithfully wrote an account of orders and battles; and the kings and prophets both had scribes working with them as normal practice. The New Testament continues that tradition.

Isaiah was told on several occasions to write things on a tablet and a scroll (Isaiah 8:1, 30:8). Jeremiah had an assistant called Baruch who helped him to record all his prophetic words to Israel and Judah (Jeremiah 36).

As I've already mentioned, I carry a portable recorder and a supply of tapes everywhere with me. If we cannot do that, we must insist there is a third person present who can both record the word and act as a witness.

This is especially important if the prophecy we are giving is correctional or directional (see Chapter 5). Very general words of encouragement may need no recording; however it is good for people to have the option of how they want to receive prophecy. Given the option most people would want either a written or taped recording, so that they can concentrate on the spirit dimension of the prophecy.

Personal and private prophecy

I believe in personal prophecy; I do not endorse or believe in private prophecy. Personal prophecy is where individuals receive a word directly into their life and circumstances from heaven. Private prophecy relates more to the method and the practice. Taking people off into a corner to give them a word; or prophesying outside the remit of meetings and the accountability of leadership is poor practice which lacks integrity. It is what my American friends call 'parking lot prophecy' and must be discouraged.

We must earn the right to minister into people's lives. If we are living our lives in a godly fashion and are seeking to behave responsibly, we have nothing to fear from accountability. People must be protected, which is the role of the shepherd; we cannot violate that principle.

Chapter 5

Guide-lines for Handling Prophecy

In this chapter we are going to look at three aspects of prophecy: Revelation, Interpretation and Application.

We need to start by understanding the difference between inspirational prophecy and revelational prophecy. Every spiritual believer is able to prophesy on an inspirational level, especially in times of worship. It's the kind of prophecy that brings edification, exhortation and comfort. It is the kind of prophecy that refreshes people, that brings encouragement into their lives; it comforts them when they are in pain, it exhorts people to carry on following after God, it motivates their spirits especially to worship which is a vital part of church life. One of the most important things we will ever do with our life is to learn how to worship God. Inspirational prophecy releases the joy of the Lord; brings peace into someone's life; causes faith to rise and brings a reverence for God. All these things are happening at this level of inspirational prophecy.

It can become fairly innocuous. At this level, people, especially beginners, find it hard to distinguish between spiritual stimulation and soulish sentimentality. This can have a particularly negative effect on congregations and meetings. Generally speaking it's useful not to have too much in a meeting, otherwise it takes over. Often the prophetic person may do everything right, but the insecurity and inadequacy in leadership can be the major problem. Sometimes prophecy is unsettling because it can lead to repentance, change and new direction. We need to put some kind of control there. Sometimes I think if this level of prophecy becomes too common, especially in our public meetings, people learn to close their ears to the prophetic and they fail to respond.

God speaks to us prophetically because he wants to do something in our lives. In order for him to do what he says he's going to do, he needs some kind of response from us. We need to get into the frame of mind that whenever we have prophetic words spoken into our lives or into church meetings, there needs to be some kind of response. One of the major elements of the gifting, particularly in leaders, is how to interpret that response; what should we be doing? It's a skill and a gift we need to develop in the church.

Any prophecy that is more than inspirational may contain elements of correction or direction.

As a guiding principle, revelational prophecy needs to be checked out before it's given. I wouldn't dream of standing up in our public meeting and giving a directional word of prophecy. It needs to be worked through with leaders beforehand. Revelational prophecy needs to have the prior approval of leaders of the church, because there is a governmental principle at stake.

God has not given me the outright overall leadership of our church in Southampton. He's given it to Kevin Allan who is one of my best friends. We take it as read that I am serving the Lord Jesus with my gift, my life, my ministry. But I am also serving Kevin with my gift and my ministry. It's very important to me that Kevin succeeds in the things that God has given him to do. I want to be part of him succeeding. If it came down to a choice between him or me succeeding, I would want him to succeed. If there was only one blessing left for the two of us, I would want him to have it. This is what kingdom life is all about. I would have to fight him for it, because he would probably be wanting the same thing for me! We are in this thing together.

There should be no such thing as enemies in the church. If there are, then it's demonic and we need to deal with it. It doesn't matter if it's people against people, the origins of it are demonic. The enemy is against us and if he can turn one of us against another then he is winning. In order for us to deal with some of those issues we have to first deal with the enemy because we are not fighting flesh and blood. Then we have to work things out together because there should be no such thing as enmity in the church.

Look up in a concordance all the 'one anothers' in the New Testament: 'love one another'; 'honour one another'; 'provoke one another to love and good works'; 'pray for one another'; 'encourage one another'; it goes on – it's a huge list. That is church life and the kingdom of heaven, where we want the same attitudes in the church that exist in the Godhead.

The Father can say about the Son, *'this is my beloved Son, listen to him.'* He promotes Jesus as the focal point of attention: *'Listen to him.'* What does Jesus do? He walks with men and says, 'I'm only doing what my father in heaven is doing. I'm only saying what my Father in heaven is saying.' Then Jesus made an astounding comment to his disciples, *'it's better for you if I go away, because then the Holy Spirit can come.'*

The disciples must have wondered what he was talking about! Surely it was preferable to continue walking with Jesus? What does he mean … *'better if I go away?'* Jesus meant that the next phase of their lives could be better handled by the Holy Spirit. The Spirit of truth will come. The Holy Spirit who is absolutely brilliant at teaching us; guiding us; empowering, releasing and building the Body of Christ.

When the Spirit comes he specifically speaks of Jesus, revealing and magnifying him. Here we have the

Godhead; all promoting, honouring and preferring one another. They are all speaking and blessing one another and talking well about one another. They are each representing the others. This is kingdom life and it is this attitude and perspective that we need in the church. I am serving Kevin with my gift and my ministry; I want him to succeed over and above my own desire to be good for God.

Judgement before delivery

Revelational prophecy must be checked out privately before it is delivered publicly. When sharing a revelational word it is very helpful to write down as much as possible. At least try to encapsulate the main headlines of the prophecy. This will facilitate the communication process and make it easier for the leadership to understand and receive the prophetic word.

We can leave the prophecy with the leaders if we understand that the accountability for the word will pass from the giver to the receiver. The leaders must now give account to the Lord for their reaction and response to the prophetic. At the very least they must take prophecy seriously enough to judge.

We must leave the prophecy with them. We are no longer accountable for it. We may want to check on its progress as the leaders submit the word to the judging process. That is quite natural and normal, because sometimes the burden does not leave us with the delivery of the word.

However, we must take care that we display no sense of arrogance, or of checking up on people. Leadership in turn needs to be gracious and patient in the process. Both parties need a large measure of humility and understanding; we must be in fellowship together in the situation.

Failure to follow that principle can generate an awful lot of strife. I've had to work in the situation over the years as part of my ministry, of going into churches and healing the damage that has been done by prophetic ministry. It's one of the reasons I set up Schools of Prophecy, because there is much damage being done in local churches in the name of prophetic ministry. A very unhealthy tension can exist between prophetic ministry and local leadership that can be exploited by unscrupulous people and by the enemy.

Tension is often an ingredient in that particular dynamic. However, tension does not always mean that something is wrong; it can mean that something is happening. There is no movement without tension. I can be relaxing in a chair and reach out to pick up my coffee cup; the part of me that is in motion is tense whilst the remainder of my body can be at rest.

This is typical of the Body of Christ anywhere in the world. All ministries bring tension into the mix of relationships, organisations and human desire. We must be careful that when tension occurs, we take the issues which potentially may divide and put them on one side. This is a time to renew our friendships, allowing the oil of the Holy Spirit to ease away the friction.

Often the enemy seeks to exploit these times of tension, his purpose being to divide and rule. God has his own agenda too, which is always rooted in love, honour and faithfulness.

We must understand that the enemy cannot sustain an attack. We must allow the Lord to bring us even closer together in these times of trouble. The enemy makes the issue seem more vital than it actually is. The Holy Spirit seeks to elevate love and friendship to new heights. This is called the unity of the Spirit and is more precious to God than any issue.

We put the issue on one side for a given period of time. We intend to take it up again, but first our priority is our love and friendship. We renew our relationships, strengthen our love for each other and reaffirm our commitment to one another.

Only when this has been achieved to the satisfaction of the Holy Spirit, can we re-examine the issue. At this point we will discover that 90% of the time it has lost its destructive power to divide. The enemy cannot sustain an attack when the love of God is uppermost in our hearts. We are all capable, in the inspiration of the Holy Spirit, to be gracious and humble; loving and kind. When these aspects of God's character prevail in our hearts, then agreement is but a short step away.

Friendship has grown between us, we have fellowshipped this thing through and now we can look at the issue and discover it has lost its power to separate us. This is so important, especially with prophetic ministry because tension will usually be an ingredient in our situation. Prophetic people create tension. When God intervenes into our orderly, calm lives, this creates a tension. We need to know how to deal with that and how to fellowship it through. Otherwise prophetic ministry can be an open door for the demonic to enter our churches.

If the leadership are not ready or willing for it, the tension from the prophecy will create difficulties. Unfortunately, it is all too easy to dismiss the prophecy and cast the prophet in the role of trouble maker. It is an easy way out of a potential dilemma, and has been used on many occasions.

It is the lack of understanding about how prophecy actually works that causes many difficulties and misunderstandings. Unfortunately it is all too easy to simply blame the prophet rather than face the issue of change that prophecy often releases into the church.

There is also a tension between the 'ideal' of where God is taking us and the 'actual' of where we are right now. Prophecy relates to the ideal and paints a new picture, broadening our horizons and lifting our vision. Leaders deal mostly with where the church actually is now.

The middle ground between the ideal and the actual is called frustration! Both parties must occupy that ground righteously. If, as the prophetic person involved we move out of a sense of frustration with events, or rejection in the ministry, then it is easier to prophesy our own opinions. Also we must ensure that we are not living with any negative influences over our own lives that can infect the prophetic word. It is perfectly possible to have a positive word about the future of the church, seeing prophetically a new horizon, with new things that God is going to bring into the work.

However, our frustration and negativity can get the better of us. Instead of prophesying blessing and showing the new things of God to lift our vision; instead of speaking out the ideal and saying 'this is where the Lord is taking you'; in our negativity and frustration we speak to the actual whilst pointing at the ideal ... saying 'I have this against you, says the Lord, that you are not this!'

Leaders too can be at fault in this area. There is a need to care for our prophetic people, to give them love, accurate feedback, loving kindness and a framework of discipleship. Above all we need to establish a leadership that has at least a basic understanding of how prophecy works. I have often been amazed at how many times the leaders of a church hosting a prophetic conference have not attended the event themselves. It is essential that we know how to handle that middle ground of frustration.

We must understand too, that these guide-lines apply to everyone irrespective of our 'status' within the prophetic ministry. We must be committed to waiting for confirmation on prophetic words we receive.

Bring in outside perspective

Some friends in another church had received a number of prophetic words internally from their congregation. These words were directional and would create an agenda within the work for some time to come. The leaders had received so many words they were finding it hard to be objective and to judge them properly. They contacted me and asked me to wait on the Lord with a view to providing some external input into their situation.

They did not tell me anything about the content of the previous prophecies. They were seeking to use my input as confirmation by laying my external perspective alongside their internal prophecies. They asked me to come and give my prophetic input at a specifically arranged meeting.

I started to pray but found that what I was getting about the church was so specific and directional I called my friend and said I couldn't do the meeting. I knew I had the platform to go and prophesy, but the things I was getting were so specific and directional I needed him to hear them first, to judge and weigh. He said they were quite happy for me to do the evening as planned. I appreciated that but was still unhappy, so I asked to see him and the elders to discuss it and decide where to go.

When I met with the leaders and shared the prophetic words I had received, a terrific excitement took hold of them. Apparently not only had the Holy Spirit confirmed many of the previous words, he had also taken them several stages further on and actually given them a whole strategy for the next five years.

When the excitement of God's blessing had cooled a little, we realised through prayer that we needed to plan a prophetic evening for the whole church, in order to create an environment where the whole work could become impregnated with the prophetic word of the Lord.

That meeting, apart from being a brilliant success, has been a landmark; a watershed in the life of that particular church, which has seen significant growth numerically, impressive growth spiritually and now has a developing influential growth throughout the area.

It is a vital question to ask within any work, 'How do we introduce significant prophetic words into the church?'

Scripture has no clear guide-lines to offer on this matter. We are left then with two extremes; the purely spontaneous, off the cuff word, and the prepared, rehearsed prophetic input. Both are equally valid. Most times it is a question of both together rather than choosing one method over the other.

Much of the prophetic ministry in the Old Testament was certainly planned and rehearsed. Many prophets had secretaries and associates who were scribes. Jeremiah had Baruch to write out his words for him. If the Lord spoke to the prophet in Jericho and gave him a word for the king in Jerusalem ... then the prophet would be praying and rehearsing that word as he walked to the city. It may have been a journey of several hours or even days during which the word would be crafted by the prophet through prayer.

It is good to have a prepared framework of prophecy through which the Holy Spirit can breathe and add to that word in a spontaneous manner.

Directional words having been judged and weighed beforehand, can receive that investment of prayer, guidance and preparation from the Holy Spirit. The people feel safe knowing that directional prophecy has already been subjected to judgement. When that word is released it will create an immediate faith impact in the hearts of the congregation.

If we work the other way and bring a directional word into the work without weighing it first, then we will not get the response that we are expecting. Firstly, this method opens the church to the danger of non-accountable prophetic gifting sowing disorder into the work. Secondly, the response can only be muted because the word still has to be weighed and judged.

There will be a gap between the word given and the word being approved. Even then we will have to plan the successful entrance of the word into the hearts of the people. It is a little like giving a plateful of mouth-watering food to a hungry man and then whisking it away to be checked that it has been cooked properly. By the time he gets the food back, it may well be cold!

If we judge the word prior to public delivery, we can safeguard the flock and create an environment that is dynamic in bringing the prophetic word into the work.

The final point to make here is that even though I had the friendship, the relationships and the platform of trust to speak prophetically into this particular work without consulting the leadership, I did not go down that route. I wanted them to have the same courtesy in their church from a visiting prophet, that I would expect in my own work. Boundaries that are set by the Holy Spirit do not quench his ministry; they help us to fulfil his purpose. Prophecy requires a response. The method of delivery must correspond in some way to the desired outcome.

Revelational prophecy and character

Revelational prophecy brings correction and direction from God into the earth. If we aspire to this level of prophetic gifting we must take phenomenal care of our character; otherwise our gifting could destroy the church. Words of correction are concerned with the morality and purity of the work; that concern must be reflected in our own lives.

'When does a prophetic person become a wolf in sheep's clothing?' It occurs when we ignore character issues that God wants to deal with. Disregarding a lifestyle of accountability produces a nature that is ungovernable and not to be trusted.

The stakes are too high to permit people with a non-accountable gifting to speak into the church. The character of any ministry must be open to view and open to comment from mature people. It is a prerequisite. We have to earn the right to prophesy, or preach and teach into the work. Leadership responsibility is to guard the flock and set an example of humility and accountability that the church can follow.

We cannot insist that an individual's character is 100% right, otherwise no-one would be in leadership or ministry. We must however insist that there is a framework around their lives for the development of their character. There must be real progress in this area before people are permitted to move out in the ministry or take responsibility for others.

It is important that we allow others access into our relationships, marriage, sexuality, finance, parenting, how we run our homes, our ministries; to speak into these areas of our life. It is always the unshared areas of our life where Jesus is not Lord. The enemy is flying around our lives looking for a landing strip; relationships of openness and honesty will plough up any fertile ground where sin may grow.

It is only through the process of accountability that we come into self-government, and we learn how to police our own lives well.

What this means is that we become governable in the areas of life that really matter, those which are private. What we do publicly in meetings often has very little to do with our actual life and lifestyle. Meetings are the least important part of church life. They are important, but really ... they're not that important. What is going on in our homes is of greater consequence. That is where the Kingdom of Heaven is established or not, that is where the reality of the Lordship of Jesus is seen or not, not our public face in meetings.

Prophetic ministry becomes difficult if we lose our servant spirit in the work because it results in us hearing God for everybody else, but not for ourselves. Accurate revelation does not equal godly character. Just because I prophesy over a few people here and I hit the 'spot' every single time and it's accurate, it doesn't mean that I am absolutely wonderful in my private life back home. The two do not equate to each other and we must not fall into that trap of thinking that they do; that just because people get revelation, everything else must be okay.

Balaam in the Old Testament had a genuine prophetic anointing when he began, yet he led Israel into great sin. Saul prophesied by the Holy Spirit and drew exclamation throughout Israel because of the anointing. *'Is Saul among the prophets now?'* was a cry heard throughout the land. He was speaking some revelatory words which provoked that kind of response, and yet he ended his life being tormented by an evil spirit. The church at Corinth had tremendous spiritual gifting, but were publicly acknowledged as being a carnal church.

We need to be so careful with people in the area of character. We have a right to insist that a certain level of character is being demonstrated in people's lives, before we let them loose into any kind of ministry or leadership.

Whenever the Lord gives me a prophetic word generally about people's future or their ministry, it may make no reference in the word to their character or their lifestyle. God's silence on a matter of lifestyle and character do not imply his approval. Just because God doesn't talk about areas of our life to the prophet, it doesn't mean he approves of what is going on. I have found that every personal prophecy has a character application, whether it is referred to or not, because all prophecy has a moral imperative. We can have a prophecy given to us about our ministry, our future, what we'll be doing, where we'll be travelling, who we're going to be releasing and how God is going to use us. The issue is, 'how do we get there from here character wise?' because the one thing that will stop that prophecy being fulfilled is lack of character development in that individual's life.

There is a protocol to be observed here. When our people receive directional prophetic input about their lives, we must ensure it is recorded, transcribed and made available to leaders and mature people. Leaders must now ensure that in order to meet the demands of the future, any changes in lifestyle, life, character, morality and relationship with the Lord, are given equal consideration alongside any ministry development and the opportunities that the Holy Spirit will release.

People who continue in blatant sin whilst exercising spiritual gifts create this ever widening gulf in their personality which results in spiritual failure, emotional collapse, sometimes mental breakdown, physical illness, relational difficulties and quite often a complete moral lapse. If we are seeing someone with gifting and ministry emerging, we have to have someone who is there to shape up their character and their lifestyle. Supernatural ministry can mean a greater intensity of satanic attack and if we compromise our character development we can become an open channel for the demonic to enter the church. Jesus said in Matthew 7:15–23,

> *'beware of the false prophets who come to you in sheep's clothing, but inwardly they are ravenous wolves ... get away from me you who practice lawlessness – get away from me, I never actually knew you. You might have had a ministry but I never knew you.'*

We must inspect the fruit of people with supernatural gifting, both in terms of ministry and character. It is important then, that we are willing to have our ministry tried and proved. Even our good track record needs watching, we must not get complacent about the ministry. I expect my ministry to be tried and proved till the day that I die and I would not have it any other way.

> *'Prove all things, hold fast to that which is good.'*
> (1 Thessalonians 5:21)

Regular pruning nips problems in the bud.

Interpretation

With regard to interpretation, 1 Corinthians 13:9 says:

'we know in part and we prophesy in part.'

The revelation can be accurate, but the interpretation can be totally off-track. Sometimes revelation comes in bits and pieces from different people and God wants you to work together.

I had a call from a guy in a church where I had a lot of contact. He had a situation in his life which the elders couldn't resolve, so they told him to call me for my perspectives. Apparently they'd had some prophetic ministry through from overseas and this guy said to 'John' that he'd had this picture of him dressed in army fatigues, walking up and down a beach with a metal detector sweeping this beach. The following interpretation was given to John by this man: The beach was the church and God had given John a ministry in spiritual warfare to detect enemy activity. He would be deliberately looking for devices of the enemy (e.g. unexploded bombs, mines and grenades). God was going to use him to sweep through the church and detect all the enemy activity in people's lives. He was going to be used to defuse enemy devices; he would be surrounded by demonic activity in the world. This would make him a target and he would have to learn how to fight off direct demonic intervention into his life and family. Not the most cheerful word he'd heard!

The problem was that the interpretation brought a tremendous amount of confusion, fear and uncertainty. There was no progression in that word from any previous prophetic words John had ever had. There was no connection from that word to anything in his ministry that he'd ever actually done before. That doesn't necessarily mean it's wrong, but there was such a sharp divide there. He had no peace in his heart about it and one or two close friends couldn't witness to it. His wife was also extremely worried about it. Then things began to happen at home; his children began waking in the night screaming; horrendous smells would come out of nowhere. The children complained of seeing monsters in the hall and on the stairs, they sometimes felt a 'presence' which induced fear.

They didn't know how to tackle this whole issue. One thing they didn't do was question the interpretation. They thought maybe this was part of the price he had to pay for this ministry. When he called he could not complete our conversation without tears. I asked him for the picture revelation only, not the interpretation, and told him I would pray.

The Lord showed me this interpretation. 'The beach is the church and the Lord was going to use John like a metal detector.' However, the word metal was in fact to be spelled as mettle. John would be a mettle detector. Mettle is an old English word derived from the times of knights, armour and sword battles. It means 'quality of spirit, courage, temperament, to encourage a person to greater effort, to release zeal and determination'. Thus the old saying 'being on your mettle' is an exhortation to be the best you can be.

Far from John looking for enemy activity and defusing enemy devices (unexploded landmines, bombs, etc.), in fact the Lord was sending him on a treasure hunt! He would be sweeping through the church looking for treasure in people's lives;. the rich deposit of Christ's love and care; the heavenly deposit of gift, power and anointing that was in people's hearts.

Some of this treasure may be buried in some people under layers of sin; low self-esteem; unbelief and ignorance. However, John would bring it to the surface and clean it off, polish it and reveal the beauty of Christ. The Lord was giving him a ministry particularly on the fringe of the church where there are many people who feel they have missed God, have lost any significance and are going nowhere. The Lord would send John to detect what the Spirit was doing in the lives of these fringe people and bring it to the surface.

When I relayed these perspectives to the elders and John, the overwhelming feeling was one of ... 'that is the correct interpretation.' We could then move forward in prayer against the activity of the enemy, confident that these things were not part of the price for his ministry but that the enemy had simply taken advantage of his situation. Words are powerful, they create things. They can bring a blessing or a curse; understanding or confusion; faith or despair. As we took authority and spoke the right interpretation into John's life, we saw God move in his situation and return things to normal.

The revelation was absolutely right, but the interpretation was completely off-track. Do not be tempted to strive to manufacture an interpretation when one is not clear. Very often we find people have the uncanny ability to mould the interpretation they prefer around a particular prophetic word.

We do need to be careful around the prophetic. Often I've found the people that are the best at getting revelation are not necessarily the best at interpreting it. This is where in prophecy we need to work in team throughout the church. If we can get prophetic ministries to work in a team, particularly with pastoral ministry, that is a brilliant combination.

If we don't have the interpretation to a particular word, we need to pray with the individual that one will come. Sometimes I give words and have no understanding why I'm saying them. I am just being obedient. I have not received the interpretation, but I know I have permission at this point in time to give this prophetic word, so I obey. The person who is receiving the word does not necessarily understand it. Other people around them may say, 'we know what that means.' Sometimes no one knows what it means! So what we have to do then, is take that particular prophetic input and put it on a shelf.

We should encourage people to have a shelf where they put words that they do not understand or that have no application for where they are in life at that moment. God has spoken something, the fullness of which will be revealed in time. We are expecting an interpretation and a greater clarity as we prayerfully wait.

Many times I have had words that were delivered ahead of time so that people may, through a prayerful response, be made ready for what God is doing. Suddenly we are pitched into a set of circumstances which are now illuminated by the light of the prophetic word given some time previously.

I once gave a man a word that his job situation was going to change for the worst, where his boss would turn against him and make his life so difficult he would want to leave. The Lord, however, was going to teach him about trusting; standing his ground in faith; resting in the Lord and fighting the enemy. He was to stand still under God's hand through this time of testing and he would inherit a place of authority.

At that time this man's cousin was his boss and they were the best of friends. His initial reaction was that I had completely missed it. I encouraged him to shelve it rather than dismiss it. Ironically the prophecy drove he and his cousin, a spirit filled Baptist, to pray for the company and so for a while everything was even better. Several months after the prophecy his cousin moved to another job. The man who took over was violently opposed to Christianity. There followed eighteen months of hell in that place as this man took every opportunity to get the Christian fired. During this time the only thing the believer had to hold on to was the Lord's promise for the situation. Two years after the prophecy was given, the manager was himself dismissed and the Christian brother elevated to fill his place!

In the early stages of that prophetic word, when it seemed that the opposite was occurring, the man needed to keep the word safe rather than dismiss it out of hand. On those occasions it is a great comfort to know that the Lord saw everything beforehand. The prophetic word becomes a doorway from heaven to earth through which the Lord steps at the appropriate time. Being able to stand in our circumstances and declare, like Peter at Pentecost, *'this is that which was spoken,'* is a powerful weapon in our hand. The Lord is often amazing in situations like that; his kindness is incredible.

Application

A revelation, an interpretation and the application, can be given by three different people. That's why it's important that we don't look to prophecy alone for guidance and why we should encourage people to have a shelf, write things down and share them with other people.

Revelation can open up a whole area of someone's life. Sometimes when I'm prophesying I don't always know what's happening in the individual's life, but the revelation can open something up that the Lord may want to touch and deal with.

There are three parts to any prophecy. There is the word of knowledge that can open up the situation, the word of prophecy that can speak to it, and the word of wisdom which comes and says, 'this is what you need to do about it.'

Very often in the application, I'm looking for a word of wisdom, 'now Lord, what do we do?' We've had a true revelation, an accurate interpretation but where do we go from here? With the application I always want to be sure about who else is supposed to hear this prophetic word. I'm always trying to encourage people, 'you must go back and share it with your leader or a mature person;' someone else is supposed to hear this or read it. That's why I like prophecy to be recorded.

Are there any action points that need to be pursued? Every time a person gets a word of prophecy about their ministry, we have to talk about their character. Character may not have been mentioned in the prophecy, that's irrelevant, we still need to talk about it.

What about timing? We have to make sure people don't rush off and start moving out of their job into their ministry before confirmation has occurred. I've seen that happen before! People suddenly jump straight into the ministry because they want it now. However, generally speaking, after the calling comes the training. When there is a prophetic call on someone's life, they have to go through a period of training and development.

Are there any obvious conditions that the prophecy may actually allude to? We need to get people thinking about the whole thing of 'what do I do next?' Timing belongs to God. Preparation belongs to us. We have to cooperate with God in the preparation otherwise we may never see that time actually come into being. I prophesied to a man, some time ago, and said, 'you should have been in this ministry three years ago but you're not because you never took care of the preparation'. The word became a call to him to wake up, repent and seek the Lord.

If we don't take care of the preparation, all that happens is the timing keeps getting put off. God feels 'I can't bring this person in now, I can't trust this person with this.' We must pay attention to areas of our life in preparation so that we can see this word fulfilled, otherwise this word may never be fulfilled. There are so many people living with unfulfilled prophecy in the church today because we've never taken care of the preparation/response factors that God is looking for.

Chapter 6

Personal Prophecy

There has been some debate in recent years about the validity of one person prophesying over large numbers of people in a given meeting.

Certainly, one person prophesying over a large group of individuals would be the norm in a lot of places. Is it right or scriptural for one person to be moving in the prophetic gift for several hours in succession?

Scripture provides many examples of people receiving personal prophecy. However, it is fairly silent on the issue of whether one individual should be doing all the prophesying. It does not say whether it is right or wrong.

In my own ministry, I am constantly amazed at the levels of expectation that people have of those in prophetic ministry. In one conversation with a church leader who had telephoned to request a date for his church, I asked him what he felt he wanted me to do in terms of ministry.

Basically, his reply was that he wanted me to visit for several days, prophesy corporately to the church in terms of its vision and ministry, and also prophesy over all the congregation! I asked him if he wanted me to teach on prophecy and do some activation workshops to get people moving in the gift. His reply was negative, 'I want you to come and do it, not teach on it!'

I asked him a second question, 'Supposing I arrive and the Holy Spirit forbids me to prophesy ... what happens then?' There was a silence for a couple of minutes ... 'But you're a prophet!' he squeaked.

Actually there have been numerous occasions over the past twenty years when I have been forbidden to speak prophetically. The latest in the past twelve months occurred during a particular church weekend. As I entered the church building, I believe the Holy Spirit said to me, 'Under no circumstances are you to prophesy this weekend.'

The leadership put me under intense pressure both in very subtle and also very crude ways throughout the time. I felt strongly impressed to speak on the nature of church, real fellowship and relational unity within the local body. On the Monday morning, after one of the most difficult weekends I have ever experienced, I learnt that the minister was going to resign over the backbiting, critical spirit and uncommitted attitudes of the elders and the flock. Quite simply, he had wanted me to come in, wave a magic wand, and prophesy a change of heart to all his people.

Instead, I came in and taught from the revealed word of Scripture, what they needed to know. He confessed his disappointment in me and my ministry. The truth is, however, that firstly if we are not prepared to obey the revealed word, we often forfeit the right to hear a now or new word of God. Secondly, we cannot, and must not, treat prophets as magicians. Prophets are not here to pull things out of a hat, make things disappear or make miraculous changes in people's character without them having to respond to the Lord.

One vicar asked me to come and speak on a subject, (nothing to do with prophecy ... great!) at his church. After prayer, I felt led to accept. However, when I arrived he gave me a hyped up introduction about my prophetic gift, which made me feel uneasy. Then he proceeded to call people in the congregation to stand to their feet, ready to receive a prophecy from the prophet.

Suddenly it dawned on me that I was not there to speak on 'Building a Pioneering Church', I was in fact there to prophesy over all his worst cases! When I protested quietly to him on the platform, he informed me that the Lord had just shown him that I had received words for all these people.

My inclination was to close my gift down and leave the church. I agreed, for kindness sake, to pray for a few people. After the meeting, one man informed me that he had been telephoned several days before by the vicar, and told to come expecting to receive a prophecy.

It is absolutely vital that we establish guide-lines for having the five-fold ministry gifts in the church. These people are not magicians, they are not here to take the place of God. When one person is expected to come and move abundantly in the prophetic gift, we could be laying ourselves open to abuse. Continuous revelation without a break will cause tiredness, lack of concentration and pressure to perform, all leading to mistakes.

There are many examples of whole groups receiving a corporate word from one individual. There are also a number of examples whereby individuals have received prophetic input from the presbytery.

What is the presbytery?

The function of the presbytery has been quite varied when we examine church history. In some places it has indicated a board of advisers which sits during times of difficulty to give the church the benefit of their wisdom on stressful situations. In other places, it may relate to people who represent their churches at a regional level to the national conference when decisions are required. They may be part of a regional denominational team (presbytery) which seeks to reflect the views of the particular churches from that area.

However, when we examine the biblical function of the

presbytery, we see something different. The Scriptures indicate that the presbytery was a name for a group of people with a prophetic mantle who prayed and prophesied over people and churches as the situation demanded (Acts 13:1–3, 1 Timothy 4:14). This group can be the team of elders in the local church, or a group of several five-fold ministries who are present within the church for a particular reason or occasion.

As well as to edify, exhort and comfort, the purpose of the presbytery is to bring direction, bestow a clear call of God into people's lives, authenticate a person's ministry or role, and to impart the word of God or a blessing upon an individual. It can be used to set people apart for ministry or leadership; to enable individuals to find fresh vision and impetus in the Lord; or to bring prophetic direction to the whole work. Presbyteries can really strengthen the faith of the church and can be a focal point for the release of key blessings into the body of Christ.

During prophecy conferences, I always use a team of anointed ministries to act as a presbytery in that event, with the permission and approval of the host church leadership.

The presbytery, just like any individual prophetic ministry, is subject to the local leadership, to whom they are accountable for what they say. In this case, we need to determine who the 'bottom line' is in the presbytery, in cases of judgement or accountability. In my own cases, I act as the leader for the whole team, and this means I carry the can if something goes wrong. In the first instance I ask people to write to the team member first (copy to me), and if they get no help or support from that quarter, or they are unhappy with the response, then they can refer it to me and I will take it up on their behalf with that team member. On the other hand, if they are unhappy with my response, then we need to call in an independent arbitrator who can determine the issue and make an impartial judgement.

Prophets in the plural

In the Bible there is a lot of mention of organised groups of prophetic ministries working together. In Samuel's time there were companies of prophets (1 Samuel 10:5–10, 19:20). In the time of Elijah, a man called Obadiah (the king's main servant), hid one hundred prophets in caves (1 Kings 18:4).

There are a number of references to the sons of the prophets at Bethel and Jericho, which seemed to be two main teaching centres for prophetic ministry (2 Kings 2:3–7). Prophets (plural), came to Antioch from Jerusalem (Acts 11:27, 13:1).

> *'Judas and Silas, being prophets, strengthened and exhorted the brethren with many words.'* (Acts 15:32)

It does not say whether these 'many words' were corporate or individual or both! No distinction is made.

> *'Let the prophets* (plural)*, speak.'*
> (1 Corinthians 14:29)

In 1 Corinthians 14:1–5, Paul makes a number of observations about prophecy. He makes the point that speaking in tongues is an intensely personal gift, unless it comes with a public interpretation that will bless the church. He also seems to imply that there is a personal and corporate aspect to prophecy. *'He that prophesies speaks to men'* (plural), and *'He that prophesies speaks to the church'* (corporate).

The Bible, however, does have more to say about everyone prophesying rather than one prophesying over everyone! (1 Corinthians 14:24, 31). I firmly believe that the role of the prophet is to train, equip and release people into the correct use of the gift; to enable the Body to minister prophetically, rather than continually come in and prophesy over everyone; to bring the office of a prophet into the church alongside the apostolic in a building capacity.

Who needs prophecy?

Firstly, there are the obvious people. Those who are not doing particularly well and who may need a word of exhortation, edification or comfort. Local leaders must always examine people's lifestyle in determining their need before releasing prophetic ministry. On many occasions it is more important that people believe and stand upon the revealed revelation of Scripture than look at prophecy to 'hear' from God.

People get themselves into a mess most of the time by ignoring or disobeying revealed truth. We must encourage people not to treat prophecy as a shortcut to God. People in the New Testament Church should not have a habit of seeking a prophetic word every time they need to make a decision. They have the use of Scripture, the indwelling presence of the Holy Spirit, the fellowship of the saints, and a personal relationship with a loving Creator.

Continually seeking out the prophet or prophecy will consign us to immaturity for it is vital we discover the will of God for our own lives. If we cannot hear God for ourselves, how can we be expecting to hear God about anyone or anything? A relationship in Christ is our immense privilege and it is our birthright in Jesus. We must take care not to violate that liberty.

The Holy Spirit will lead us into all truth. He is our truth inspiration. When people come seeking prophecy, I normally will ask several questions regarding their relationship with God, their lifestyle and their prayer life. Many times I have been led to give advice and counsel concerning intimacy with the Lord and pray for blessing ... but not to prophesy. I have, over the past few years, included a seminar on 'knowing the will of God' as part of the curriculum, for the Prophecy conferences.

When is it right to prophesy and when to open the Scriptures?

The answer to that question, for a prophet, is always in asking for a context in which to speak. I ask the Lord for background information (hidden knowledge of circumstances); this helps me to determine whether I should ask the Lord for Scripture or a prophetic word.

One teenager asked me to pray for him and release a prophetic word because the enemy was really oppressing him at work, at home and in the church. He felt he was on the verge of breaking through into a new realm in God and that these situations were being used by the enemy to hold him back. He felt that a prophetic word from me would release him in the Spirit.

When I asked the Lord for a background check to determine context, I was shown several pictures. One showed this lad being late for work. His mother hated the early mornings because he would never get out of bed. The lad was often abusive and blamed her for his being late. Another picture showed me that his bedroom looked as though a herd of pigs lived in it. The third picture showed him stealing money from his mother's handbag. The scripture from Exodus 20:12, a commandment to, *'honour your father and mother that things may go well with you,'* came into my spirit.

I had to inform this young man that it was not the enemy nor people who were against him in his current situation. It was in fact God who was opposing him, on behalf of his mother. He did not need a prophetic word, he needed to repent and change his lifestyle.

Leaders, ministries, people doing well

All need prophetic input to help them do even better. We are in the business of raising up champions. Men and women of great significance who want to give their lives for the heavenly cause.

The great problem, particularly in the western world, is that we have developed a needs-orientated church. People are being inadequately birthed into the kingdom. The Gospel in a nutshell, is: 'Jesus Christ is Lord, what are you going to do about it?' People are not presented with the true claims of Jesus being both Saviour and Lord. People are presented with a watered down message that exhibits a Jesus who will meet all your needs and solve all your problems. This is patently untrue.

Not even Jesus made those claims about himself. He stated clearly that those who follow him will have opposition. We may lose our parents, family and friends. People will seek to imprison, wound or kill us for our faith. Believers must be prepared to lose their life (literally and figuratively), for Jesus' sake. He said openly,

> *'I have not come to bring peace but a sword.'*
> (Matthew 10:34)

and

> *'In this world you will have trouble, but be of good cheer, I have overcome the world.'*   (John 16:33)

The Gospel is trouble. It is also redemption, peace and forgiveness, cleansing, restoration and love. Nevertheless, the Gospel will get us into trouble (please God!), because it brings us into conflict with a world system that is anti the kingdom of heaven. So the need is to raise up people of real quality, who will make a stand and lead others forward. These people will always be under attack the most, because they represent a life that the enemy is dedicated to destroy.

The church makes two great mistakes in this area. Firstly, because it has a needs-orientated gospel, it spends most of the time in pastoral, maintenance and motivational ministry. The people with needs get all the attention, those who apparently have no needs get very little help or support. The people helpers in church seem to get the least help and support of all. The only time they get quality input is if they go down themselves. So we have a system that makes victims of our heroes.

Our second mistake is that we have almost no training, equipping or empowering structures in our churches. We are not actively in the business of raising up champions, people who can go further and do more. Prophecy has a classic part to play in this scenario. People who are doing well should be targeted for input, prayer, further training and equipping, and should also be on the receiving end of prophecy, specifically aimed in their direction.

If we are to prevent our heroes becoming casualties, we need to rethink how we use and support them. Continual use of a gift can blunt it. Prophecy puts an edge back into the lives of our loyal, trusted and committed people. It will help to establish them even more in areas of gift, responsibility and influence.

Prophecy can also release people from doubt and unbelief into seeing God's perspective. It can open up new opportunities to serve. It can increase the vision of an individual as well as the corporate man. It will give to the revealed word a sense of impetus that will cause faith to rise and expectation to blossom. Prophecy results in an enlargement, the creation of new room in our hearts for the Lord, for faith, for understanding and for service.

In responding to God's prophetic word, we must recognise that there are three characteristics that are true of all personal prophecy. However the prophecy is worded, it will always be either incomplete, ongoing and developmental, or provisional and dependent on our obedience.

We need to understand each of these qualities in order to see God's word fulfilled in our lives.

Prophecy is incomplete

The apostle Paul declared,

> *'We know in part and we prophesy in part.'*
>
> (1 Corinthians 13:9)

A word of knowledge is only a tiny, infinitesimal part of God's total knowledge. In similar fashion, a prophecy gives only a small insight into God's will for our lives.

Deuteronomy 29:29 says,

> *'the secret things belong to the Lord; whilst revealed things belong to us and our children for ever, that we observe to do the works of the law.'*

That is a lovely look at truth. God has things hidden, as yet to be revealed. The truth he does reveal to us, he expects to be owned by us. It should 'belong' to people and also to their descendants. Truth should be generational; handed down through our children. The whole point of having truth is that we make a response to it; we *'observe to do'*.

Prophecy is truth also; it reflects the accuracy of God's heart and purpose. He is truth, so anything that speaks of him accurately is automatic truth.

God only reveals what we need to know in order to do his will in that particular time and place. The things that he does not wish us to know, he keeps secret from the one prophesying. Elisha said,

> *'The Lord has hidden it from me!'*　　(2 Kings 4:27)

In other words, 'I don't know.'

There were many prophecies spoken about the life of Jesus by a wide variety of people. Many of them had different parts of the prophetic jigsaw to speak out. One saw him as servant under the affliction of the lash, enduring hardship and death; another saw the victorious rule of Jesus; yet another spoke of eternal reign and rule for God's son. There are times when continuous prophecies about someone's life are like a jigsaw. You need all the pieces to see the full picture.

Personal prophecy will not tell us everything. Often it will go into detail in one area, have a couple of comments concerning another aspect of our life, but may say nothing about other parts of our life. There are times when a prophecy may trace a number of steps or phases that our life may go through.

Oddly enough, a prophecy will give us positive highlights about our future role or tasks, but may say nothing about any pitfalls we may encounter. It may not refer to enemy opposition, people letting us down, or any crushing disappointments that we may experience as we attempt to be faithful to our call. Sometimes in retrospect, I have wished that some prophetic words had told me of the tribulations that I would face. At least I would have been prepared and perhaps more able to endure and challenge some situations.

Joseph's dream (Genesis 37), gave him no idea of the horrible turn his life would take after he recounted it to his brothers. It was whilst musing on the positive highlights of his dream which concern him ruling over his brothers, that he was suddenly flung headlong into a pit. From there the nightmare scenario continued, with his being sold into slavery and eventually ending up in prison, facing execution in Egypt. It was a long time, some 24 years, before he saw the full picture.

When David was anointed by Samuel to be king (in time) – 1 Samuel 16 – there was no mention of his spending half his life in caves with malcontents. It did not divulge that he would live with and work for the Philistines. It left out that his own people would pursue him all over the wilderness to kill him. The prophecy did not point out that he would feign madness in order to get out of a tricky situation, or that he would lose his best friend!

Prophecy always reveals a part of God's purposes for our lives. Do not despair if the prophecy fails to mention particular things that are of concern to ourselves.

The mercy of God never condones sin

If we have hidden problems, sins, areas of bondage or disobedience in our lives, and yet the prophecy we receive is wholly positive, we cannot conclude that the Lord fully approves of us and is condoning our sin, or the present state of our lives.

Moses was in a similar situation in Exodus chapters 3 and 4; he had received the prophecy regarding the deliverance of Israel from bondage, and the promise of Canaan as the promised land. This prophecy was also supported by demonstrations of God's power. The staff becoming a snake, and his hand becoming leprous, were both signs attending the prophetic.

Moses, after a little deliberation, eventually moved off in the direction of Egypt. Along the way, God met him and sought to kill him. Why? Moses had sinned against God by not having his son circumcised (Exodus 4:24–26). Moses, as the deliverer of God's people, could not have an effective ministry himself, if he had not fulfilled the covenant relationship with the Lord fully. Circumcision was a vital part of that covenant. In his disobedience, he had broken faith with God. So even though he had a prophecy and a purpose, he was still in opposition to God, because he had not obeyed the revealed word!

His prophetic encounter with the Lord had shown nothing of the hidden circumstances of his life. The failure in the prophecy to mention sin did not mean that the Lord was sanctioning his disobedience. Moses' failure to obey the covenant of Abraham had put him on the wrong side of God.

We have no doubt seen this many times in the modern church, where leading ministries are falling into sin. I have shared platforms with some people, have watched as others prophesied into their life, and yet several months to a year later, I have witnessed a moral fall that had its roots in ungodly activity, going back years into their life.

I have had close friendships and working relationships with key people who have fallen badly through immorality or fraud. The roots of sin had been strongly in place throughout our friendship, yet I had never seen or heard.

Looking back, I can see a common thread of behaviour in these people. They all believed that because their ministry was anointed and successful, because prophetic words made no mention of their ungodly ways, their conclusion was that God was not concerned about it!

Once that mindset begins to be entrenched in our thinking, we may leave the Lord no alternative but to shout things from the rooftops. Not one of those people confessed their need and asked for help. They were all exposed by events. Not one accepted the discipline of the church, nor any real humility. There was remorse because they had been found out, but also resistance to the outworking of new checks and balances on their lives.

Sometimes, prophecy does not speak into the part of our life that we want it to. It is important that we do not react out of disappointment. Prophecy speaks into that part of our life that the Lord may most want to stimulate. Therefore we need to pay attention to the Holy Spirit.

Sometimes our lives may be in a real mess and all sorts of trouble, yet the prophecy speaks a clear word about our future. Well, at least we know that if we allow the Spirit to move, we are going to get out of the mire somewhere along the way!

Prophecy is ongoing and developmental

The Lord will never speak the totality of his heart to us in a single prophetic word. Rather he speaks words that will give us a focus for now and the immediate future. As we work within those prophecies and allow our lives to be encouraged and shaped by them, we can see that prophecy builds from one word to another.

Each of the prophecies I have received, from a wide variety of sources which are mostly unconnected and unrelated to one another, have built successively a picture of where God has been determined to order and direct my paths. Each word has confirmed and strengthened the goal. At times a new word has been released that opened up a different horizon. Occasionally, the prophecy has re-emphasised something told me a long time previously, that I had possibly forgotten or was not living in its full strength.

When prophecy is ongoing, the concept that we need to understand is that the Lord is establishing a covenant with us. He does that via the revealed truth of scripture. However, he uses prophecy to do this too. Looking back, I can see the covenant heart of God at work in the prophetic ministry I have received over the years. To really understand this concept of prophecy, we must examine the first time it occurs in scripture. Generally speaking, the first time God does something, he sets a precedent. He provides a model, a pattern, a standard that can be followed.

The classic study in this instance is the life of Abraham, father of many nations, a patriarch and the one with whom the Lord makes a consummate covenant. Abraham is the model for a covenant relationship, so it is only right that we examine the prophetic words over his life. As we do so, we will see a distinct pattern emerge with each successive prophecy.

As each prophecy builds on the previous word, we will

see words of **confirmation**, words that **re-emphasise** previous prophecies, some words of **instruction** of things to do, other words that **re-establish** prior promises, and finally new revelation that opens up a different area of activity.

The **first** word occurred when Abram was seventy five years old. He was given a great promise that from him will come a great nation and through him all the nations of the earth would be blessed (Genesis 12:1–5). He was told to leave his present home and go to a land that God would show him.

Abram received a **second** word when he reached Canaan (Genesis 12:7). This was a word of **confirmation** that this land would belong to his descendants.

After he and Lot went their separate ways, Abram received a **third** word, (Genesis 13:14–17). This word **re-emphasised** that the land was his and his descendants. He was given **instruction** to *'look up and see'*, to all points of the compass and also to, *'go, walk through the length and breadth of the land'*. Instructions like this in prophecy are usually put in to encourage us to go and explore, take possession of what the Lord is giving. In this case, Abram was taking possession both for himself and future generations. He had to exercise the right of possession by obeying the instruction.

He also received new revelation about his nation, that it would be as *'numerous as the dust of the earth'*. Expressions like this are spoken by the Lord in order to expand our thinking. Most of our thinking is too small. Our concept of God is too small. Many times in prophecy, the Lord will use expressions that cause our mindset to grow, our understanding of God to broaden, and our faith in God to increase.

At the age of 83, Abram received a **fourth** prophecy. This word contained specific new insights, plus a re-strengthening and establishing of previous words (Genesis 15). Abram was childless and felt the pain of it. God gave him a word about a son, *'from your own body'*. A very clear word; your own son, not adopted, but from your own body. This was a **new** word that also carries with it a **re-emphasis** of a previous word. Previously, the prophecy said, *'as numerous as dust of the earth'*. Now his offspring will also be *'as numerous as the stars in heaven'*.

Again, there was another word **re-emphasised** from 15:7, *'I will give you this land as a possession.'* This was restated, but with the additional words establishing the territorial boundaries of the land of promise (15:18). This does make it all the more difficult to comprehend the unbelief and disobedience of Israel at Kadesh Barnea (Numbers chapters 13 and 14).

Not only did Abram's fourth prophecy clearly delineate the boundaries of the land of promise, it also identified the specific nations that would be overcome in the subjugation of that land.

At this point, the prophetic word stepped forward over 400 years of history. It foretold Israel's slavery, their deliverance from and the punishment of their oppressors, and their paid expulsion!

This whole prophetic scenario was sealed with a covenant that was initiated by the Lord. Progressive prophecy inspires covenant making. It binds us to the Lord and to our destiny. This type of ongoing and clearly continually developing prophecy, is a viable and significant part of the prophetic ministry.

At the age of 99 years, Abram received a **fifth** prophetic word where several new and important elements were added, (Genesis 17).

Firstly, he received a **new** word: *'be blameless'*. God was beginning to set out his terms for prophecy to be fulfilled. Secondly, there was a re-emphasis and re-establishing of the previous prophecies (Genesis 17:2–8). What is interesting, too, is that there was a triple emphasis concerning *'many nations'* coming out of Abram. This signifies the absolute intention of God! In the midst of this, Abram's name was changed to Abraham, meaning Father of many, which clarified and solidified the resolve of God towards Abraham. Every time he heard his new name, the phrase *'father of many nations'* would be hammered home in his thinking. In giving the name, God safeguarded the promise. The fulfilment was in the name and the name was the promise! Just like the name of Jesus – ask anything in my name and I will do it! (John 15:16).

There has been an **expansion** in this prophecy from father of one nation, to father of many. Again, the land was **re-established** as his possession (Genesis 17:8).

Also, there were new elements in this latest prophecy that were also **instructional**. Abraham is given specific details of a new covenant that the Lord was making with him. A feature of progressive prophecy is that it becomes more personal and intimate as it proceeds. There is a setting apart for God that is typified in the act of circumcision.

Also, for the first time in 24 years, Sarah was specifically mentioned as the mother of this promised heir. Her name change, from Sarai to Sarah (princess, queen, mother of a nation), reflected the fact that she was very much a part of all the prophecies spoken over her husband. She would bear the son!

In this prophecy, we see a good mixture of new revelation, confirming words, strengthening and re-establishing of previous words, and a strong element of instruction. All of these add up to progressive prophecy, that is ongoing and developmental.

The **sixth** prophecy (Genesis 18:17–19), was given in the context of Sodom and Gommorah. It appears almost to be an indirect prophecy ... not actually spoken to Abraham, but spoken in his presence. It is as though the Lord was speaking to the other two men about Abraham. I have included it as a prophecy because it did reflect the heart and intentions of God to Abraham. It is a fascinating insight into God's mind and shows his thought processes in line with the prophetic words that he utters.

In prophecy, we can have the initial excitement of hearing the prophecy spoken. Then we have to exercise faith in the ensuing circumstances. This situation shows the Lord living with the prophetic words over Abraham and owning them for himself.

In twenty years of prophetic ministry, I have met hundreds of people who let go of prophecy and took hold of their circumstances instead. I believe that the Lord never lets go of what he speaks. When he speaks, he creates. His word is event, it produces. He never forgets a prophecy.

In this word, we see again the **re-establishing** in v. 18 of the two themes, *'great and mighty nation'*, and *'in Abraham all the nations will be blessed'*. There is a new revelation aspect also in v. 19,

> *'I have chosen him, **so that he will direct his children and his household**, by doing what is right and just, so that the lord will bring about for Abraham what he has promised him.'*

This is the nerve centre of fulfilling prophecy. Our intention should be in life to do *'what is right and just'*. In that context God always fulfils his word, both the revealed word of scripture and his prophetic utterance.

What does the Lord require of us?

> *'To act justly, to love mercy and to walk humbly with our God.'* (Micah 6:8)

The **seventh** and final prophetic word occurred (Genesis 22:15–18) in Abraham's life after his test with Isaac, where he has to offer his son as a sacrifice. In all of our prophetic situations with the Lord, testing is a vital ingredient. The Lord has to know what is more important to us, our destiny and calling, or relationship with him.

The test is an absolutely crucial issue in the fulfilment of prophecy. When Abraham passed the test, the prophecy turned from being a promise to a fixed and ratified oath.

> *'I swear by myself, that because you have obeyed me, I will bless you.'*   (Genesis 22:16–18)

This prophecy was now taken into a new dimension, out of the provisional/conditional, into the absolute/unconditional. It **would** be fulfilled because God's own name (*'I swear by **myself**'*) is now at stake. Abraham proved himself, he has passed the test. It was now up to the Lord to keep his word.

In this context, again we see a **re-emphasis** of the same words that were given nearly 50 years before. *'I will make your descendants as numerous as the stars in the sky and as the sand on the sea shore.'*

There is a new element also in the promise that *'your descendants will take possession of the cities of their enemies'*. A reference to the conquest of Canaan and beyond. How interesting that their first battle in Canaan involved the conquest of a city based on a prophetic word to Joshua (Joshua 6). So the progression continued through Joshua's life. He received much of the fulfilment of Abraham's words about his descendants and the land. How wonderful, to fight a battle whose outcome had already been determined over 400 years before!

It is an amazing and powerful thing to be living in the unfolding of prophecy. To come to the place where, like Peter, we can say,

> *'This is that, which was spoken.'*   (Acts 2:16)

I am living in the unfolding of prophetic words spoken over me in 1974. In all of the prophecies I have received since, I can trace the progressive nature of God's heart towards me.

From Abraham's life we can see that many personal

prophecies can be given over a lifetime, in order that God can reveal his whole plan. The timing and fulfilment may be long and drawn out, taking many years. However, the Lord keeps the vision bright with progressive prophecy.

Abraham and Sarah waited 25 years for Isaac; David waited more than 20 years to be made King in fact; Joseph waited 22 years for his dream to be fulfilled. In 1976 I received a prophetic word that I would be working in America and influential in the national church scene. In 1992, after 17 years of waiting, prayer and preparation, I finally gave my first talk in America. Instant Christianity is the enemy of persistence. Instant Christianity will not endure the times of testing. Instant Christianity will never produce mature men and women of God.

Prophecy is provisional and dependent on obedience

There are no unconditional personal prophecies. Personal prophecy refers to the possibility, not the inevitability. If our response is poor and full of unbelief, or our lifestyle is one that continually grieves the Holy Spirit, we may not expect those prophecies to be fulfilled. At the least, the prophetic words may be remodelled or significantly reduced. It is possible that they be repealed altogether, as King Saul discovered, and also the children of Israel in the wilderness. There must be a high level of response and co-operation from the recipient.

That is why I believe that every personal prophecy should be followed up by mature people. If the prophecy does not mention any conditions, or the prophet does not give any instructions, then the leaders should pick it up and follow it through.

I have seen many instances when immature prophetic people gave words to people that concluded with the phrase, 'you won't have to do anything, God is going to do it all for you!' This is clearly unscriptural in personal prophecy. All personal prophecy has a moral imperative. The words are spoken to illicit a response, either verbally in lifestyle, or relationally.

The lack of that response can cancel a prophecy, as Israel discovered on their journey to the promised land from Egypt (Numbers 14). The whole prophetic word spoken by Moses in Egypt was cancelled and then reactivitated for the only two men who made a positive response – Joshua and Caleb.

God is continually monitoring our response to all his overtures through teaching, dicipleship and the prophetic. As my friend, Graham Perrins, said in the prophecy class of 1980, 'God is looking for a ... "because"'. The word **because** can signify that a positive response has been made that was anticipated, looked for, and expected. Alternatively, it can signify that a negative response was made that does not please the Lord and incurs a negative response from him in turn. It literally means, 'on account of' (your response); 'owing to' (your response); and 'since' (you have responded) ... then I will fulfil my part too ... or not, as the case may be.

In Scripture, we see that this word is used throughout to denote that people were either blessed and increased, or suffered loss due to their actions and unwillingness to obey the Lord and his word.

Again, let us look at the first time the word is used in this context (Genesis 3:17). Adam had received a word from the Lord concerning not eating any fruit from the tree of the knowledge of good and evil (Genesis 2:16, 17). Adam disobeyed that word and was evicted from the Garden of Eden because of it. **Because** he had listened to his wife and not to God, he was forbidden to remain in the garden. Everything that came so easily before would now be earned by sweat, toil and hard labour.

As we have already seen in the case of Abraham's test with Isaac, the word because is again the fulcrum point in his situation (Genesis 22:16–18). **Because** he has not with-held his son, then all the previous prophecies now become a yes and amen! At this point, the promise becomes a fact as God swears by himself that these things will come to pass. There comes a point at certain times in prophetic situations, when the conditional promise becomes an unconditional fact. The prophecy changes from promise to an absolute – cannot be stopped – reality; because *'you have obeyed my voice'*.

Interestingly, too, when Isaac was in a time of famine some years later, the Lord spoke the same word to him that he spoke to his father Abraham (Genesis 26:3–5). The word came true for Isaac **because** of his father's obe-dience. This is worthy of note. Some prophetic words are not just for us, they can be for our family too. I have had several words that the prophetic line will continue in my family through my children. That makes me examine all the more closely some of the words I have received in recent years. I jokingly said to a friend that I would have to live to be 150 in order to fulfil all the prophetic words I had received. Some of those words refer to my offspring and family. I have not come to any conclusions yet, but the possibilities are interesting.

Hebrews 6:11–15 refers to Abraham's situation and urges people, *'not to be sluggish, but be imitators of those who through faith and patience inherit the promise* (the prophecy).' It then cites Abraham as a positive role model in this regard.

Today, more than ever, we need such role models to exemplify the type of response that the Lord requires when his prophetic word has been spoken.

King Saul was another character who, unhappily for him, failed to receive the fulfilment of prophecy because of his disobedience. He defied some specific instructions given to him by Samuel (1 Samuel 9, 10). The result of that rebellion was that his kingdom was torn away from him (1 Samuel 13:13, 14). Again, the word **because** is a feature of his indictment.

In a second situation, a little later on, Saul again defied specific instruction given by the prophet. He was told (1 Samuel 15:3) to utterly destroy Amalek and put everyone and everything to death, including the livestock. His failure to obey that prophetic instruction was a further nail in the kingship coffin, culminating in him being told that his rebellion and insubordination was equal to witchcraft and idolatry.

> '**Because** you have rejected the word of the Lord, he has rejected you from being king.'   (1 Samuel 15:23)

Again in the New Testament, we see a reference to David, Saul's successor, as being *'a man who will do **all** my will'* (Acts 13:22). In Judah, Asa was a king who followed the Lord wholly (2 Chronicles 14). When outnumbered two to one by an Ethiopian army numbering a million men, he cried to the Lord. God heard his prayer, saw his trust and routed the enemy, giving him a great victory.

Later on, the Lord sent the prophet Azariah to give Asa this prophecy:

> *'Listen Asa, the Lord is with you when you are with him. And if you seek him, he will let you find him, but if you forsake him, he will forsake you.'*
>
>   (2 Chronicles 15:2)

There were other things spoken of, but this was the centre-piece of the word.

Years later, Baasha, king of Israel, came up against Judah to do battle. Instead of seeking the Lord as he had before, Asa sent gold and silver to Ben-hadad, the Syrian king, in order to form an alliance and make a treaty against Israel. The treaty was made and worked very well in resolving the problem. However, Hanani the prophet was given this prophetic word to speak to Asa:

> '***Because*** *you have relied on the king of Syria and have not relied on the Lord your God, therefore the army of the king of Syria has escaped out of your hand. Were not the Ethiopians an immense army? ... yet because you relied on the Lord, he delivered them into your hand.* **For the eyes of the Lord move to and fro throughout the earth, that he may strongly support those whose heart is completely his. You have acted foolishly in this. Indeed, from now on, you shall have wars!'** (2 Chronicles 16:7–9)

What could have been a time of extended peace became a time of war and bloodshed.

In Jeremiah 25:1–9, we see Judah being delivered over to banishment and exile. For 23 years Jeremiah had prophesied to the nation about turning away from evil. Numerous prophets had given similar messages. This particular word ends with,

> '***Because*** you have not listened to my words, I will summon all the peoples of the north and Nebuchadnezzar my servant, and bring them against this land...' (Jeremiah 25:9–12)

We can see the principles of hearing the prophetic voice and obeying the Lord are both vital for the fulfilment of prophecy. Prophecy is conditional upon our response.

When people prophesy that we don't need to do anything, that God will do it all, they are prophesying falsely. Mostly this occurs out of genuine ignorance. People misunderstand the Scriptures that say,

> '*you will not have to fight in this battle, the battle is not yours but God's.*' (2 Chronicles 20:15)

In this particular episode and with this precise prophecy, there were very definite instructions given that required a distinct response. Firstly, not to be afraid. Secondly, to march out against them. Thirdly to take up positions, and fourthly to stand firm. The prophecy did not say that they had to do nothing, it gave precise instructions which required obedience. There is always something for us to do in personal prophecy.

Another reason why people make this basic error in prophecy is because they do not understand the difference between conditional and unconditional prophecy.

As we have seen, all personal prophecy is conditional. It requires a response from the recipient. All personal prophecy has a moral imperative. The prophecy does not have to mention that we must be pure and not sin, that we must be holy and righteous. We take this as given. **Of course** we must be those things. The whole of the Scriptures declare these truths! We do not have to be restating these things in prophecy, though sometimes in particular situations it is helpful to mention specific acts of right behaviour which may be required.

For example, I once prophesied over a church leader that his leadership would go through a severe test both from within and outside the work. In this time he was to humble himself and keep his spirit clean. He was told that to meet an accusation with an accusation was to do the work of the accuser. He was instructed to be like Jesus who stood like a sheep before his shearers and opened not his mouth. Better to be quiet and get fleeced than open your mouth and become a wolf!

He went through 18 months of hell with all kinds of people, including many local church leaders, commenting openly on his work, without bothering to ask first. Rumours abounded, misunderstandings were monumental, yet he kept his spirit clean. Today, several opponents are gone, their churches closed. He himself has seen tremendous growth, to the point where he has the biggest church in the area.

The prophecy gave him strict instructions about his morality. Most personal prophecies will not do that ... they should not have to! Our lives are fixed on Scripture and the Bible is very clear about righteousness and godly character. Personal prophecy is provisional and conditional.

There is some prophecy, however, that is **unconditional**. It depends solely on God himself for fulfilment. Normally it relates to the overview of his plans and purposes for mankind as a whole. There are some areas of life that personal prophecies won't touch or change. The march of nations, the rise and fall of earthly powers, and the rule and reign of kings and sovereigns all comes under the overview of God's heart for the earth. He sees the end from the beginning.

> *'He sits upon the circle of the earth and its inhabitants are like grasshoppers ... he reduces rulers to nothing.'*
> (Isaiah 40:22–25)

There have been times when the Lord has spoken out his purposes for nations through his prophets, for example Daniel's interpretation of Nebuchadnezzar's dream, (Daniel 2:26–45). The head of gold on the statue was symbolic of Nebuchadnezzar himself, who was the Babylonian ruler. The silver chest and two arms illustrated the Medo-Persian empire which overcame Babylon in 539 BC. The belly and thighs of bronze represented the Greek and Macedonian rule under Alexander, which overthrew the Medo-Persian empire around 330 BC. The legs of iron symbolised Rome which conquered the Greeks in 63 BC.

The feet of clay and iron spoke of the splitting of the Roman empire into many nations, some strong, others weaker. The rock cut from the mountain represented

God's kingdom which would outlast and rule over all others.

This is an unconditional prophecy, because it depends entirely on God's power for fulfilment. It does not matter what these nations do or don't do. When God decrees a change of government, then the governments must change. Nothing and no-one can prevent that from happening.

When we look in the book of Revelation, the same principle occurs. We see the unconditional word of God occurring because of his incredible and inexhaustible power. Nothing can prevent the end times occurring in the manner in which they have been prophesied. Ultimately, all of God's enemies will be defeated, the nations judged, the Lamb will marry the Bride and there will be a new heaven and earth.

However, there is an interface between unconditional prophecy and the response of man which must not be overlooked. Things are rarely black and white, especially in prophecy. We must remember that the mercy and kindness of God is from everlasting to everlasting. He is both just and kind and will not turn away from people who are making the best response to him that they can.

The most common reference used in scripture to depict this is in the book of Jonah. The Lord decreed the end of the Assyrian empire and Jonah was despatched to Nineveh with the prophetic word. Assyria was a great and evil empire and the sworn enemy of Israel. The Assyrians were a cruel and heartless race who displayed their power with a terrible savagery; it is no wonder that Jonah chose to run in the opposite direction! Eventually he gave the prophetic word and to his consternation, Nineveh repented. Because of their response to the prophecy, the Lord changed his prophetic agenda and adjusted his calendar.

Fulfilment of the prophecy was postponed. Jonah was most unhappy, he wanted vengeance on Assyria, not mercy. The repentance of that generation did not transfer to successive generations, and so there was a gradual slide into sin and depravity. One hundred years later, the prophetic word first given to Jonah was now re-activated and given to Nahum. The Assyrian empire was smashed, its conquerors and tormentors were destroyed and the nation never rose to prominence again. Nineveh itself was so completely destroyed by the Babylonians in 612 BC that its remains were not discovered until 1845 (nearly 2,500 years later!).

Conditional prophecy depends upon man's response for fulfilment. There is always something for us to do. Unconditional prophecy, however, is dependent only upon God's power and purpose, which cannot be stopped. Occasionally it can be postponed for a while, but it cannot be cancelled. It will be fulfilled; the mouth of the Lord declares it!

PART 2:

Prophecy in the Church

Chapter 7

Judging and Weighing Prophecy

SECTION A – THE MAIN TESTS

We cannot be too careful when scrutinising prophecy. Scripture encourages us to *'examine everything carefully'* (1 Thessalonians 5:20–21). This can be quite an exhaustive process as there are a lot of things to consider.

To avoid confusion in having to read what could be an overlong section, I have split this chapter into two parts. The first deals with the **main tests** of prophecy, and features the main judging criteria. If the prophecy falls at any one of these hurdles, it must not be allowed to stand. Part one is the microscope section where we examine everything in detail. If the word fails, we must trace it back to source and work through the difficulties and anomalies with the people concerned, for their sake and for the welfare of the church.

The main criteria we will examine together are the following:

- The biblical pattern
- Does it edify, exhort and comfort?
- What is the spirit behind the prophecy?
- Does the prophecy conform to Scripture?
- Does the prophecy glorify Jesus?
- Is it manipulative or controlling? If so, what are the signs of manipulation and control?

- How do we handle negative prophecy?
- How do we apply the tests?

A basic grasp of Scripture enables us to see that within the New Testament church, the exercise of prophecy is not on the same footing as it is in the Old Testament. Under the old covenant, prophets were sometimes a single voice speaking a righteous word to a corrupt and rebellious nation. They were often hounded individuals, living lives of immense hardship as they shared the joys and often the bitterness of life with the people.

Who cannot fail to be moved by the life of the prophet Ezekiel? He was told from an early age that he was being sent to a people who would not listen. At the start of his ministry he received a prophecy that the Lord would make his forehead like flint (Ezekiel 3:9), and all his life, he contended with rebellion. He had to speak, whether they listened or not (Ezekiel 3:11). An object lesson here for any aspiring prophet who feels frustrated at not being heard!

In the New Testament, the prophet is essentially a member of the body of Christ. Therefore, he is obliged to function in fellowship and co-operation with other related members. This places certain restrictions upon him which are good for the ministry and for the body of Christ.

As fellow members of the body of Christ, we have a right to insist in local church, that prophetic ministries coming to us are held accountable for their gifting. We have a right to ask them the hard questions, such as, 'are they rooted in a local church?'; 'are they accountable within that to the leadership?'; 'is there covering for their ministry and gifting while they are away from home?'; 'what redress have we got if things go wrong?'. These are the questions we ought to ask. The very least we will find is that people may not come to the church to minister, which probably won't be a bad thing. If they do come, they may not prophesy, which probably may be even better. What we don't want is non-accountable people coming into our work and speaking the word of God, when no-one is speaking it into their own lives.

It is a brave man or woman who will put their head into that kind of noose. However, it should not only be the prophet who submits to that level of accountability. The evangelist, teacher, pastor and apostle should have accountability frameworks for their lives and ministries that are tangible and real. The problem is, of course, that it is not only the prophet who moves in prophetic ministry. An evangelist, pastor or teacher can move in prophecy and cause problems and difficulties, yet it is the prophet who often gets tarred and feathered! This is also exacerbated by the fact that all believers can prophesy, which increases the pressure on the prophetic ministry.

For many years, I have been conducting schools of prophecy throughout the world. In each new place, I have to fight through a whole host of suspicion, wariness, mistrust, subjective poor experience, and antagonism. In many cases, when I ask questions in return, I discover that I am the first prophet they have personally encountered. Most bad experience has come through poor body ministry within the life of the local church, or from evangelistic, teaching and itinerant ministries that have moved in the prophetic without proper lines of accountability being established. We will look at that issue in detail in Chapter 15, 'The Prophetic Partnership'.

In the New Testament, the prophet is obliged to function as a fellow member of the church universal, not as a superstar ministry, and we must insist on that. In all passages referring to prophetic ministry in the New Testament church, we read about plurality of prophets. It may not be a plurality in the local church, but we need to make sure that if we have any strong prophetic figures in the work, they are relating to other prophetic figures with whom we feel comfortable. Iron sharpens iron, and sometimes prophetic people need to be together to sharpen each other up within a process that is governed and accountable.

I have a number of people with prophetic ministries, within a variety of churches from across the denominational spectrum who work with me on schools of prophecy and at conferences. This has the blessing and approval of those local churches involved. In a number of cases, I have established prophetic guide-lines and practices in those churches and have been instrumental in the Lord redeeming prophetic ministries that had gone off the rails.

The implication in Scripture is that an individual prophet is a member of a group and, therefore, his ministry is co-ordinated with others. It is clearly and emphatically stated in Scripture that all prophecy in a New Testament church is subject to judgement without exception:

> *'Let the prophet speak, let others pass judgement.'*
> (1 Corinthians 14:29)

> *'Don't despise prophecy. Examine everything carefully and hold fast to that which is good.'*
> (1 Thessalonians 5:19–21)

The biblical pattern

There are two extremes of thought regarding prophecy in the church currently, both of which are wrong. The first extreme rejects prophecy altogether for today. Prophecy, it is believed, belongs to another time and dispensation. We do not need prophecy today because we have the Bible. Prophecy has been replaced by teaching, preaching and Bible study; which are deemed to be the only authentic means of communication from heaven to earth. The Bible, it is argued, is the sole means of revelation today.

The other extreme is that which accepts all prophecy

unreservedly without judging or weighing it. Of course, this is made more difficult by the actions and antics of some so-called prophets, who are locked into the 'man of God' syndrome. This attitude declares, 'I am the man of God, you must listen to me.' Any venture at accountability, request for explanation, or attempt at judging their word is seen as an insult to their integrity. I have come across many cases where the local pastor has felt pressured, intimidated and subtly bullied into accepting revelation. Many leaders are not equipped to resist these indirect strong arm tactics. In prophetic terms, we cannot allow an Old Testament hierarchy to prevail in a New Testament culture. Prophets cannot pull rank on local church leaders; the five-fold ministries operate under a team concept, designed to provide safeguards for the church at large.

The New Testament pattern is that we are open to the prophetic gift; we give respectful attention to prophetic revelation; we submit each prophecy to careful scriptural scrutiny; and we only accept that which passes the test. Most importantly, we deal with prophecy that does not pass muster.

We must be allowed to go back down the line to ask for redress when prophecy is dubious. It is the job of leaders to protect the flock. All credible prophetic ministry will understand and co-operate with that important aspect of the pastoral role.

Many leaders feel they cannot approach the prophet because it seems they are questioning their credibility as prophets. Others sweep the mess under the carpet because they know that confronting the prophet may be more trouble than the situation is worth. I believe the responsibility is on the prophet to establish the right kind of relationship with the local church during the visit.

Church leaders should be put at ease by the prophet's behaviour. We are neither lording it over people, nor going cap in hand with a subservient spirit. Lines of trust, love and friendliness should be established, which are rooted into a firm structure of accountability. Church leaders should feel at ease with visiting prophets; likewise prophets should feel relaxed and not under a microscope where everything they do is lit by a glaring spotlight.

Every prophet should have an established framework and routine of accountability. Every itinerant ministry **and local pastor** should be answerable to someone. A prophet by himself (i.e. with no answerable framework), is unbalanced. However, a pastor, teacher, evangelist and apostle by himself is equally unbalanced.

I want to suggest that more errors in doctrine and practice, more abuse in terms of control and manipulation, and more people's lives have been ruined by non-accountable pastors than have ever been damaged by the prophetic. In both denominational and new church cultures, the pastor's word is law and cannot be questioned without people being labelled as difficult or rebellious.

The answer always to mis-use is not non-use but proper use. Every leader and ministry must take it upon himself to establish lines of credibility and integrity so that the whole body is safeguarded.

Allowing prophecy without testing it is against New Testament teaching. It leads to abuse within the ministry, a discrediting of the gift in general, a poor model for local believers to follow, and frustration of the purpose for which true prophecy is given.

Although prophecy is supernatural, it is up to us to know how to handle it. In 1 Corinthians 12, Paul writes about the gifts of the Spirit. In the next chapter he tells us to use love as the basic ingredient behind all supernatural manifestations. Chapter 14 explains how to handle them.

Allow the prophets to speak and follow up with judgement. Be aware of the dangers of making any adjustments in the life of the church or an individual before the judging process is complete. Separate out what is good by

sound, objective testing. Deal with words that do not pass
the safety check.

Unjudged prophecy produces shallowness in the gift
and ministry. It encourages a poor model to be established, with a low level of ability flourishing. Unjudged
prophecy will allow the charlatans to grow fat and thrive
on our ignorance. This will mean that prophecy continues
to be treated with contempt and mistrust. This is incredibly damaging to responsible prophetic people and to the
church, because the work of God can step back from
ownership of this vital gift and ministry.

The tests

Does it edify, exhort and comfort? (1 Corinthians 14:3)

The true purpose of prophecy is to build up, admonish
and stir up, encourage and release from pain and discom-
fort, and to enable people to know and understand the
heartbeat of their God for themselves.

If it doesn't achieve that, it is not true prophecy. It
needs to fall within those limitations. If the effect of prophecy is confusion, condemnation, or discouragement,
then the prophecy cannot be accepted and in some cases,
I would suggest it needs to be forcefully rejected to prevent a curse taking hold on someone's life. There is a very
thin dividing line between the gift of prophecy and the
spirit of divination as we'll find out later. We have got to
make sure that people are coming into blessing in God,
and not into a curse.

The final purpose of prophecy is always positive, not
negative. Very often prophecy has to be negative. There is
a negative aspect of prophecy that is right and proper in
the economy of God. Jeremiah's prophetic ministry (Jeremiah 1:5–10), was to 'root out, to pull down, to destroy
and to throw down'. Those are four negatives. It doesn't
stop there, thank God! His ministry was also to, 'build

and plant'. Sometimes you have to pull down something in order to replace it with a positive. We sometimes need to have the negative coming out, because there are things that God wants to tear down, root out, pull down and destroy; but in order to replace them with something that he wants to build and plant. The first part can be negative, but the final part has to be positive.

It is important to remember that there is a clear principle regarding the ministry of the gospel; the exercise of spiritual gifts; and the use of leadership. The principle in all those areas is that we are building, building, building. We are edifying people, we are building up the church.

In all aspects of our work in the church, we are always in a building context. On two occasions, Paul wrote about his authority from God. In 2 Corinthians 10:8, he writes about *'the authority that the Lord gave me for building you up, not for destroying you.'* In 2 Corinthians 13:10, he says, *'for this reason I am writing these things,'* and he wrote some very hard and very difficult things to the Corinithian church,

> *'for this reason I am writing these things whilst absent, in order that when present I may not use severity in accordance with the authority that the Lord gave me for building up and not for tearing down.'*

So, although we have some negative things to say, the whole motivation behind those words is that we want to build the work up.

It is the same principle we find in 1 Corinthians 14, which deals with the correct use of the vocal gifts, tongues, interpretation and prophecy. The key word in that chapter, which is used on seven occasions, is the word, 'edify', to build up.

Test the spirit

The second area of test is the need to test the spirits.
1 John 4:1–3 says,

> '*Beloved, do not believe every spirit, but test the spirits to see whether they are from God, because many false prophets have gone out into the world. By this you know the spirit of God. Every spirit that confesses that Jesus Christ has come in the flesh is from God. Every spirit that does not confess Jesus, is not from God, and this is the spirit of the anti-Christ of which you have heard that is coming, and now it is already in the world.*'

Behind every prophecy there are three possible sources, the Spirit of God, the spirit of man, or an evil spirit. We need to keep in mind that prophecy communicates spirit to spirit, as well as speaking into our mind and our intellect. We need to discern the spirit behind the prophecy, before we discern the words. At the moment, in the church at large, it is the other way round. We look at the content of the words and we examine that, but we don't always examine the spirit behind what is being said. We must weigh the spirit behind the words, then we look at the accuracy. Prophecy must line up with Scripture and also the spirit, because there is a spirit to prophecy.

Even if the word contains some inaccuracies, we can still receive the spirit of the word and the spirit with which it is given. Then we can isolate the word and we can examine the content, and the accuracy.

During a ministry tour, I prophesied to a man in the Caribbean. The Lord showed me a picture of him at the age of eight. His mother had forbidden him to swim by himself at the beach. Disobeying her one day, he had got himself in difficulties in deep water. He cried out to God for help; a huge wave came out of nowhere and deposited him back on the beach. Running off home, he told no-one about his experience. Twenty years later, the Lord showed me all that had happened and I was able to encourage him that the Lord had saved his life at that tender age for a purpose. The Holy Spirit then outlined in prophecy what that purpose was to be. Later, the man came to talk with me to thank me for the word and to explain that he had a question. His query was that part of the word had been inaccurate. He had not been eight years old, but seven. He asked, 'Does this invalidate the prophecy?'

I explained about the need to judge the word by the spirit and Scripture, and the interpretation of mature, gifted people with wisdom. A friend, overhearing the conversation, asked him for his correct age at that time. He replied that he had been seven years and eleven months old, or 'nearly eight' as he put it. I don't think the Lord would mind me being a month out in terms of the detail on that occasion! We can receive the spirit of the word despite one or two slight anomalies on detail.

People who get hung up on accuracy and content **before** weighing the spirit of the word are liable to make huge mistakes. We need to do both. However, I want to suggest that as a priority we adopt the following procedure as a baseline guide. That is, if any of the following areas are wrong, then we must immediately challenge the situation:

- What is the spirit behind the prophecy?
- Does it conform to Scripture?
- Does it glorify the Lord Jesus?

What is the spirit behind the prophecy?

The testimony of Jesus (Revelation 19:10), that is, the word content, is the spirit or the essence of prophecy (i.e. the heart and the will of God expressed through people). Does it lead us to the feet of Jesus? We must ask questions about the spirit in which people are speaking, otherwise we could easily be deceived. Acts 16:16–18 deals with this very scenario –

149

> *'It happened as we were going to the place of prayer, a certain slave girl having a spirit of divination met us, who was bringing her masters much profit by fortune telling. Following after Paul and us, she kept crying out saying, "these men are bond servants of the most high God who are proclaiming to you the way of salvation," and she continued doing this for many days. But Paul was greatly annoyed* (or he was troubled in his spirit)*, and he turned and said to the spirit, "I command you in the name of Jesus Christ to come out of her," and it came out that very moment.'*

What she was saying was 100% accurate. The content could not be faulted; however it was not the Spirit of God and Paul was aggrieved in his spirit. He weighed the spirit behind the prophecy and was grieved. That was his reaction. If he had weighed the content and the accuracy only, he might have been deceived.

How many people and churches have been led astray by not judging the spirit first? Paul, at that time, was in a multi-religious culture. The girl's words were almost reverential, *'they are bond servants of **the most High** God.'* She elevated the Lord to people around. Also, her word contained some evangelistic overtones: *'they are proclaiming to you **the** way of salvation.'* We cannot fault the accuracy, but this is the enemy at his best; masquerading as an angel of light.

The counterfeit will always be close to the real thing, like the tares growing up with the wheat. The enemy has invaded the church with false prophecy as he has with false teaching, poor evangelistic presentation of the gospel, and a spirit of independence and rebellion, to name but a few.

One hundred per cent accurate; however it was not the Spirit of God. This same thing is happening today all over the world. In many cases, I have had to take authority over occult spirits and release churches and people from divination and false prophecy.

In the episode recorded in Mark 1:23–26, the demons said to Jesus, *'we know who you are!'* They recognised him before the disciples did but Jesus commanded them to be silent.

We must weigh the spirit behind the prophecy. Our own spirit will be a good indicator. The Holy Spirit makes his presence felt by his fruit. Love, joy and peace will be present when he is moving. Conversely we can feel uneasy and lacking in peace with some prophetic utterances. The words clash with our spirit and do not readily find a home. That initial 'witness of the spirit'; is an important guide; a demonic presence will make itself felt. The gift of discerning of spirits can also be used at times like this.

To be effective in the area of spiritual discernment, we need to understand the culture of judging and weighing. Firstly, that it is scriptural and right to do so. Secondly, that no person's ministry is exempt from the judging process. Thirdly, that it is not disrespectful or disloyal to weigh the words of others. Fourthly, that local leaders as well as international ministries are to submit themselves for judgement. Fifthly, that the judging process is vital because it removes any enemy influence, whilst cementing the purposes of God into our conscious minds.

Does the prophecy conform to Scripture? (Isaiah 8:20)

It is vital to note that we are building our lives on Scripture and not on prophecy. In the event of a clash, we always abandon the prophetic word in favour of Scripture, the revealed word of God. We must be especially careful that the substance of extra biblical revelation does not contradict the Bible, but is in accord with the revealed message.

Prophecy must not be used to establish new doctrine or practices. We must make a further distinction here. When talking about **new**, I mean previously **unheard of** doctrine and practices. As I mentioned in Chapter 5, 'Guide-lines for Handling Prophecy', it is possible to receive prophetic input that opens the church up to seeking God's word in a particular area in response to a revelatory word. The prophecy acts as a stimulus and a catalyst to receive the revealed word of Scripture, thus causing a change of practice or a new approach to life in God.

For example, I once prophesied to a man that God was calling him to intercessory prayer. At that time he had a deep longing to go further in prayer and was quite frustrated at his inability to progress. At the time of the prophetic word he had never even heard of intercession. In praying and talking the matter through with him and his leaders, we were able to point him towards some teaching resources that got him started.

It has to be said that this is a subtle minefield, full of devious traps and pitfalls. When in doubt, check it out! Prophecy should never be used to govern the understanding of Scripture. Never get carried away by remarkable accuracy in prophecy. We can get excited and thankful to God for revelational prophecy, however, the moment we step into teaching, preaching or matters of doctrine, we need to sharpen our concentration. Scripture is the dominant test of all doctrine and practice.

Sometimes, though, it can be difficult to put a prophecy alongside a particular Scripture. Some aspects of weighing prophecy against Scripture can be quite straightforward. Whenever prophecy contradicts or challenges Christian doctrine and foundational truth, then the prophetic must be renounced; that much is clear.

Then there are the greyer areas where there are no specific Scriptures that we can use to weigh the prophetic. We must do our best to weigh the prophecy against the general context of Scripture. Where does faith in this prophecy take us? Does it lead us to the feet of Jesus? Is it causing disruption in the body?

This last question is particularly difficult. What does a

prophet do when faced with immense needs in church people who are being governed by a corrupt and avaricious leadership? How do we bring words into churches where the chief problem is a leadership riding rough-shod over the people? Obviously we can speak to the leadership privately, but what happens if there is no movement? Do we opt for a quiet life, safeguarding our reputation, pursuing a policy of non-involvement? It is incredibly difficult to keep silent when hearts are being broken and lives ruined all around you.

This is the other side of the prophetic coin that most people do not appreciate. Where leadership is having a difficult time because of the hardness of the people, the issue is clear both prophetically and scripturally. However, very often prophets have to stand in a gap of a different kind. If we speak out we may bless and release the people, but we will open ourselves to accusations of disruption and labelled as 'off the wall' by the leadership. In most cases where the word of the leader is accepted, the opinion of the prophet is never sought.

There can be grey areas where there is no specific, clear word of Scripture to help us determine whether a prophetic word is right, and there can be a limitation in this area. If I give a prophetic word to a city, for example London, Frankfurt, Chicago or St Petersburg, what Scripture do I weigh them against? These places are not mentioned in the Bible; this is a limitation.

We must do all that we can to confirm or deny the prophetic by proper use of Scripture. However, we need to recognise that on some occasions this may be difficult to achieve. There will be times when the prophet speaks into situations which are not covered by the Bible. The word cannot be dismissed, nor authenticated by Scripture. We cannot reject and deny the word in these circumstances. We must submit the word to the complete battery of tests and see how it fairs.

To further complicate matters, there are situations

when prophecy is spoken into an issue for which people already feel they have an answer from the Bible.

I once gave a word to a man that was a warning not to take a job he was about to be offered, but rather to wait for the Lord to move. I felt strongly that the company he was about to join were not ethical in their business practices and he would be asked to do things that contravened his walk with God. The problem was that he had been unemployed for two years. The whole church had been interceding and were seeing this job offer as an answer to their prayers.

I arrived on the scene to do a meeting, knowing nothing of the circumstances, and picked this guy out prophetically. The church did not feel the word was a blessing. They even had Scriptures about this man's current job offer. He was encouraged to take the job; I was told I had missed it. Subsequently, a few weeks into his new employment, he was asked to lie in order to get a particular order. This continued for some time, causing havoc with his health and nervous system. Meanwhile a job that was within the scope of his capabilities came and went whilst he was out of town on business. It was advertised and snapped up within a week, while he was away.

He soon had to leave his employment because of the double standards, and was again unemployed. He found it difficult to get welfare because he had left work voluntarily. The church did not handle the situation well; there was no apology, nor any offer of help. There is now a disillusioned man with no job, no money and no church family.

In this case the church had been praying for months; people had received 'words' and Bible verses; a job had appeared to become available and an offer of employment was made. Everyone was feeling euphoric: situation over; chalk up another win. Into that mix came a word of warning that seemed to clash with the Bible verses people had received. I said at the time that the Bible verses were correct, but not for **that** particular job. They were correct for the second job opportunity, not the first. The prophetic word and the Bible verses were not in opposition. It was the 'timing' that was causing the difficulty.

The prophetic input I gave was judged on the basis that the church had received Scripture. My word clashed with theirs; they felt they had been praying long enough and that an answer had been given. Anyone familiar with intercession will know that it is the final furlong of a situation that is the most dangerous. Issues will seem to be on the way to being resolved and our vigilance and concentration is slackened as a result.

There is usually a period of vulnerability in warfare, prayer and intercession. Perseverance is maintaining a focus right to the very end. Always play to the final whistle. Let God be the guide, not the circumstances. The enemy sometimes has one final attempt before he gives ground. We can lose right within sight of the winner's tape.

Does the prophecy glorify the Lord Jesus?
(1 Corinthians 12:3)

The prime ministry of the Holy Spirit is to bring glory to Jesus (John 16:14). Any prophetic utterance, dream or vision should accomplish that aim.

Any word or ministry that exalts man's ministry at the expense of the glory of Jesus, must be considered unworthy. Prophetic ministry should also teach us how to hear God for ourselves. In this way we do not create any sense of dependency upon the ministry of the prophet.

Many people are often seriously disappointed and depressed when they fail to receive a prophecy. The main reason for this is because all their hope is in the ministry, not the Lord of the ministry.

All the five-fold ministries are given that the wider body of Christ may be equipped to do the work of the ministry. The pastor equips people not just to be released in counselling, but to be able to counsel others. The teacher expounds the word of God, but also releases people to search the Scriptures for themselves in rightly divining the word of truth. The evangelist not only handles missions and revivals to the unsaved, but also equips the body to do the work of evangelism. The apostle builds up and establishes the body of Christ and releases people into a process of self-government and church planting.

In similar vein the prophets speak the word of God but also release people to hear God for themselves. In each of the five-fold ministries, the central aim is Christ and his Lordship; the creation of a people who will come to fullness in Christ and grow up in all things to be like Christ the Head (Ephesians 4:13–15).

Is it manipulative or controlling?

(If so, what are the signs?)

Manipulation and control are two curses in the body of Christ. Prophecy can be used for these purposes: to make people do what we want; to get them on our side in a situation; for dishonest gain or ulterior motive. Sometimes, even just making people indebted to our ministry and not to Jesus.

The word 'control' has two distinct types of meaning. Firstly, it relates to supervising, overseeing, leading and guiding; the whole emphasis is upon governing well in situations. All aspects of leadership, from government of the country; management of organisations; church leadership; parenting and school administration; involve creating areas of control. In these cases, the control elements are safeguards designed to benefit others who are less mature, powerless, or in need of particular levels of help and support.

Secondly, its other distinct meaning is to wield power over; abuse others; direct people against their will; dominate and rule; repress and curb; engineer events and circumstances; manoeuvre people and exert a bad influence.

There is a very thin dividing line between the operation of these two distinctives. The only means by which we can walk the line effectively is through a process known as accountability. Responsibility and accountability are the two sides of the leadership coin. Without these twin characteristics, governments become oppressive, managers become deceitful and demanding, church leaders tend towards repression and lordly behaviour, parents become domineering and school provides a repressive regime. It is a principle of life and democracy as well as scriptural and godly behaviour, that all leadership must be accountable.

Sadly there are many churches and ministries where the leader's word is law. Fear of man has reached epidemic proportions in some areas of the body of Christ. All ministry without accountability is ultimately wasteful. A man can have a wonderful ministry for years and yet fall into sin or error because no-one is speaking into his life. The fall from grace of people in places of power and anointing is never just personal. There is always a corporate fall-out too, where people become embittered, hurt, disillusioned, not only against man, but also the church and ultimately with God.

It is into this mix that we bring prophetic ministry and prophetic revelation. We have to examine the motivating, driving force behind each person speaking prophetically.

Words are only a means of communicating spirit. Prophecy communicates spirit to spirit. In Hebrew, the same word is used for breath and spirit. There is a difference between the spirit and the content of what is being said. Both need to line up together.

There is a thin dividing line between Holy Spirit led prophecy and a spirit of divination, control and witchcraft. Control and manipulation have their roots in the whole area of witchcraft. The nature of witchcraft is to control. The nature of a wrong spirit is to bring control and manipulation. We need to be aware of any control being exercised through prophecy. Prophetic ministry is to bring release to people, not bondage. It enables people to find the will of God for their own life; it doesn't tie them to the prophet.

Galatians 5:16–21 warns about witchcraft being a work of the flesh, involving control and manipulation which can lead us into spiritual domination by the enemy. These are some of the areas of manipulation and control which can be exercised through ungodly leadership and false prophetic ministry.

Usurping the will of others can occur very easily in connection with prophecy. Without proper accountability, people get used to behaving like some form of oracle, although they do not have the blessing or the approval of God for that ministry. When humility goes out of our life, it leaves a big hole into which arrogance, self importance, egotism and complacency can descend to fill the space. If we do not actively encourage others to judge and weigh our ministry, we lose the sense of discipline and meekness which should characterise the life of the prophet. Moses was the meekest man on the earth at that time, yet he led a whole nation to freedom. Meekness is not weakness, it is strength under control.

Without it, we can confuse God's will with our own needs and desires. I received a call from some church leaders with whom there had been no prior contact. They spoke to me about a prophet who had been a great blessing to them over a four year period. This man had been wonderfully accurate and timely with his prophetic ministry and clearly they respected and admired him. However, towards the end of his last visit, he had taken aside one of the young women in the church, and prophesied to her. She was an extremely attractive woman and the prophecy told her that God wanted her to marry this prophet! The prophecy went on to say that as she obeyed the Lord, there would be tremendous blessing for her.

The leadership were in a quandary (as was the girl); the prophet had always been right before, he had a very good track record, yet this last prophecy really concerned and alarmed the leadership who were calling to ask my perspective. It is always helpful to get an external outlook on areas of difficulty. I have benefited enormously from having an objective frame of reference sitting outside of the day-to-day operation of the ministry.

In determining a way through this dilemma, let us take the most difficult path. Let us assume that the man is right and God does want him to marry the girl! He is completely out of order in going to the girl and prophesying to her alone. This is a directional prophecy which should be shared with the leaders first. They should have opportunity to judge and weigh the word. In these cases, leadership should act as a filter between the prophet and the people.

Moreover, this is a directional prophecy from which the prophet stands to gain something ... a wife! This is doubly dangerous and needs very sensitive handling and proper protocol. This prophet broke all the guide-lines for revelational prophecy. He should have spoken to leadership first, he should not have spoken to her alone, he should have recorded the word for the benefit of others. He did none of these things; he was out of divine order and clearly wrong.

What was interesting too, was there had been no declaration of love from the man to the young woman. The young lady herself felt a certain respect and admiration for the man, but no real love other than in a brotherly/sisterly sense. She was, however, very confused, because of the nature of his ministry, his excellent track record and the esteem in which he was held. Should she obey the Lord and trust that love will blossom? Should she marry a man she does not know personally and move away from family and friends?

Her will has been usurped. The power of effective decision making has been lost. She feels confused and frightened. Her distress revolves around two fears.

Firstly, the fear of obeying the Lord and ending up in a loveless marriage. Secondly her fear of not obeying the Lord and missing his plan for her life.

Even if the prophet is right, he has acted wrongly. The word must be renounced for the girl's sake. This subtle manipulation of her will must be broken. She must be set free to pursue her life and romantic involvement without fear. Had the prophet spoken to the leaders privately, they could have shared the burden and prayed effectively into the situation. The unfolding of love could have been allowed to run its course naturally, and the word of God could have confirmed the match once the relationship had been thoroughly established.

In this instance, we cut the girl off from any word of influence that would affect her right to exercise her own will. She is now happily married (to someone else), and has two children.

Pulling rank is another sign of control and manipulation. It originates in a superior attitude that will only receive input from a person of peer level. We can easily disregard the words of God from people we feel are not our equal. On that basis, Naaman the Syrian would not have been healed, had he refused to listen to a slave girl.

We pull rank on others when we elevate our status to a point where they cannot express themselves for fear of upsetting the man of God! There are many leaders who will not stand for being questioned. To ask for explanations or an interpretation is seen as rebellion and defiance. 'Don't question me, I'm the man of God,' seems to be the attitude. Some people deliberately cultivate a separateness, a distancing between them and the people; they make themselves unavailable for comment or discussion.

We must beware of **prophecy and flattery** which is another sign of the subtle manipulative process. There can exist a variety of soul ties between people, not all of which are good and honourable. A soul tie can exist between parents and children, husband and wife, best friends, relationships in the church, disciple and mentor. David and Jonathan had a good soul tie, as did Paul and Timothy. We are encouraged to allow God to knit our hearts together and our lives to be fitted and framed as one (Ephesians 4:16).

I have a number of people that I am personally discipling into areas of character, lifestyle, ministry and leadership. There is a tie between our lives that is right and proper. It is a spiritual tie and also an emotional link, because friendship is emotional. It is a soul tie; God is fitting us together and knitting our hearts. The very act of knitting is taking two threads and weaving them together. There is an inter-twining which takes place.

A soul tie is good where there is a flow between people of love, affection, blessing and a sharpening of each other's life and gifts. We want each other to succeed and grow in God, in order to fulfil his purposes. There is honour, dignity and a desire to both speak well of each other and want the best.

If I try to use a relationship to usurp another's will, tell them what to think, order them around or dominate their personality ... then the soul tie has become negative and I am moving that person into a place of bondage.

So, when the traffic from one person to another is solely one-directional, the relationship can become domineering and controlling. We have all seen overbearing husbands, strident wives, unhealthy friendships, domineering parents, and soulish, manipulative relationships in the church.

When one person tells another continually what to think, or how to behave, a bad soul tie exists. When an individual is afraid to take any initiative for fear of disapproval, then that is evidence of a soul tie gone wrong. When an individual captures another's heart by illicit means, then the soul tie has become warped. These ties need to be severed and deliverance promoted. The people must be set free to be themselves before that soul tie can be re-established properly.

Nowhere is this area more prevalent than in the relationship between men and women. There is a dynamic about close proximity between the sexes that can produce an illicit relationship all too easily. Bosses and secretaries are an obvious areas, pastors and administration staff another, the prophet and people can also become a disturbing relationship.

In prophecy we need to have a sensitivity to people and the Holy Spirit. We must have our hearts on the same wavelength as the Lord's. It is so easy in the context of the prophetic to tune into people's vulnerabilities and areas of weakness. I have seen so many occasions where men have simply tuned into a woman's loneliness or pain. With a few choice words we are all capable of detecting pain and sadness. If we are not careful, people will jump forward to receive much more than the prophecy!

A special relationship may come into existence between the woman and the prophet which can be exploited by the enemy. This is why it is so important for men (in particular), in ministry to be accountable for their sexuality. This will help us to avoid carnal relationships and the kind of 'soulish' activity which attracts and entices people. This is yet another reason why private ministry (one to one), should be prohibited. The sexual dynamic is too strong in some cases. It provides an opportunity for the enemy, and that is reason enough to abandon the practice.

Giving **dire warnings** is another subtle form of controlling people. When prophecy is used to gain control of people, it often carries with it an element of threat. For example, 'if you don't do what the prophet says, you may suffer terrible consequences' (your family may be hurt, you may lose your job, etc.). There is an implied threat that the blessing of God may be removed because we have not listened to the voice of the prophet.

The other more extreme and overt threat is that of

giving people over to Satan to teach them an appropriate lesson. The apostle Paul did not do this because someone did not rate his prophetic gift. It occurred because a man was persistently blaspheming, was resisting counsel, and needed to be dealt with on a different level.

The threat (implied or otherwise), is designed to elevate the ministry to an inviolable place where it cannot be opposed. Why is it that the delightful, 'come with us and we will do you good,' can become the more sinister and insidious, 'don't come with us and we will do you in'?

Not allowing any outside perspective is another form of spiritual abuse within prophetic ministry. This may often happen in leadership. It can be very unhealthy for people to be locked in to one person's viewpoint and have no access to the perspective of others. In the early church, we can deduce that it was never intended to happen. With their apostolic teams and missionary journeys, key people often stayed in a location for a prolonged period and so this type of abuse seldom occurred.

In today's environment of advanced communications and ease of travel, it should be even less of a problem. In all aspects of church life, we often need access to external dialogue. Every church should seek to be less exclusive and more open to outside comment that is reliable and trustworthy.

Prophecy is never a matter of personal interpretation. We must actively encourage people to invest in the opinions of others. Collectively our leaders should be talking things through with people who have an objective opinion and who therefore have no flag to wave, nor axe to grind. This is particularly true when prophecy has come to the corporate body of believers, giving direction and enhancement of vision.

Before a church embarks on wholesale changes in response to prophecy, it is wise to run a check by other mature ministries or prophets. When we forbid outside input, we have to rely on our own internal resources which may not be strong or wise enough to handle the situation. Exclusiveness is a great aid to deception. Openness, honesty and humility are great aids to the truth. Some leaders resist outside perspective for fear it will undermine their status and authority. If they are that insecure, they are probably right!

The use of the phrase **'the Lord told me'** can be very unfortunate. In a lot of cases, it is said by well-meaning people who sincerely believe that it is the right way to phrase the prophetic. In sharing a truth generally, a lot of people will say, 'the Lord showed me this'. If we happen to disagree with the person, it can be somewhat embarrassing for them to hear the words, 'actually what you've just said is not scriptural'.

Most people have no ulterior motive in using this phraseology. To the pure, all things are pure. Nevertheless, it does give the enemy an opportunity to manipulate something to our detriment. Mostly the use of the phrase highlights a degree of immaturity or insecurity. We are not always confident about revelation and how to handle it. We sometimes want other people to look up to us a little, so we use the phrase to give a boost to what we are saying.

However, the enemy is very good at manipulating words. If we use this phrase when sharing a general truth, the people we are conversing with may not have the confidence or the relationship to come back on something they disagree with. We can then assume that the revelation we are sharing is accurate and that we are hearing correctly. In this way a little kink of deception occurs which can be strengthened and developed over the passage of time. Deception does not come overnight; it is drip fed into our lives in small doses, over a long period of time.

Revelation requires accurate, sensitive and godly feedback. People must be lovingly corrected and an environment must be created in which good feedback can occur.

Where feedback is irregular or absent, then pride can enter in, causing people to become resistant to authority.

With the prophetic word, feedback is absolutely essential. The content, the heart attitude, the method of delivery and the results achieved must all receive comment, at every opportunity. What people have to say (the content), can be completely spoiled by how they speak it (the delivery), mainly because their attitude was not right. People need to be instructed in what they did right and in what they did wrong. Feedback is a vital part of the learning process which, if neglected, will only store up trouble for us later. The lack of proper feedback allows the enemy to put his hands on people's ministry and create disorder.

Young Christians and people being freshly inspired by revelation or the moving of the Spirit are a particular target for attack from the enemy. We need to allow him no room. The use of the phrase, 'the Lord told me', should be discouraged, until people are mature enough to handle its use properly and effectively.

Mostly, it is a style that we have learned or borrowed from other ministries. Instead, let us simply borrow another style that is less open to manipulation and control. To avoid confusion and even the appearance of control, it is best to modify our language. I believe it is more rewarding to use the much more humble phraseology, 'I believe the Lord is saying', or, 'I think God wants you to know'.

It is absolutely vital to identify the motivation behind the prophecy, in other words, 'what is the spirit of the man/woman?' Often the use of the phrase, 'the Lord told me', can be another sign that the individual may be trying to engineer something that is not of God. It means that the only way forward into clarification and understanding may be through confrontation. When someone declares, 'God has shown me', it gives the listener very few options. It robs people of the initiative to respond with a question if one is necessary.

People of little confidence will feel that they cannot possibly respond contrary to the prophecy. It can be used quite ruthlessly by some people. It can be a complete departure from the gospel of grace and kindness. The gospel is redemptive and prophecy is intended to liberate people into a wider expression of God's love. Most people prefix their prophecy with that phrase because they have very little confidence in the prophecy itself. They are trying to invest the message with an authority they themselves do not possess.

They are also trying to make it difficult for people to counteract their word. They are seeking to endow their own life and ministry with an authority that the Lord has not given them. As well as being incredibly arrogant and ill mannered, the constant use of this phrase may reveal an immaturity and an inadequacy that is quite desperate.

Revelation has a power all of its own. In general, it does not need to be prefixed with, 'the Lord showed me'. Our spirit will always recognise truth. The Holy Spirit, the Spirit of truth, has his own way of impacting our spirit with truth. He does not need help from us in this regard.

I am always amazed at people who use this form of expression. In many cases the needs of their own life seem blindingly obvious. If they are hearing God tell them things, how is it they have never heard some basic truths for themselves? Why didn't God tell that man to love his wife, or father his children properly? Why didn't the woman hear God say that worry, anxiety or bitterness should be exchanged for trust, faith and forgiveness? Why didn't those people hear God talk to them about giving financially, being faithful and committed, the need to stand with their leaders, the importance of giving the gospel to the lost, and about the Holy Spirit and his work amongst the poor?

People are selective about truth. We take on board things that will bless us and push away those truths that will cause inconvenience or disruption to our normal routine. If we are not prepared to hear the Lord speak the whole truth and order our lives on a regular basis, we should not dishonour him by prefacing things we do hear with, 'the Lord says'.

It is this kind of **superspirituality** that is anathema to God's Spirit and can be a major factor in control and manipulation. Where there is no grace, there is control. Where there is no love, there is an outlook that sees people as objects to be moved around according to our own purposes. We manoeuvre objects into places where they will have the most use for us, just like we place our home or office furniture.

It is a major crime against the body of Christ when we fail to see the value of all people; to look upon them as God sees them; to see the best in people and bring the life of Jesus to the surface.

A superspiritual attitude is hell-bent on preserving its own life. It seeks to make everything deeply spiritual and mystical. It cannot bear the thought of others knowing what it knows. It seeks to make the gifts and knowledge of God inaccessible to people. The very thought of equipping and activating the saints so that they can do the work of the ministry is an abomination to such people. The very root of this disease is found in control and manipulation; and in a desire to dominate others spiritually so that they become dependent upon our ministry. People with such an attitude need serious help to realise the love of God in a deeper way. They may require deliverance from inadequacy, insecurity and a dominating lifestyle.

Prophecy seeks to release people into the fullness of God's desire and purpose for them. Prophecy will always co-operate and be founded upon the glory of revealed truth. It is an awesome thing to sit before the Lord with an open Bible and have the Holy Spirit speak through those pages, bringing confidence, joy, real change, and renewal. It is a sheer pleasure, a great delight, to sit in a teaching meeting where there is anointed exposition of Scripture. Look around in those meetings and see the concentration and the joy of learning.

Revelation releases joy. The entrance of personal revelation has always left me wanting to adore Jesus, to kick off my shoes and dance, to shout with joy, to beam with pleasure in God's direction. Sometimes it's good to have the teaching before the worship so that when revelation has come, we might have more reason to bless the Lord.

How do we handle negative prophecy?

The gift of discerning of spirits enables us to determine the spiritual origin or source of actual events, or of the spoken word. There can be an immediate 'witness' in my spirit to something that is said or done. This must be confirmed in other ways too; by Scripture and by agreement with people of maturity.

Where there is no inner witness to prophecy, we must exercise our hearts more cautiously. In this caution, we are attempting to discover the following:
• Is the source of the word an evil spirit?
• Is the word originating out of this person's human spirit? Is it the spirit of man?

With words of judgement, we must understand that true prophecy does not produce slaves. Words that are negative, judgemental and condemning can create wrong fear. There is a fear of God which is right and healthy, but this type of prophecy won't produce that. A prophet must be good news, even if that news is 'repent', and words that highlight sin must contain a clear call to repentance. There is a way to deal with negative prophecy that is wholesome and positive and achieves the purposes of God. Revelation chapters 2 and 3 contain several prophetic words to the churches in Asia. They were not all complimentary! We need to note the context, the words and the response required from each church.

Revelation 2:2 (the church at Ephesus),

> *'I know your deeds and your toil and perseverance and that you cannot endure evil men and you put to the test those who call themselves apostles and they are not, and you found them to be false and you have persevered and have endured for my name's sake and have not grown weary.'*

That is good; it contains some good, positive contributions into the heart of the word. This is what you are like, this is why we love you.

In order to bring an effective word of judgement that will really achieve God's purposes, we must have an idea of the situation and circumstances. Negative prophecy must be rooted into the context of what is happening. It is vital that we understand the context, that is, how hard things are for the church or individual people.

We must give commendation to people in areas where they are doing well, or bearing up in a godly fashion under intolerable strain.

We can then highlight the area that God wants to touch and that will require change, giving a clear call to repentance. As we move on in the prophecy to the church at Ephesus, we see those distinctives emerging.

'But I have this against you, that you have left your first love.' It is negative. *'Remember, therefore, from where you have fallen and repent.'* Come back, change your mind, turn around, come back to God. *'And do the deeds that you did at first, or else I am coming to you and will remove your lampstand out of its place unless you repent.'* There is a double negative in the prophecy but the end result is, we want this situation turned around. We are speaking a negative in order to achieve a positive and that's very important.

The pattern in negative prophecy should be:

- Understand the context of what the church is facing;
- Express areas where commendations are relevant;
- Highlight the area requiring change;
- Give a clear call to repentance.

We can see the protocol very clearly again in the prophetic word to the church at Pergamum (Revelation 2:12–17):

> *'I know where you dwell, where Satan's throne is, and you hold fast my name and did not deny my faith, even the days of Antipas, my witness, my faithful one who was killed among you where Satan dwells, but I have a few things against you. Because you have there some who hold the teaching of Ballam, who kept teaching Balak to put a stumbling block before the sons of Israel to eat things sacrificed to idols and to commit acts of immorality. Thus, you also have some in the same way who hold the teaching of the Nicolaitans. Repent, therefore, or else I am coming to you quickly and I will make war against them with the sword of my mouth. He who has an ear, let him hear what the spirit says to the churches.'*

So we can see there is a negative there, but as before, the end result is this; we want to see this thing turned around and we want some positive repentance.

There is nothing wrong with negative prophecy if the outcome is to turn us back to God. Negative words that contain no positive way forward and just leave us feeling totally condemned should be resisted, or we may allow the enemy to get a foothold in the church. That kind of negative prophecy is ungodly, and it's unscriptural; it's unspiritual and it needs to be dealt with. Negative words should produce repentance, not condemnation.

We need to beware of those people who **prophesy their opinions**. They give a negative word that may contain elements of truth, but is really a platform for what they think. They tag the 'you need to repent' message on the end to give it some kind of credence. There may well be some areas that do require attention and it is always good to let the light of God shine, no matter who seems to be holding the torch! Never dismiss truth because you don't like the truth giver. Our allegiance must always be to the truth.

People add the repentance message on, in order to feel spiritual and safe. Any opposite response to their word can be called rebellion and disobedience; pride or arrogance. Some situations simply do not deserve the weight of that kind of prophecy and people will rightly reject that type of word.

Some people cannot differentiate between their own opinion and the word of the Lord; they cannot tell the difference between a righteous anger and the gall and bitterness of their own frustration. These people need help and support to enable them to mature. Again, the place of feedback is vital; we must not let people get away with things in prophecy, if we do we are storing up trouble for the church.

If we have a negative word to bring, there is a procedure to follow which will glorify God.

Firstly, we must get our own attitude right. Get rid of the plank in our own eye before sharing the word with responsible people. Secondly, come to fasting and prayer. This is a wonderful way to purify our motives and enable the Holy Spirit to filter out our opinions, frustrations and resentments. Try holding onto frustration whilst your stomach is growling! Thirdly, during this time before the Lord, we need to become obedient ourselves. Make sure we have nothing against anyone, put things right if we have problem areas with people. Finally, share the word with leaders and mature people, and allow them to judge it prior to it being delivered.

There is a peculiar responsibility in negative prophecy,

which we must carry out with integrity before the Lord. In lots of cases, he gives us a negative word as part of his process of bringing change into our own lives. If we find it easy to give negative words, then there is something wrong with us; we may require ministry ourselves. Be careful with negative prophecy; truth always rebounds!

I would not allow people to give negative words in the first few years of their development of the prophetic gift. We must earn the right to bring that type of word. We do that by our character, our service and by demonstrating our love for God and his church. It is good to keep people on a diet of edification, exhortation and comfort words until they really know the tenderness of God's heart toward his people. I would encourage such people to filter negative words through mature people who may well give that prophecy themselves if it is proved out. Of course, we can always credit the source.

Allowing a person to deliver a negative word should mark the change in their ministry and in their maturity. It is evidence to all that this person is 'growing up' in the gift and can be trusted by their local leaders.

There is a cost in giving negative words. It should not be easy; pain is involved; heart searching is necessary. Being right before the Lord is a pre-requisite.

How do we apply the tests?

When we go into the doctor for a full medical examination, we experience a battery of tests designed to check our fitness and health. One or two positive results do not guarantee a clean bill of health. There is a priority series of tests which are given to determine any major health problems. If we fail these tests, we are in trouble; we cannot proceed any further. It is a similar rule with prophecy. If the word fails these basic tests in Section A, we cannot take the word any further. We must go back down the line to the one who prophesied, to ask some specific questions and try to get some resolution.

In the medical, if a person gets through the initial major test series, they are subjected to another battery of different tests in order to determine the general level of fitness. Similarly, in prophecy there is a further series of observations that need to be made with regard to determining some of the finer points of the word. This second series of checks will enable us to determine what kind of word it is and the appropriate response we can make. It will also provide us with some idea of the wider issues involved in judging prophecy.

SECTION B – THE SUBSIDIARY TESTS

Section B will enable us to understand some of the wider issues with judging prophecy. In Section A we examined prophecy under a microscope to determine the main areas of testing. We can view this section as the magnifying glass segment. We are seeking to understand some of the finer detail around the word. The prophecy may have passed part one and so has been broadly accepted. However, it may need fine tuning so that any irritating or offbeat elements are screened out.

Section B is a final filter through which we strain the word. We can view this second section as **subsidiary testing** in order to refine a word that has passed the main tests. It will help us decide certain things that will enable us to present the word in the best possible light.

The subsequent areas of test and concern are as follows:
- Focus on the outcomes.
- Recognise all prophecy is partial; what part is the prophecy speaking into?
- What type of prophecy is it? Is it a now, future, confirming or new word?

- Distinguish between false prophecy and poor prophecy.
- Don't make adjustments too early.

Focus on the outcomes

With prophecy our main emphasis has to be on prior judging. With words of correction and direction, the prophecy needs to be checked out before it is delivered in the public arena. There is also a retrospective testing that goes on; because a prophecy may pass all the main tests and the subsidiary ones; yet may take years to be fulfilled. Caleb waited 45 years before his prophecy from Moses was fulfilled and he came into his own land of Hebron (Joshua 14). David waited 24 years before Samuel's word about being king finally came to pass.

In 1975 I received a prophetic word about having a significant ministry in the American Church. In 1992, after having prayed and believed God for 17 years, I finally was given permission by the Holy Spirit to take up some opportunities to speak. In all that time, we have to face the issue and the battle of whether the prophecy is true and if the timing is of God.

The temptation is to feel that if the word does not happen within a specific time frame, then it cannot be of God. This thinking can lead many people to let go of the word. I will deal with this aspect more thoroughly in the chapters on hindrances to fulfilment and responding to prophecy.

Suffice to say here, that we cannot just spend our lives waiting for a word to come to pass. We must get on with our life and be involved in doing God's work for now, whilst at the same time using the prophecy to keep us in touch with God's agenda for our future. Prophecy always gives us a prayer agenda. In my own circumstances, I continued to work in the United Kingdom and Europe, doing Prophecy Schools and building up churches. At the same time, I continued to pray for America. I continually asked the Lord to speak to me about that great country.

Now obviously when the Lord spoke to me about the American church, I had no outlet to speak those prophetic words. So I have spent many hundreds of hours in prayer, speaking those words back to God in confidence. The prophecies gave me a prayer agenda for the United States. When I first began visiting America, I was delighted to see that many of the things I had been praying about for years were now beginning to happen. Such things as embracing the apostolic ministry; understanding the role of Ephesians 4:11 ministries; cell group dynamics; non-religious Christianity; evangelism by church planting; the restructuring of church government; the fire of heaven falling on key ministries and churches; the purifying work of the Holy Spirit; the return to preaching the kingdom; and the training and development of the saints are all high on the agenda of the American church. The result of all that prayer is that I feel completely at home in the United States and have been received wonderfully well wherever I have ministered.

We need to focus on outcomes as far as time will allow us. Has the prophecy produced any negative elements? What are the positive things that the Spirit is highlighting to us?

> *'If a prophet or a dreamer of dreams arises among you and gives you a sign or a wonder, and the sign of the wonder comes true concerning that which he spoke to you, saying, "let us go after other gods whom you have not known and let us serve them," you shall not listen to the words of that prophet or that dreamer of dreams. For the Lord your God is testing you to find out if you love the Lord your God with all your heart and with all your soul. You shall follow the Lord your God and fear him. You shall keep his commandments, listen to his voice, serve him and cling to him, but that prophet, that dreamer of dreams, shall be put to death because he has counselled rebellion against the Lord your God*

> *who brought you from the land of Egypt and redeemed*
> *you from the house of slavery, to seduce you from the*
> *way in which the Lord your God commanded you to*
> *walk. So you shall purge the evil from among you.'*
>
> (Deuteronomy 13:1–5)

We must learn to work with prophetic ministry; both the gifting we are growing internally, and the prophetic input we receive in from outside the work. Internally we need to change the way that prophecy is administrated. The government of the church cannot be usurped and the flock cannot be damaged. Yet at the same time the word of the Lord must be given free rein, no matter how unpleasant the word of God is to the local leadership.

True prophecy promotes obedience at all levels of church life from the leadership through to the youngest believer. It should bring a closeness to God even if we have to turn 180° through repentance. The prophet and the prophecy must exalt Jesus and promote a godly response.

Accuracy in prophecy is not enough. Miracles, signs and wonders, are not the evidence of a true prophet. If any prophetic word is accompanied by signs and wonders, **we must still judge it** by the criteria we have established in Section A. The key issue is, where does faith in this prophetic word actually take us? Does it take us away from God's purposes, away from his morality? I know people today, who ten years ago were given a prophetic word that they would have a particular ministry and travel to certain places. At the time, nobody else really witnessed to it, but nevertheless they held on to it and they have now become isolated from the body of Christ. They are no longer in any church. They are in isolation, on their own. The outcome of that prophecy has been profoundly negative, but they are still holding on to it.

To a real prophet, the glory of God is absolutely essential. We live to see him glorified, honoured and his name uplifted. The model that John the Baptist displayed, i.e. 'He must increase, I must decrease', is the hallmark of a true prophetic spirit. We simply must glorify the Lord Jesus.

The primary ministry of the Holy Spirit is to reveal and glorify Jesus and we have to guard against any revelation that emphasises a person or a ministry more than Jesus. True prophecy always wants to reproduce the character of Jesus in people. It is always the nature of prophetic ministry. We've got to reproduce the character of Jesus. In my conferences I don't apologise because we hammer the necessity of character. True prophetic ministry has to be concerned with the nature and character of the work; the morality of the work; the righteousness of the work; and the holiness of the work because that is who God is. It is such an essential part of prophetic gifting. Romans 14:17 talks about righteousness, peace and joy being the main products of life in the Spirit. Ephesians 5:27 says that *'the fruit of the Spirit is in all goodness, righteousness and truth.'* Galatians 5:22, 23 speak about the nine forms of the fruit produced by the Holy Spirit.

Where that fruit is not evident in the life of a person, we must be careful. In Matthew 7:15–16 we are told, *'you'll know them by their fruit.'* It's important that in any kind of ministry, especially prophetic ministry, that we always insist on character before gift.

Does the prophecy arm rival factions? Is it divisive? Is it anti the vision? Does it speak against the leadership? There may be problems in the church but prophecy is not the way to solve them! Using prophecy in this way will bring the displeasure of the Lord down upon our heads.

We prophesy in part

1 Corinthians 13:9 says that,

> *'we know in part and we prophesy in part.'*

All prophetic words speak to only a part of our life and circumstances. It is important that we don't throw away any previous prophetic words that we have received. This latest word may be different from the others because the Lord is providing revelation for a different part of our life.

Where we are unsure about prophecy but we feel that the spirit behind it is good,we may need to put it on a shelf and wait. We should encourage all our people to have a 'Holy Ghost shelf' in our lives where we put things that we don't understand. It may be that further on down the line we can work it out. We can pray in the meantime and keep taking it down off the shelf; blow the dust off and bring it before the Lord.

Some prophecies have fallen off my shelf altogether. They were given by well-meaning people, but actually produced nothing in real terms. The Holy Spirit will always bring things that he has spoken to us to our remembrance by way of revelation through Scripture or direct through prophecy. This is not a problem to God and we can afford to be gracious to people.

Prophecy can be in part; sometimes because of mixture – part man, part God. The revelation was of God, the interpretation maybe had too many human insights. Prophecy speaks a part word into an area of our life that God wants to stimulate. That's why God speaks to us, because he's speaking to a part of our life that he wants to encourage and bring into life. This partial word may not speak to the area that we want! God knows what he's doing and he speaks this prophetic word into the part of our life that he wants to quicken right now.

I spoke prophetically to one man, that the Lord wanted him to love his wife more. She had been neglected by him as he pursued his ministry and the Lord was unhappy. He told me after the meeting that he had been convinced that God would speak to him about his ministry in the church. As we talked, I tried hard to show him that God had done just that in an indirect way. We are told to love our wives as Christ loved the church. The correct inference, I believe, is that if we fail to love our wives and give ourselves to them for their benefit, how can we love and give ourselves adequately to the church which is the Bride of Christ?

If a man cannot love his wife in a way that glorifies the Lord, has he any business being involved in ministry within the church? Sadly this man went away convinced that the prophet had missed it; he was disappointed.

We still need to keep our hearts open. We can't afford to let a sense of disappointment come into our spirits. We need to let this new area that God is looking at receive prayer and attention. God may be opening up an area of life that he wants to deal with and if God wants to deal with an area of our life, we need to let him in now, first time, because there's always inflation, especially in the truth. If God wants to touch an area of our life and we don't let him, we go round the wilderness one more time and come back to that very same point; that very same issue; that very same place. Like Israel at Kadesh Barnea, we come back to the very first place, but this time with inflation; it's going to cost us a little bit more to put it right. Why? Because we have had a year, maybe, of disobedience or whatever it is; the problem has got more entrenched in our life and it is going to be that much more difficult to move.

There is inflation in the truth, and so we must face what God wants to do now and let him deal with our lives. If we don't, it is round the wilderness one more time. God is open to reason! He may not change, but he is happy to talk to us. As the prophet Isaiah said,

> *'Come let us reason together, though your sins be as scarlet, they shall be as white as snow.'*

God won't change, but he is happy to talk.

There are different categories of prophetic words

All prophecy will normally fall into one of four types. We may even find that some prophecy can contain elements of all four.

There is a **now** word that will address us right where we are currently in life and ministry. It may refer to our past, but has implications for the present. It may provide us with an agenda for change and can be used as a catalyst for other people to minister into our life.

Remember, prophecy always provides us with some kind of agenda to work/pray through.

This is why it is so important that we share the prophetic word we have received with mature people. Prophecy is never a matter of personal interpretation. It may require other people to see the things that we cannot see for ourselves, and help us through. A now word stimulates the area that God wants to work in at this moment. Lack of response could mean our life going on hold for a while until we allow the Holy Spirit to have his way.

A **confirming** word will establish and strengthen people in what they know to be right. Continual use of a gift can blunt it. In these circumstances, prophecy is used to 'sharpen people up' again. People can become legitimately tired **in** the work. However, without some form of prophetic confirmation or encouragement, they may become tired **of** the work. I gave a word to one friend that was simply, 'carry on doing on earth what in heaven you are famous for.' It brought a renewal of joy and faith that released new strength and confidence in that person to continue the work they were doing. A confirming word builds faith because people know they are in the centre of God's will for their lives. It brings a fresh initiative and impetus to fight the enemy. It gives new heart and perspective in the slog of life.

Then there is a **future** word. it will speak about the next phase or the next few stages of the future. It will give us context and meaning to what we are going through now and what we are to encounter next. It has that essential link with the present that will tie it in effectively to our life. Although speaking about the future, it has a sense of 'fit' within the present.

It may map out a particular course as well as helping us to see that we are on course right now. It may contain suggestions for training and development, or areas of preparation, that need to be considered to meet the demands of the next phase.

It can be given in the present tense. For example, Gideon received a prophetic word that related to his future, although the angel of the Lord spoke it in the present tense.

> *'Hello Gideon, you mighty man of valour!'*
>
> (Judges 6:12)

At that point he was in hiding and feeling anything but mighty. However, as he responded to God, it actually became his real experience. God's view of the future is not the same as ours. His view, though, is just as sure and just as certain as the present tense in which he speaks, because he sees the end from the beginning. When God speaks, it is an event; it is a creative word that causes an event to happen.

Finally, we have a **new** word. The Lord has things in his heart for us that have never entered into our minds. We could never think or imagine it at all (1 Corinthians 2:9, 10). It opens up new areas and creates opportunities for us to serve God in other ways.

It is different from a future word in that a new word may have little or no link with the present. Sometimes it can be so far off into the future that it can be difficult for us even to comprehend it. In 1973/4, I received several prophetic words that said I would one day be raising up prophets all over the world, speaking to kings and governments and people in high places prophetically. At that time, not only had I never prophesied, I didn't even know what prophecy was, and I had never encountered the gift! However, within six months I had begun to prophesy. Twelve years after that prophecy, I began running Schools of Prophecy in Great Britain. Today I am doing prophetic conferences all across the globe and have spoken prophetically to Prime Ministers and people in high places.

Initially, the prophetic word was beyond my wildest imagination. I could not conceive it in my mind or heart. Yet it shaped the direction of my life from that point on.

Prophecy opens up new horizons; it provides us with a long term aim. We can use the prophecy like a compass heading, to keep us on track in the will of God. it will provoke us into seeking the Lord; requesting discipleship; pushing us into areas of training and preparation; ultimately it provides us with a long term vision which breeds a certain restraint into our lives. We cannot do other things because we have a particular vision, rooted in the prophetic, shaping our lives.

For years I drove from England to Wales one evening a month to be in the home of Graham Perrins, an anointed prophet and Bible teacher. Those times of study and prayer were well worth the two hundred and fifty mile trip in one evening! Graham gave me such a love for Scripture and Bible exposition. I was probably the quietest member of the group, but I would like to think that I have done a great deal with what Graham taught. I soaked up everything he said like a sponge, took it away and pondered it closely. Never did I just take notes and file them away at home. I worked everything through each month and came back for more. Graham was and still is, regarded by me as a father figure in my training on prophetics.

Obviously there are overlaps between all the categories, especially between a now/confirming word and future/

new word, and all shades in between. Some prophecies can contain elements of all four categories.

Examine the track record

I can appreciate that at times it may be difficult to apply this to the person prophesying. It may be someone who is just starting to move out in prophecy on a regular basis, or alternatively someone from outside the church with whom we are not familiar. However, in the latter case we must try to get a recommendation for their ministry from a reputable source if we can.

Asking for recommendations from others is an important and worthwhile thing to do. Leaders must always be protective of their flock. However, please bear in mind that it is not just the track record of the prophet that we should worry about. We need to examine the track record of all ministries: the teacher; the evangelist; the itinerant preacher; the deliverance ministry; the healing ministry ... anyone who has a public ministry needs to have a track record that is observable.

It is important to note with new people that we must be gracious and allow for their learning experience. Good quality and loving feedback is absolutely vital. Don't let them get away with anything, not even the smallest mistake. Do put every correction in the context of love, kindness, approval and a desire to see them grow and develop. This is called fathering. We must look to develop people in the prophetic gift and into the prophetic ministry. Please note these two are quite different! In terms of gifting, everyone has prophetic potential that needs development and training. However, we need more than potential to develop the gift into a ministry. We need hard evidence! We need positive proof that their words are coming to pass and that God is with them in a ministry capacity.

In Deuteronomy 18:20 we read,

> *'if it does not come to pass, it is presumption, God has not spoken.'*

People must have a track record of their words being fulfilled. If there is no confirmation after judging the word, or no fulfilment of the prophecy, we must go back to the person who gave the word.

Other people who may know us may witness to the word, yet that is not necessarily confirmation. A witness is a good indicator that will inspire us to press on in judging the word correctly.

Distinguish between false prophecy and poor prophecy

False prophecy at its heart is deceptive. It involves a subtle and often deliberate attempt to lead people away from the Lord. It may well raise up men and women in place of God. It will move people away from the vital place of humility before God that all of us should enjoy. Humility of heart is a major characteristic of any public ministry in the body of Christ. Some people confuse boldness with arrogance, or meekness with weakness.

Boldness comes from a confidence in God that arises out of our intimate knowledge of who he is and our inheritance in Christ. Meekness is simply strength under control. Humility and confidence go together. They are both sides of the same coin. Sadly we seldom see them paired together in people.

A humble heart is one that is dedicated to the truth, however costly. It seeks out the truth like a lover. False prophecy creates idols often by putting something or someone in between the people and God. Anything in prophecy that makes God one step removed from his people must be disregarded.

Poor prophecy on the other hand, needs to be understood. Prophecy can be impure because it mixes our own thoughts and opinions so that the word can become distorted. People can put some padding around the word that can devalue the prophecy. A lot of this can be attributed to style and upbringing. If we live amongst people who are long-winded in prophecy, we may well take on those characteristics. If that is the case, we may not know how to handle a short word from God. Some of the most profound words I have spoken have been one-sentence prophecies.

Sometimes prophecy can be poor because we have borrowed a style and a language from someone else. In some Pentecostal circles, I am not regarded prophetically because my style is so different. I do not clamp my hand on people's heads, roar some prophetic words in an archaic language with spittle flying everywhere! I use the same language and tone of voice in prophecy that I do over dinner. Let us try to be ourselves. We are normal people in touch with a supernatural God. When we really touch God's heart completely, we discover that he is the most normal, sane, well balanced person in the universe. Except when he isn't!

After all, who would send one elderly gentleman into the most occult kingdom on the face of the earth, to speak to a despotic ruler, and demand that three million people be released from bondage to go and serve their God? Who else would reduce one man's army from 32,000 to 300, just to give the enemy a fighting chance? Who else would instruct an army general to order his men to keep quiet whilst walking around a city for a week, then get them to shout on the seventh day, after which all the walls would fall down!

Get the message? God is normal, except when he is

being extra-ordinary. We misunderstand God so much. This is seen particularly in how we handle the prophetic.

Some people have to dress up their prophecy in fancy language; or by raising the volume; or by speaking for a certain length of time. This is not evidence of the Holy Spirit.

Weak prophecy can also occur. This happens when we move out on a feeling or just a couple of words. There is a school of thought that says, 'if all you have are a couple of words, then you must step out in faith, open your mouth, and God will fill it.'

They often quote the verses of Mark 10:18–20, Luke 12:11, 12 and Luke 21:12–15, which at first glance seem to say, 'take no thought for what you should say, I will be with your mouth.' However, we take these Scripture out of context when we use them in connection with prophecy. All these Scriptures clearly refer to situations where people are being dragged before synagogues and rulers who are demanding an explanation for the preaching of the Gospel. In those circumstances, God will give us wisdom (not prophecy!), that will be difficult to resist. It is the same promise that God gave Moses (Exodus 4:10–12), in connection with instructing Pharaoh to release Israel.

Many people think it is wrong to plan or rehearse the prophetic. Clearly we cannot manufacture prophecy, but then neither should we kiss our brains goodbye! The definition of a lot of prophecy in this post charismatic era is, 'an empty thought passing through an empty head!'

In the Old Testament, if God spoke to the prophet in Beersheba and gave him a word for the King at Jerusalem, it would have taken him several days to get there. In all that time he probably prayed, rehearsed and planned the delivery of that word, particularly if the word to the king was not very encouraging . . . it could mean the prophet losing his head. He might even have written it out before he got there! Over a third of the Old Testament is prophecy, written down and recorded.

There is a place for spontaneous prophecy. However, the Scripture has at least as much to say about planned and rehearsed prophecy. The reality is, that we need both methods to be judged and weighed effectively. One is not better than the other; they are both different.

Everyone has to grow up through the baby phase of moving in prophecy. This mindset thinks that because our heart is pounding like a trip hammer, because our palms are sweaty, because our hair is standing up on the back of our necks, because we have these few words going around in our mind, and because we have this sense of the presence of God ... then we must step out and speak!

We must always ask for God's permission to speak

Never assume! Very often, in my experience, when I have encountered those same feelings, it has simply been God trying to get my attention. It is often his way of letting me know that he wants to say something to me personally. It does not indicate at this point that he wants to speak through me to others!

Our priority is to ask the Lord, 'what are you saying to me?' Or as Samuel was instructed to say, *'speak Lord, your servant is listening'* (1 Samuel 3:10).

We may have to determine some things at this time. Is this personal? Is it for someone else here? Is it for the whole church? Is it correctional, or directional, or simply inspirational? What type of word is it ... a now word; a future one; if it is a confirming word then what is it authenticating; or is it a new word? Does it fit in with the meeting? Does it cut across the meeting? Does it have any negative element or warning? There are so many things to think about here. The crucial issue which will often cut across all the questions is ... 'do I have permission to speak now?'

On numerous occasions the power of the Holy Spirit has come upon me in my own congregation; sometimes so strongly I can barely stand up. The Spirit has begun showing me several things; sometimes there has been a complete understanding; at other times a partial revelation for the church; on many occasions the Lord did not give me permission to speak that word in that meeting.

Sometimes he wanted me to go away and pray about the revelation for several days/weeks. At other times, the revelation birthed a time of fasting and intercession for the situation. I never got to speak some prophetic words, because my job at that time was to intercede only. Prophecy always gives us a prayer agenda.

On some occasions I received a strong prophetic revelation in my own church, but had no freedom to speak. Several weeks later, after much prayer, I delivered that same word to another church, thousands of miles away on another continent. It exactly fitted their circumstances.

My point is this: if we move out solely on the basis of something we feel, or because we have a few phrases or a picture, we may end up in front of a microphone with precious little to say. To cover our embarrassment, we may turn to volume or repetition to pad out our 'word' and make it more acceptable.

It usually results in individuals talking subjectively about how they 'feel'. The prophecy becomes weak as it moves into a more soulish dimension. We, ourselves, are in the grip of something powerful, but cannot articulate at this point what we are seeing or feeling. It could simply be a matter of timing and not having sought permission to speak. The prophecy floats over the heads of the congregation and never finds a home, leaving them confused and ourselves discouraged.

The Lord may simply be saying to us, 'I want to speak to you ... come aside!'

We have all had situations where someone has spoken 'prophetically' and a spirit of 'naffness' has descended on the meeting, causing some embarrassment. For the uninitiated, the word 'naff' is a good old English expression which indicates that something with a 'high cringe factor' has just taken place! This is weak prophecy. Mostly it occurs towards the end of a meeting. It can cause some confusion. I want to suggest that possibly this week's last minute 'prophecy' that didn't achieve anything could in fact be the word that we use to begin next week's meeting. In the intervening period, we have a week to pray, polish the word and discuss with the leaders what we believe the Lord is saying.

Sadly, it seems that in the process of bringing prophecy into the church, **many people** seem to kiss their brains goodbye. Rather than educating the **whole** church (leaders included), about prophetic protocol, all we see is the introduction of platform policemen whose main role is to discourage oddball prophecies from being heard. More about them in Chapter 14.

In distinguishing between false prophecy and poor prophecy delivered by immature gifting, we will not make the mistake of rejecting a prophecy because of the vessel that brought the word.

Our embarrassment at the method of prophetic delivery will not deter us from hearing the truth it may contain. It is a well-known fact that the enemy will use all means possible to prevent us receiving input from the mouth and heart of God.

Subsidiary testing helps us to shape the mouthpiece as well as the prophecy. We intend to produce people who can hear accurately and deliver properly the prophetic word. Section B will provide us with a few guidelines as part of the process of judging the word and the giver.

Don't make any adjustments

It is important not to make any adjustments before the judging process is complete. We need to wait for confirmation that, a) the word is right; and b) that the timing is **now**.

The word may well be right and correct, but the timing could be several years or more later. The critical question in this instance nearly always surrounds character and preparation. More about this in Chapter 9.

It is so important that we always bring in mature and gifted people to judge and weigh the prophetic word. Prophecy is never a matter of private interpretation. We cannot go off the rails if we submit each word to the judging process. In the first instance, we need the microscopic testing of Section A, followed by the magnifying elements of Section B in order for us to thoroughly vet and understand the prophetic word.

Chapter 8

The Role of the Christian Prophet

The major thrust of this book is dedicated to the practical development of the gift of prophecy, its reception into the local church and the understanding required to handle prophecy effectively.

This chapter is concerned to address the wider issue of the prophetic ministry and the office of a prophet. This would normally be the subject of a book (or two) in itself. I am not proposing to give any detailed exposition in these pages, simply to provide an overview that will help us put the prophetic gift into its wider context

The gift of prophecy

Prophecy is like a swimming pool (Figure A). There is a shallow end that all can safely use. This is inspirational prophecy where our aim is to encourage, build up and

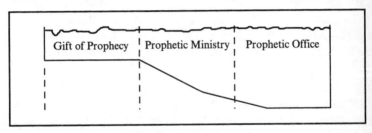

Figure A: *Swimming Pool*

comfort people. It is non-directive, not correctional and seeks to bless people and glorify the Lord in simple terms. When Paul declared that he desired that all would prophesy (1 Corinthians 14:1, 5) it was this level of prophecy he had in mind. It was not a general call for everyone to become a prophet.

The prophetic ministry

After the shallow end there is a middle section where the water gets progressively deeper. So, in prophecy there is a time when some people must push on in a gradually deeper expression of the heart of God. Prophetic ministry is quite different from the gift of prophecy. Many people will experience prophecy as a one-off gift for a particular time and purpose.

Continual use of the gift of prophecy will begin to push us in the direction of a ministry rather than just a casual use of the gift. Being able to lay a few bricks in a straight line does not make me a bricklayer. However, if I continue the craft, laying bricks continuously to increase speed and proficiency plus take some specialist training, then my improved talent would promote the new title of bricklayer.

Moving in the prophetic is very similar. It means getting into deeper water in terms of our faith, i.e. believing for more specific and revelational words instead of the general, inspirational type. It will broaden our use of the gift to include a wider range of people, situations and activities. We will need to consider a more extensive set of issues than just handling prophecy in the local church.

That is why we cannot see prophecy as just timely preaching of the Word into a particular situation. Prophecy isn't just having special insight into the Scripture. Obviously that is a part of being prophetic. Yet there is a dynamic about prophecy that takes it out of the ordinary and into the supernatural.

Preaching and teaching can speak to our minds, our emotions and our spirit. Inspired preaching can unlock our faith, free our mind, create a depth of understanding and evoke a response to the Lord. Prophecy is much more than this however. The Scripture can provide **general** guidelines on a multitude of things that pertain to our lives, relationships, fellowship with God, marriage, work, home, church and ministry. Prophecy can supply **specific** detail to general principles. For example, the Bible can tell us how to live but not where. It can tell us how to meet together but not the specific location of our church building. It can remind us of the need to be employed but not with whom, nor volunteer information on the type of work we should do.

A friend told me the story of how his church were seeking for a new building to purchase having outgrown their rented accommodation. As they met for prayer they received Scripture that God would give them a place. As they continued to meet and pray one of the members had a vision/picture of a long, low warehouse type building with blue fire doors. Their next meeting was attended by a visiting prophet who gave them a word of prophecy during his talk. Speaking about the division of territory of the tribes (Joshua 18) he moved into a prophetic anointing which declared, 'God is giving you a ministry amongst the poor and needy, particularly to those who live in high rise apartment blocks, and your new building will be located close to six apartment buildings.'

The next day they drove to the part of the town where there was a high rise development. Next to a cluster of six tower blocks was a long, low warehouse building with blue fire doors! They walked into the office to speak to the Manager who informed them that he had just received a telephone call from the owners 'informing him that he should put the building up for sale because they had found a larger property!' The prophet was from overseas and had never been to that church or indeed that part of the country before.

We need the dual revelation of the general word of Scripture, which gives life principles and guidance, to be allied to the specific word of prophecy, which supplies the fine detail to the broad brush strokes of the Bible.

Prophetic ministry is concerned with the church, and it is concerned with the direction we take, as well as who will lead and how we will get to our destination. Every church has times of testing, battles to fight and things to over-come. Prophetic ministry brings God's perspective, releases vision and calling and undermines the enemy. It is concerned to see the church fulfilling its call. It draws attention to the majesty and supremacy of God in times of trouble. It has one hand in the past and one in the future, but is able to bring both elements into the present to help us make sense of what we are going through. Prophetic ministry sees the continuity of God's purpose from our past to our future. The knowledge of both these things helps us to come to a different and often radical perspec-tive of current events. This prophetic perspective ignites faith and hope and gives us the energy to fight on and break through.

The office of a prophet

The office of a prophet would continue along that same line but going ever deeper into the supernatural realm of hearing God and being his mouthpiece.

The prophet is concerned with holiness and purity and is seeking to prepare the Bride of Christ. The end time theme will be uppermost as they build the church and establish kingdom values and practices for Christ's return. The prophet has a kingdom perspective that will motivate the church universal towards a practical unity of the Spirit.

The prophet will speak to churches, cities, regions and

nations. Their words will be heard by all in authority; church leaders, kings and governments. Their words will be accompanied by signs and wonders in healing miracles and clear signs of the supernatural presence of the Lord and his hosts. They will invest the church with supernatural faith as they both **forth tell** the word of the Lord and **foretell** his purposes.

The importance of development

These things do not just happen. We must look at our prophetic ability and practices and plan to upgrade them. I am constantly amazed at how many churches send and encourage people to attend one of my conferences and yet never think to send a delegation from the leadership.

People need training in prophecy as much as they do in prayer, warfare, worship, sharing their faith and praying for the sick. At the shallow end there is a large mixture of our thoughts competing with the mind of the Spirit (see Figure B). As we receive training, discipleship and opportunity to move in the gift, we develop our listening potential. We learn to filter out our own thoughts, discern the voice of the enemy and hold on to the word of the Lord. In prophetic ministry there is less mixture; we are growing

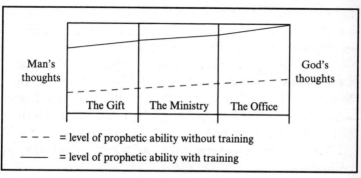

Figure B

into the gift and establishing credibility and a good track record.

As we move into the Prophetic Office, we come into a greater flow of revelatory anointing and responsibility on the national and international scene. All ministries must grow. If we halt our development our ministry will hit a ceiling and level off.

Without adequate training, our gifting will not reach beyond a certain level. One of the main causes of difficulty in the prophetic realm today is the lack of development, training and discipleship.

Everyone has aspirations. That is why church is such a great place to be; it's full of wonderful people who want to be bigger and better for the glory of God. Sometimes church can be hard, difficult and awful. It can abound in bitterness and frustration. However, scratch a frustrated person and we discover uncultivated aspirations. As my friend Gerald Coates says 'aspiration turns into achievement through development'.

The five-fold ministry gifts (Ephesians 4:11) of apostles, prophets, evangelists, pastors and teachers have their main function *'to equip the saints for the work of ministry'* (Ephesians 4:12).

There are varying kinds of prophets with different types of anointing. It is the same with church leadership. There are different anointings and ministries, and we cannot make everyone act the same or be involved in similar ministries across the church.

Methods of operation and the end product will contrast, sometimes quite sharply, between individuals. I know prophetic ministries that are rooted in evangelistic and pastoral situations. Others use their gift to open up difficult issues because their prophetic ability is channelled through the word of knowledge. Some are clearly involved in forth telling, using Scripture messages to inspire congregations with a timely and relevant word. Others move particularly in revelatory prophecy in a predictive manner. Some move only in personal prophecy while others are more happy speaking corporately.

We cannot all fit into the same mould, therefore we must have the attitude: 'vive le difference!' Some people can only move within one specific sphere of endeavour while others are comfortable across a wide range of prophetic activity. The important rule is to allow people to learn their specific sphere of influence. Knowing the boundaries is just as important as locating the territory. Influence and activity will expand through relationships and by development and opportunity.

Features of Old and New Testament prophets

In his ministry the Lord Jesus said at times *'you have heard it said'*, then he would quote a verse from the Old Testament. He would follow that (Matthew 5) by saying *'but I say to you'*. These new words brought change, a different understanding and new practice.

There are many things which flow out of the Old Testament into the New Covenant. There are some things which clearly do not, such as animal sacrifice, polygamy and stoning people caught in sin.

When we examine the prophetic ministry through both Covenants there are areas of similarity but also of difference.

Similarities

Both are called by similar titles, prophet, man of God, servant of the Lord and messenger of the Lord.

There are many similarities in terms of their function as prophets. In both Covenants, they would act as spokesmen and the mouthpiece of God. They would be engaged in forth telling and foretelling. They would pronounce judgement and interpret the law. They would communicate their prophecies in the same way by word of mouth, in dreams and visions, by action and symbolic drama, strange burdens and also by the written word.

They both have prophets of vision with Daniel and Zechariah in the Old, and John (Revelation) in the New. There are prophets of judgement in both covenants. There are prophets of Scripture such as Isaiah, and in the New Covenant many of Paul's Epistles are written with a strong prophetic influence.

Prophets in both covenants are concerned with the morality of the Church, and are actively preparing the Church to be the Bride of Christ. There is also a strong spirit of justice at work in all prophets that speaks out against all moral, social, governmental and political corruption and injustice. They are a part of that kingdom voice of God that calls all men everywhere to repent from idolatry, sin and unfaithfulness to God.

Differences

The Old Testament prophets were also called seers, a term not applied in the church. Under the Old Covenant prophets gave guidance to people who came looking for a word from the Lord. In 1 Samuel 9:4–10, Saul and his friend went to enquire regarding the whereabouts of a certain donkey, and Saul found a kingdom instead!

Enquiring of the Lord and seeking guidance from the prophet is a major function of the Old Covenant which is completely outlawed in the New.

Under the terms of the New Covenant we have all received the Holy Spirit and can enjoy an intimate relationship with the Lord. Guidance is the by-product of a right relationship with God. In the Old Testament the priests represented man to God and the prophets heard from the Lord and spoke to men.

Now, we have Jesus the great High Priest and the Holy Spirit, who is our helper, resident within our lives. No New Testament prophet was ever used to give or to bring prophecies that guided, steered or governed people in the will of God. Instead they are used to give confirmation to people. Even when receiving new or future words we are instructed to judge and weigh them and wait for confirmation.

There is a check on this kind of activity in the church by the process of examining every prophetic utterance. Christian prophets do not tell people what to do, they confirm what God is saying. To go to a Christian prophet for direction and guidance is to violate the New Covenant which gives us direct access and approach to God through Christ by the Spirit. People do not 'need' a prophecy, they need the Lord Jesus. There is absolutely no need to seek a prophecy. New Testament people receive guidance, direction and oversight of their lives from Scripture which is infallible, and the indwelling presence of the Holy Spirit. Prophets as well as other witnesses and ministries can confirm what we receive personally from the Lord.

We need to understand the difference between guidance and directive prophecy. Guidance occurs when people seek out the prophet and ask for prophetic insight into their life and situation (e.g. 1 Samuel 9). This is an Old Covenant approach because the Holy Spirit came upon people.

In the New Covenant the Holy Spirit resides within people and teaches them to know the voice of the Lord for themselves. A directive prophecy is therefore an unsought for word, sovereignly imparted by the Lord into our lives to bring either confirmation or indeed to completely open our lives to some new purpose. The initiative lies completely with the Lord. However, we are to judge and weigh everything in a responsible manner.

Christian prophets when asked for guidance should ask questions to examine the quality of the individual's walk with God. We cannot take God's place in this area but must point people towards an improved relationship with the Lord Jesus through the activities of the Holy Spirit.

In the Old Covenant the prophets were some of the main historians and were used to write infallible Scripture. This aspect of their ministry was given to the apostles in the early Church who like John may have had a very strong prophetic element to their gifting.

In the Old Testament, prophets were very forthright in rebuking, warning and chastising people, and were often used to denounce people and their sin. In the church, prophets minister the word by exhortation, teaching example and confirmation. The Gospel is redemptive, and we are serving a God of grace and mercy therefore our prophetic utterances are tempered by the kingdom message.

Christian prophets should not have the function or personality of their Old Testament counterparts. Prophets were feared before the time of Jesus. They were eccentric, intimidating, authoritarian individuals who gave messages of great portent often with a foreboding or a sense of impending doom, which seemed to hang around them. They were strangely independent, not easy to receive and at times deeply unpopular. Whether their lack of acceptance was due to their presentation, personality or their message (or a combination of all) is perhaps open to question.

By contrast the Christian prophet must be exhibiting the fruit of the Spirit with all grace and humility. They must be accountable members of the body of Christ and living under authority while acting as a team member not an individual ministry.

In the Old Testament the prophets were mainly a blessing ministry which over the centuries represented the heart of God to man. In the New Testament the prophet is a building ministry working with the apostle to lay foundations and establish the Church as the house of the Lord. For that reason the prophetic ministry is subject to the apostolic and comes under its authority (1 Corinthians 12:28, 29).

The last prophet of the Old Covenant, John the Baptist, laid his life and ministry at the feet of Jesus who is the first in a new line of New Testament prophets.

Sadly far too many people are displaying an Old Testament ministry and personality in a New Testament Church setting. This, I believe, accounts for the large number of horror stories, misunderstandings and misrepresentations which belittle the prophetic ministry and discredit the gift. I have seen it on so many of my Schools of Prophecy, where those with embryonic gifting and limited understanding are seeking an Old Testament anointing.

People with immature gifting are trying to understand negative words, judgements and pronouncements with neither an accurate understanding of grace or how to handle their own frustrations, rejections and lack of humility. It takes time, effort and specialised training to sort these things out and develop Christian prophets fit for the New Testament Church.

The Christian prophet

Ironically the purpose of a New Testament prophet is not primarily to prophesy! Firstly, it is to train people to hear the Lord for themselves. Secondly, it is to teach believers how to find and live in the will of God for themselves. Thirdly, it is to instruct and train people in the gift of prophecy and to help churches establish the right framework and protocol for the gift. Fourthly, it is to bring the word of the Lord either in inspired preaching or by supernatural prophetic utterance.

Obviously these areas are not necessarily in this order. Much may depend on where the local church is placed in spiritual terms when the prophet comes to visit. I have put them in this order to illustrate the importance of people hearing God, knowing his will and being trained in the prophetic gift, for themselves.

The New Testament prophet is called to a working relationship with the apostolic ministry. This interaction will provide adequate checks and balances for both ministries.

The New Testament prophets act as a **catalyst** within the church, they make things happen. God is full of plans and purpose for his church. A prophet will envision and call the church and individuals into an understanding and receipt of those plans and purposes. God still reveals his secrets to his servants the prophets.

God is always speaking; unfortunately the church is not always listening. People who cannot discern the voice of the Lord often have words in their heart of which they don't know the origin. Many times I have prophesied to people and it has been like switching on a lamp. Suddenly illumination comes: 'so that's what it means!'

People get preoccupied with something new and fail to do anything about what the Lord has already spoken. Often I have prophesied to people and their response has been 'Oh but I knew all of that, tell me something I don't know.' People always want to hear something new. This preoccupation with new things can really prevent us from hearing the Lord in a fresh way. We need a new response to a previous word. Here I am, a complete stranger, prophesying all these things into their hearts and people don't realise the importance of what is happening!

Actually the issue should be 'if you know all that, why has God sent me to tell you these things?' It could be that the timing is right for these things to begin to happen. After every calling and envisioning comes a time of death and burial. It is called preparation, as the Lord puts our call on the shelf and deals with who we are as people. During this 'in the ground' time, the reality of the call leaves us for a time. Therefore, when suddenly someone begins to restate our call prophetically it may be the time when the Lord is opening doors and making things happen.

Alternatively, we can prophesy things that people already know simply because they have not co-operated with the original word. God does not speak for novelty value, his word should create something in us that will guarantee a fulfilment.

Perhaps one of the answers to the 'I already know that' impatience/disappointment of some people is to ask them what they have done with the original word.

Prophets are also active in terms of **preparation**. They are making ready a people prepared for the Lord as in Isaiah 40:3; Luke 1:17. Also they are working with other five-fold ministry gifts to prepare for the second coming of Christ.

Part of that preparation is the receiving and imparting of specific revelation to the earth. The apostle Paul and presumably the prophet Silas, his team mate, both enjoyed receiving revelation as part of their office (Ephesians 3:1–7). A true revelation will always cause revolution.

There are many words that must be fulfilled before Christ's return and we will need prophetic revelation to interpret those signs. Where there are credible and active prophets the church will not stumble in ignorance. God does nothing unless a prophet knows about it (Amos 3:7).

It needs a prophet to interpret these signs correctly. The Scribes and Pharisees did not discern the greatest sign of all, the Messiah walking in their midst. It required John the Baptist to say.

> *'Behold the Lamb of God who takes away the sin of the world. I have seen and testified that this is the Son of God.'* (John 1:29–34)

Prophets are also preparing the Bride of Christ, literally 'making ready a people for the Lord'. These are the people, a peculiar people (isn't that the truth!), who have been bought with a price: the blood of Jesus. It is this body of people that God is sanctifying and cleansing (the rite of purification), to present it with no spots, wrinkles or blemishes. A people of holiness and glory (Ephesians 5:25–27).

The Bride must be in the prime of life in terms of beauty and preparedness. With no spots of adolescent immaturity or the wrinkles of a staid and elderly senility. Jesus is marrying a redeemed church of people made in his image, filled with righteousness and grace (Hosea 2:19, 20), a chaste virgin (2 Corinthians 11:2).

Prophets are **activists**. They are part of the *'equipping the saints for the work of the ministry'* team that every church must have access to in these days (Ephesians 4:11).

Timothy was instructed to *'not neglect the gift which was given you by prophecy'*. This gift had been imparted with the laying on of hands by the prophetic presbytery (1 Timothy 4:14). It is vital that we put the saints to work in the church and the world. Some people are church people in that all of their focus and influence is within the body of Christ. Other people are Kingdom people who have their main sphere of influence across the wider body or in secular tasks. Some are called to be policemen, teachers, politicians, newsmen, media artists, involved in social action and justice.

It is interesting to note that when an anointed member of the church discerns gifting in other people, prophecy can draw that gift to the attention of the individual. However when an apostle or prophet lays hands on people for those giftings to emerge, there is an impartation which takes place.

Currently we have a malnourished body of believers across the world because the Ephesians 4 ministries have not taken their rightful place in much of Christendom. These ministries equip people to be joined and knitted together by what every member is contributing. As every member is activated to be effective in the work so the church grows up (Ephesians 4:16).

Real prophets promote ministry and have a passion to train and release others.

Prophets also have a role in declaring the word of the Lord i.e. **forth telling**. This is communicating the heart of God for the present. This declaration can come via teaching, preaching, the spoken prophetic word, vision and interpretation and symbolic acts. It will exhort, edify and comfort as well as admonish, provide warning and bring reproof (Revelation chapters 2 and 5).

Another aspect of the prophetic role is in predictive prophecy, called **fore telling**. Communicating the future as it is perceived in the mind and heart of God. This is used to shape the direction of the church; to cause a desire for godliness; to empower and release people. Often the Lord has enabled me to understand a church's history, see its future in terms of vision and call; and then to bring both those things together into the present in a way that helps people to make real sense of what is currently happening.

I spoke to one church about their having a spirit of reconciliation upon their ministry in terms of working with the poor; broken homes and marriages; and working for unity across the local churches. Before I spoke the Lord showed me that their history contained several instances of splits and divisions. Also I saw that currently there were frustrations and difficulties within the work.

Putting all these things together I declared a time of prayer and fasting for the church. During that time we successfully rid the church of a number of demonic influences that had plagued the work. There is nothing like a spot of fasting to undermine the enemy.

Prophets should work closely with other of the five-fold ministries. There are a number of **partnerships** that the Lord can bring together at different times. In the early church a number of prophets travelled together as a **team** (Acts 11:27). In my experience working in a team produces a better quality product that working alone. Iron sharpens iron. Obviously more things can happen with a team. During a recent conference in Germany, my team came under a spirit of prophecy where several hundreds of people received prophetic input, and there were evidences of healings and deliverances taking place throughout the auditorium. Prophets together will ignite each other to a greater anointing.

Working in a team enables us to encourage and strengthen the church as Jude and Silas did in the book of Acts (15:32). Personally I would love to see churches in every region operating a School of Prophecy and encouraging people to come together in this ministry.

Prophets and teachers came together (Acts 13:1–3) at Antioch. They were instrumental in releasing Paul and Barnabas to their wider call and ministry. This is an interesting combination, both parties love God's word, though they seem to approach it from different angles.

Teachers want to stop and consolidate the word ensuring that people are practising what has been taught. My friend Martin Scott says that nothing has been taught unless it has been caught.

The prophet is always working to move forward into new revelation and is looking for challenges, battles to fight and things to overcome.

A prophet may release a word unfolding the whole prophetic panorama of what the church is to do in its locality. There may be a number of aspects to the vision but no clear steps emerging to say how we get there. A teacher will come along and with strategy begin to pick out the relevant stepping points along the way where we can equip and prepare the church for its future role. Teachers make things accessible.

Similarly teachers need prophets to open up that new horizon, which in turn inspires them to receive revelation.

Prophets also can take teaching and give it a prophetic application that results in a response from people to what the Lord is saying.

Some prophets can make use of the teaching gift also, though not necessarily to the same degree. Likewise teachers can prophesy though perhaps not with the same authority and power. There need not be any friction between these two ministries if they understand each other's role and have respect for one another.

Apostles and prophets are clearly linked together in Scripture (Ephesians 2:20). Adequate foundations in the church cannot be laid without this partnership. The prophet will see the end product in terms of the building God is erecting. The apostle as a wise master builder is gifted to build the property line upon line and brick by brick.

At every stage of the work prophecy and wisdom will be needed to put things in their rightful place. There is a dual role of building and erecting the church and equipping and releasing the saints so that the church can be further built up. The bigger the house the more we need to release people.

It has often been said that **prophets and pastors** do not mix. I believe this to be a lie. It is true that there may be more tensions in this relationship than any other. However, I firmly believe that tension does not only mean there is something wrong. It could indicate that something is happening. Prophets have a way of ploughing up the ground and causing disturbance. Sometimes this is sorely needed. I know many pastors who, when encountering hard ground, simply lay a patio and cover everything up! Prophecy is attacking, stimulating and provoking by definition. Pastoring is about restoring calm and order. Prophets challenge, pastors soothe.

They do need to talk to each other. Prophets need to brief pastors and share their burden. Pastors should have access to prophetic revelation, not to water it down but to bring their wisdom to bear in the situation. Then together they should present a united front to the church: a partnership which should be seen and noted. Too often a prophetic word has been spoken without prior consultation. The pastor becomes defensive and people are very quick to spot tension and disagreement. Some will take sides with the prophet, others will align themselves with the pastor in the hope of avoiding any consequences. This is how splits and factions appear.

Co-operation and prayer before, during and after the prophecy will ensure that everyone takes it on board, the plans of the enemy are thwarted and the church moves on purposefully. Pastors do need access to prophetic ministry in the aftermath of prophecy being given.

When a piece of ground is ploughed up all manner of things can surface. Consequences do result from prophecy and it is only right and proper that the prophet should give a hand with the clearing up. Extra local prophetic gifting should always make time for adequate liaison with local church leaders, pastoral ministry and resident prophetic people.

If I know I have a fairly serious word, directive or corrective prophecy to bring to a church, I will ask in advance for time to meet certain people during my visit. I want to make sure that when I leave, the prophecy I have deposited is in good hands. I also want to ensure that they have access to me for questions, discussion and planning. Strategy is formed at times like this which can be invaluable on the ground in the situation.

We are all in a team when we are together and need to act accordingly. Prophets should form working partnerships that glorify the Lord, undermine the enemy and build up the body of Christ.

Chapter 9

To Be or Not to Be?

'To be or not to be?' is the question that Hamlet asked himself in Act three, scene two of Shakespeare's tragedy. Hamlet was deliberating on whether it was better to live and fight in his circumstances, or to give up and die.

We probably need to ask ourselves a similar question with regard to prophecy spoken over our lives. Do we let it live, or allow it to die? Clearly, our response to the Lord when we hear his word is so vitally important. This is why James warns us about being hearers but not doers of the word (James 1:22–24). Such people are prone to delusion because they continually forget what God has said.

It is so easy to forfeit some sense of the power and the glory, the marvel and the miracle of hearing God speak into our lives and situations. Almighty God, the absolute Creator, has a heart so huge he can be personally acquainted with hundreds of millions of people. He finds time to hear, speak and respond to countless millions of prayers daily. He speaks countless messages of love, peace, truth and blessing on an hourly basis.

When God speaks, he does so with purpose; to create life, hope, faith and an awareness of himself in the lives of his people. He wants to bring change, adjustment, correction, direction, renewal, restoration and encouragement. His words are always strategic, contain real purpose, and reveal his heart and plans for us. In all of this, he is looking for a response from us. This chapter will look at the elements of our response and examine some of the consequences of our failure to respond to the word of the Lord.

Christian fatalism

Before we examine those issues, we need to lay to rest the, 'God said it, so it is bound to happen', mind-set. People become fatalistic very easily, because it suits their purpose, and it absolves them from any responsibility.

Over the past twenty years in prophetic ministry, I have continuously been confronted by the, 'God will do it all, man does not have to do anything', brigade. They have regularly quoted the following passages of Scripture to me, in proof of their argument.

> *'Blessed be the Lord, that has given rest to his people Israel, according to all that he promised: there has **not failed one word** of all his good promises, which he promised by the hand of Moses his servant.'*
>
> (1 Kings 8:56)

> *'For I am the Lord. I will speak, and the word that I shall speak **shall come to pass**, it shall be no more prolonged; for in your days, O rebellious house, will I say the word, and **will perform it**, says the Lord God.'*
>
> (Ezekiel 12:25)

> *'... so is my word that goes out from my mouth. **It will not return to me empty**, but will accomplish what I desire and achieve the purpose for which I sent it.'*
>
> (Isaiah 55:11)

Let us take each of these passages in turn, beginning with 1 Kings 8. Firstly, we must agree that the promises did not fail. They were wonderfully fulfilled in their entirety. However, they were fulfilled by the second generation, not the first who received them in Egypt. These prophetic words spoken first by Moses in Exodus 6:6–8, were cancelled in Numbers 14:20–23 on behalf of that first generation of freed Israelites.

The issue at stake here is not that God's words were fulfilled, but **who** received the promise!

What is also interesting to note in the passage from 1 Kings 8 are the following verses (57–61), in which after speaking about God's word not failing, Solomon declares that there are four requests/responses plus a command, that need to be uppermost in our hearts.

(1) For God's presence to be with us (v. 57);
(2) For our hearts to be turned to him, that we may obey him in all things (v. 58);
(3) For our prayers to be heard and our needs met (v. 59);
(4) For God's glory to be seen by all the earth (v. 60).

He then goes on to say, *'But your hearts must be fully committed to the Lord . . . '* (v. 61).

Moving on to Ezekiel 12, verse 12 is given in the context of Israel being a rebellious nation. They had eyes to see but did not; they had ears to hear, but did not, for they were rebellious (v. 2). The prophet had been speaking prophetically about Israel's coming exile to Babylon as captives. The people's response was, *'this prophecy will not be fulfilled for years yet'* (v. 27). In other words, we do not need to respond right now; it can wait!

In this instance, their lack of remorse and repentance ensured the fulfilment of the word of judgement when normally our lack of response removes the blessing.

When we come to examine Isaiah 55:11, we must do so with two things in mind. **Firstly** that there is a difference between the prophecy of Scripture and personal prophecy. **Secondly** that we must not confuse the issue between human free will and the sovereignty of God.

The prophecy of Scripture relates to God's ultimate purposes for the earth and his people. He declares the end (Revelation), from the beginning (Genesis), and from all ancient times ... his purpose will be established and his good pleasure accomplished (Isaiah 46:10).

All of those words relate to God's eternal covenant with his people. Having given us his Spirit, he declares that his word will never depart out of our mouths, nor our descendants for now and forever (Isaiah 59:21). In that context, Jesus declared that, *'heaven and earth will pass away, but not my words'* (Matthew 24:29–35).

The prophecy of Scripture, contained in Isaiah 55:11, always points to an unchanging God who is the same yesterday, today and forever. He has a fixed purpose and so gives fixed prophecies that will undoubtedly be fulfilled, though not necessarily to the generation who first received them.

We cannot put prophecy to individuals in that same category. Isaiah 55:11 undoubtedly refers to the prophecy of Scripture, the ultimate desire of God for the earth and mankind. In that context, God's word will come to pass, his purpose will be achieved.

However, I believe it also contains the element of God's ideal for the individual. If we were to ask God's intention for every personal prophecy spoken to individuals, I believe he would point to this verse as the evidence of his desire for us. We know, however, that **God's intention and desire** will not override our own free will. He does not impose personal words on us by his sovereignty. He graciously speaks out the possible, not the inevitable.

As we have seen in Numbers 14, a prophecy was cancelled for two million adults and reactivated for their teenagers and children. Saul had his personal word cancelled in 1 Samuel 13. In fact, the Lord said to Samuel that he regretted making Saul king, because Saul had turned back from following the Lord and had not obeyed his words, (1 Samuel 15:11). At this point, God is expressing sorrow, not admitting that he made a mistake. His **intention** was that Saul would receive the full promise; the reality was a source of grief to Him.

For twenty-three years, Jeremiah prophesied continually to Israel, proclaiming the message, *'turn back, each of you, from your evil ways and practices'* (Jeremiah 25). Numerous prophets had spoken continuously the same message into the nation. The intention and the desire of God was to see Israel turn around. For twenty-three years, the word of the Lord had been graciously spoken, but met with no response.

Going further back into the history of Israel as a nation, we discover some foundational principles that undergird every prophetic utterance given to that people group. Leviticus 26:14–33 expresses in great detail the penalty for not obeying God's words, rejecting his statutes and breaking his covenant. From ill health; destruction by their enemies; a hard land and cast iron sky; plagues; wild animals; pestilence; rationed food; cannibalism; and desolation in their cities and throughout the land, culminating in exile and banishment. In their history, Israel suffered all these things.

Deuteronomy 28 continues this theme, beginning with the blessings of obedience to God's word, followed by the curses of disobedience. Verse 14 is pivotal in this chapter:

> *'do not turn aside from any of the words which I speak to you, neither to the right hand or the left.'*

When God speaks prophetically to us personally, it is his intent and desire that these things should happen. However, there can never be any room for fatalism in the heart of the Christian. We must not fall victim to the Doris Day syndrome, 'whatever will be, will be!' Personal prophecy always speaks to the potential, never to the inescapable. We must make a positive response.

There are three points that we must consider in

responding to God's word and avoiding potential hindrances to fulfilment of prophecy.

A. Acceptance and Acknowledgement.

B. Absorption and Assimilation.

C. Actualisation and Attainment.

If we are going to get straight As in our response to the Lord, we must consider these points carefully.

SECTION A – ACCEPTANCE AND ACKNOWLEDGEMENT

Section A concerns itself with the issues of creating a favourable reception to prophecy. It will also explore the need to agree the appropriate terms in responding to the word by a confession of faith and owning the word with thanks. We will also examine the importance of fighting to hold onto prophecy and consider obstacles that will prevent fulfilment.

In order to make a good response to prophecy, we must make sure that we **hear the word correctly**. With the reception of prophecy, it is an all too common mistake to hear only the elements that are applicable to our current life and circumstances. The main parts of the prophecy could possibly relate to a time in the future and may have very little to say into our present situation. This is why the recording of prophecy is so very important. It will allow us a more objective look at the word and help us to select the parts which are for now from those which are for the foreseeable future.

Very often our immediate reception of prophecy is at a very subjective level and our response often follows that pattern of behaviour. Make sure the word is recorded and then pay the best attention to what is being spoken.

Established opinions hinder response

Many people live with preconceptions about themselves and the Lord; their theology can often prevent a good response to the prophetic. A prime example is in Matthew 16:21–21, where Peter disagreed with Jesus about a prophecy he had just given! Jesus was speaking prophetically about his death, burial and resurrection. The disciples did not understand him; the word he gave brought confusion, consternation and misunderstanding. Jesus was not causing those things to happen. We cannot always blame the prophet or the prophecy if confusion comes. The confusion was caused because the word of the prophet clashed with an established mind-set.

Peter stood and rebuked Jesus, saying, *'not so Lord'*. In other words, you are wrong and you have missed it. Why? He resented and denounced that prophetic word because it didn't agree with his personal goals for Jesus. It didn't agree with his preconceptions about the Christ. The Jews had a political concept of the Messiah's coming and any word contrary to this, even a prophetic word from Jesus about death and burial, was incomprehensible and, therefore, unacceptable. It did not compute with their own understanding, so they rejected it. It clashed with their mind-set.

There are many similar problems around today. I once gave a guy (a minister in the Anglican denomination), a prophetic word which had three words of knowledge in it about his childhood. I couldn't possibly have known those details. He looked at me and said he could not deny the accuracy of what I said, but that he did not believe in prophecy! Prophecy was needed to get the church kick-started two thousand years ago, but in his opinion we don't need prophecy now because we have the Bible. Some people seem to elevate the Bible to almost the point of it being the fourth member of the Trinity. The Bible is not the Word of God. Jesus is the Word of God. The Bible is Scripture.

The Bible clearly says in Revelation 19:13 when speaking of the Second Coming of Christ,

> *'He was clothed with a robe dipped in blood and his name is called "The Word of God".'*

The gospel of John opens with that amazing statement,

> *'In the beginning was the Word, and the Word was with God, and the Word was God. He was in the beginning with God.'*

In 1 John 1:1, we are again told about the things we have handled, seen and heard from the beginning, concerning the Word of Life.

> *'And the Word became flesh, and dwelt among us, and we beheld his glory, the glory as of the only begotten of the Father, full of grace and truth.'* (John 1:14)

John bore witness of this person, the word become flesh, man, Jesus.

The Bible is quite clear about who the Word of God is! It also says about itself,

> *'All scripture is given by inspiration of God, and is profitable for doctrine; for reproof; for correction and for instruction in righteousness, that the man of God may be complete, thoroughly equipped for every good work.'* (2 Timothy 3:16, 17)

The evangelicals amaze me at times with their willingness to defend the Bible. I admire them for it. What a pity then, that so many don't actually live what they defend. If we lived the Word as ferociously as we defend it, we probably would not have the abuse within the prophetic ministry that we have today! How ironic that our lack of understanding and experiencing the revealed word of Scripture should have such an appalling influence on our reception of the prophetic.

It is not some red-lettered edition of the Bible that will return on a white horse at the end of days. It is Jesus, with a sword in his mouth. Jesus, the living embodiment of the Word of God.

The Bible is Scripture and quite wonderful. To be able to read about the heart and character of God; who he is; what he is like; the things he can do. What a wonderful gift the Lord has left us. All Christians should have a profound love of Scripture. We should however save our adoration and real reverence for the person of the Living Lord Jesus. The Bible is not the fourth member of the Trinity. How sad that many people put the Bible before the person of the Holy Spirit. They elevate Scripture to a level where they deny the person and the work of the Spirit in today's church.

The Anglican minister I had given the prophecy to did not know what to do with it. He called me asking several questions. He said, 'I don't know what to do. Should I put this prophecy into the back of my Bible and start something new in the canon of Scripture?' Because it clashed with his established opinions and thoughts, he checked it out with his Bishop who said it sounded suspect and recommended that he reject it. The minister did. He called and said he could not accept it because it clashed with his opinions and thinking. He's a poorer man for it. He could not fault the accuracy, for the prophecy contained things he'd never told another living soul about his dreams and aspirations over many years. He was in tears on the telephone. God spoke a word into his life, but it clashed with his thoughts.

Witness of the spirit

There is an initial witness of the spirit that we need to pay some attention to in the first instance. We need to recognise God's voice; to have that 'witness of the spirit'. Where we recognise not just the voice of the prophet, but spiritually tune into God's presence, and have an awareness that God is speaking. Prophecy will communicate heart to heart and spirit to spirit. When someone is speaking prophetically, your spirit witnesses to it, you know there is something inside that keys into it. That is recognising God's voice. It is not just receiving words into our minds, it's allowing our spirit to interact with the Spirit of God and it will go beyond a mere understanding to awaken recognition within. We will be aware of that when God is speaking, as opposed to just man. It's all part of our response, our receiving of the word of God.

We need to formally take receipt of the word. When a parcel or registered letter is received, we are used to signing for it as we take receipt. I like people to formally accept and acknowledge their prophetic word in the judging process.

Parable of the sower (Matthew 13:9–23)

The four types of soil represent the different responses to the Word of the Lord. People respond in different ways because their heart is in a contrasting state of preparedness. Some hearts are hard; others are too shallow; others have been contaminated by the worry of life; others are open and ready to receive. It is important to identify where we are in this regard and make appropriate adjustments.

This parable gives some useful insights into receiving 'words', whether they are from Scripture or prophetically spoken. The word can be **snatched** away by the enemy (v. 19).

The word can be received with joy but opposition and trouble can cause us to lose hold on the word (v. 21). With some people, their ability to hold on to the word is determined by the cares of the world or the riches they may have gained (v. 22).

When a person hears and takes steps to understand the word, it produces fruit at various levels, 100%; 60%; or 30%; dependant upon the strength of our response and will.

Disobedience prevents us from hearing the Lord

Hardness of heart helps the word to bounce off our life. It won't actually influence us; it won't penetrate, go beyond the exterior of our lives and, therefore, there's no possibility of it creating anything. Hardness of heart can be due to a lot of different things: fear; previous bad experience of prophecy; misunderstanding of God's heart for us; confusion or deception; a fixed mind-set; unsubmissive attitude; or disobedience to previous things that God has been saying. I often find that when people say, 'I'm not hearing God', it is not because God isn't speaking, it's because they are not being obedient in life. God isn't going to speak if he knows you're going to be disobedient. He's not somebody whose word is void. It's going to accomplish something; it has meaning, he wants us to obey.

Often, when people tell me that they cannot hear the Lord, I ask questions about lifestyle, their relationship with God, areas of bitterness or resentment, attitudes of unforgiveness. People who cannot hear God are either being attacked, in which case we may need a word of authority rather than prophecy, or there may be lifestyle or character issues which will require a word of Scripture rather than prophecy. In these circumstances, the best question is, 'Are you being obedient?' I fully appreciate that it is a question some people may not want to face, particularly if they are in disobedience! Their first response may be denial; however, the gift of discerning of spirits (i.e. the truth in God's spirit; man's spirit; or the presence of an evil spirit), will enable us to witness to the truth of that response. The witness of the spirit and the gift of discerning of spirits operate from the same root source.

The world lives in such lies and deception, which is part of the spirit of the age. The church of Jesus Christ has been so seduced into the spirit of this age that sometimes we just cannot hear God on issues that are vital to life. We become so used to living in what we've accepted, which God may be quite unhappy with, that our mind is not open to really hearing him. We need to be listeners and not just hearers, to have a teachable and an open heart and we need to be sure that we are living in obedience to what God has previously spoken because very often he's not going to add to it. He's not going to add disobedience to disobedience. He's not going to put us in that place of testing.

Register the elements of truth

The elements of truth and revelation that really impact during the prophecy must be registered in our hearts. They may offer subtle indications regarding where we are to prioritise our response.

All prophecy must receive a response ... even if it is simply one of thanksgiving and praise. Words that really mean something to us, need us to go over them thoroughly at the first opportunity. God is not the author of confusion. He always speaks for a purpose. He speaks to clarify our situations; his heart towards us; and give us a hope for the future.

If we receive a prophetic word and we fail to understand what God is saying to us, we may have to question whether it is the Lord who has spoken. We cannot always determine this for ourselves. We may be living in denial in an area of our lives and when a corrective word is given, we reject it out of hand. Sharing the word with responsible people will help us to avoid that pitfall.

What happens when the opposite of the prophecy occurs?

In the parable of the sower, Jesus stated that persecution and tribulation can come because of the word you have received. This is as true about prophecy as it is about the reception of revealed truth. The enemy always contests the word of the Lord. *'Has God said?'* is the first recorded act of temptation and warfare against the word.

There is a vivid portrayal of this in the book of Exodus. Moses met the elders of Israel and prophesied to them all that God had shown him regarding their deliverance from Egypt. The prophecy was supported by the demonstration of the signs (e.g. the rod becoming a snake; the leprous hand, etc). The people believed and worshipped the Lord (Exodus 4:29–31).

However, after Moses had spoken to Pharaoh, the net result was that their labour was made more severe. Now they had to make bricks without the benefit of straw being supplied. They had to both gather their own straw and make the same quota of bricks. Far from being set free, the exact opposite had happened (Exodus 5:6). When Moses came to prophesy again in Exodus 6:6–8 (the famous 'I will' prophecy), we discover that their initial reaction was one of disbelief and discouragement. The latter prophetic word was fulfilled in part to that generation. However, only two adults, Joshua and Caleb, received the total fulfilment (Numbers 14). Everyone else over the age of twenty did not inherit the completion of the prophecy.

We see exactly the same scenario at work with the life of Joseph. He related his prophetic dream about ruling over his brothers only to find himself staring up at them later from the bottom of a pit!

Far from ruling over them, he found himself sold into slavery; then made to serve as a criminal (Genesis 37, 39). He received the fulfilment of his prophetic word as he held on to the Lord in his circumstances. He did not allow his situation to determine his response to the prophecy. In fact, the prophetic word about ruling was fulfilled in the slave home and the prison as Joseph held on to the Lord!

Receiving prophecy brings you into the orbit and attention of the enemy. I have to confess that this gives me a real sense of excitement. Prophecy puts us on the cutting edge of life between the clash of two kingdoms. I would rather be attacked by the enemy than left alone by God. Have you ever wondered why the exact opposite from what the prophet said seems to happen?

I once prophesied over a man during a conference in the UK, that he was moving into a time of unparalleled prosperity where God would bless him with finance in abundance. Less than a week later this same man called me at the office to inform me that I was a false prophet.

Clearly upset and angry, he told me that he had just been made redundant for the first time in his life. He was now unemployed, about to go on welfare in an area of 25% unemployment! He was quite rude and adamant that I was a false prophet.

After hearing him out, I told him that I felt there were three possibilities to consider in this situation. Firstly, **had the prophet got it wrong?** In some way I may have completely blown it and missed the heart of God altogether. If this was the case, then I would have to return to his church to speak to him and his leaders. I spoke the word publicly; the least I could do is make a formal apology in public. Not only that, I would want to invite him to sit in a panel of his leaders and mine to discuss the appropriate action for my ministry. If I had indeed missed it, I could need help and counsel to put me right. I would certainly want him to feel safe and covered from my mistake.

Another possibility is that **the enemy was trying to snatch the word away**. Jesus said in Matthew 13:19 that this was possible. Personally, I am not sure of exactly how much power the enemy has in this matter. There were several hundred prophetic words about Jesus, his birth, life and eventual death. If the enemy had really understood about his death on a cross, he would have chopped down every tree in Israel. Stealing the word is a possibility, but probably not all the time. It needs, however, to be considered.

The final possibility is that **God knew beforehand** that this man would be made redundant. He has therefore been kind enough to give him a prophetic word to hold onto whilst he is going through the circumstances of redundancy and finding employment.

I asked him to talk those things through with his leadership and get back to me. When he returned the call, it was to apologise for calling me a false prophet and to agree that the third possibility had received a genuine witness with himself and his leadership.

At that point we prayed together over the telephone. He notified me that he had a meeting to discuss his redundancy pay-out in a few days. Apparently everyone in the company was getting the same amount of £2,500. As we prayed, I believed the Lord said he was to ask for £5,000 and the company car! He was initially reluctant to do so because he was convinced that the company policy of everyone getting the same, would prevail. I said I felt there was no harm in asking, after all they couldn't fire him twice! He finally agreed, and we prayed together for God's blessing.

When he arrived at the interview he found not his finance manager, who had been taken ill, but a very harassed finance director. The director was busily engaged in trying to sell off parts of the company and so asked for another date to discuss the pay-out because of pressure of work. When my new friend politely declined, the director asked him point blank how much he wanted. He replied, 'I want £5,000 and the company car'. The director said, 'done', shook hands and promptly signed the contract release form. My new friend was the only one in the whole company who received that pay-out. Then again, he was the only one in the company with a prophetic word about prosperity.

Over the next few months we talked together several times as he sought new employment. Eventually, after a temporary contract, he found a job with nearly three times the salary he had been earning before redundancy.

This man made the typical and common mistake of allowing the circumstances to challenge the prophecy, rather than using the prophecy to attack the circumstances. God knows everything that is happening in our lives. He sees the end from the beginning.

This man was about to lose his job anyhow. The Lord was kind enough to give him a word about financial blessing before his redundancy, so that he had a promise to hold on to during the situation. When God speaks, he reveals the absolute intention of his heart towards us. He does not speak for a novelty value. He speaks to challenge our circumstances. The prophetic word turns everything upside down, that is part of its nature.

The Lord is moving us into things that are impossible for us. Every church will have to take on projects that are impossible. Many of these projects will have their roots in the prophetic. The Lord is in the business of delivering his church from a 'safety first' Christianity. The Spirit of God is leading us into risk taking. There are times in our church life when we need to step out of the boat into something unreasonable. Faith is a walk in the unseen realm. Prophecy opens the door to that realm.

There will be a contesting

The contesting will happen on two fronts, spiritual and circumstantial. The **spiritual** battle will occur because prophecy puts us at the flashpoint between two kingdoms. When God speaks a directional prophetic word into our lives, his intention is to draw us further into a kingdom perspective, to involve us in extending his kingdom. Whenever we allow ourselves to respond to that challenge, we become an object of interest and attention to the enemy.

The enemy has not the time or the manpower to afflict every Christian personally. He mostly uses the flesh and the world to keep us out of God's will. Whenever we resist those two areas by living in the Spirit, we usually come into personal confrontation with the enemy.

In these situations, we have to learn appropriate responses and behaviour. Everything that challenges me is a direct challenge to the Lordship of Christ. Why? Because I am **in Christ!** God has put me into the one place, the person of His Son, where the enemy finds it the hardest to overcome my life. That is why the great need today is to build men and women who will stand in Christ. In warfare we do what we know to do, pray, believe, be clean, have an expectation of God ... and we stand, not allowing ourselves to be moved away from the unchanging God of the gospel.

The enemy would much prefer us to be apathetic and passive, that way he can control our lives. When the prophetic spirit moves upon us, God stirs our hearts to become active. At this point warfare of a different kind takes place. There is a clear link between prophecy and spiritual warfare.

Paul wrote to Timothy, saying,

> *'By these words previously spoken to you by prophecy and the laying on of the hands of the presbytery, fight a good fight.'* (1 Timothy 1:18)

He was encouraging Timothy to examine the substance of his prophecies and to clothe himself in them, literally to put them on, to wear them. He was advising Timothy to battle against the enemy, using the prophecies as a weapon of warfare. Stand on them, quote them, use them in the fight. As the enemy contests the ground of our life, we use the prophecy against him.

The prophetic word turns everything upside down and right side up. The contesting will also be **circumstantial**. Every prophecy that has a directional context will have a physical and practical out-working. God is intensely practical. He made clothes for Adam and Eve. He made sure the Egyptians paid Israel to leave, so providing them with the funds to launch their economy in Canaan. He had breakfast flown in every day on their journey through the wilderness. In the midst of stressful and challenging situations, his attention to detail is awesome.

The introduction of prophecy into our lives will probably herald a change in our circumstances. Sometimes our circumstances will appear to be adverse. They're not; it may be that God wants to change them. Things may look as though they are going into reverse. This is when we need to examine the content of the prophecy. It may well give us clues regarding where and how we are to hang on to the Lord.

We must not allow ourselves to get drawn into a debate with the devil regarding our current situation. We need to challenge the circumstances with the prophetic word or the opposite will happen by default. We will find ourselves standing in our circumstances, taking issue with the prophecy.

This is where the role of prayer plays a very important part in holding on to the prophetic word. We need to draw close to the Lord and cry out to him; 'Lord, you spoke this word. It looks like everything is going into reverse. I'm under attack from the enemy. By your grace and strength I am going to walk in the light of your word.

By your anointing and the power of the Spirit, I will see fulfilled the word you have put upon my life.'

We contest the same ground in prayer and we learn how to stand firm in the Lord and the power of his might.

Examine your faith for a good confession

It is always good to take time to re-evaluate our current faith level. What are we believing for today? In terms of my relationship with God, what am I in faith for today? Regarding people; issues of church life; progress for the future; what am I **consciously** believing for? What am I asking for? Where is my level of expectation? Am I giving a lead of faith to people around me? Can they see the muscle of my faith growing and becoming stronger? These are all important questions to ask.

Prayer is finding out what God wants to do, then asking him to do it. In a similar way, prophecy reveals God's heart and intentions to us. Prophecy then, gives us a prayer and a faith agenda.

When God spoke to Israel in Egypt, through Moses, he declared his heart and intention. In Exodus 6:6–8, the prophetic word gives Israel a seven point prayer and faith agenda:

- I will bring you out from under the yoke of the Egyptians;
- I will free you from slavery;
- I will redeem you with an outstretched arm and
- with mighty acts of judgement (the plagues!);
- I will be your God;
- I will bring you to the land I swore to give to Abraham, Isaac and Jacob;
- I will give it to you as a possession.

This prophecy begins and ends with a statement of identity, **I am the Lord**.

When the spies went out to survey the land and report back, only one man really went out and came back in faith. Only Caleb realised that the prophecy spoken in Egypt had power in their present circumstances. Caleb spoke out alone at that initial report-back meeting. Joshua said nothing at first, and then the following day decided whose side he would fight on.

Initially Caleb stood alone, not just against the spies, but against over two million adults also. Small wonder that the Lord calls him, *'a man of a different spirit'* (Numbers 14:24).

His initial response to the bad report of the other spies and the silence of Joshua, is to make a positive declaration which interrupts the negative message of the others.

> *'We should by all means go up and take possession, for we can certainly do it.'*   (Numbers 13:30)

The next day both Joshua and Caleb make a joint stand against the growing unbelief of the Israelites. The main points of their positive stand against unbelief serve to remind us throughout the ages of the dynamic ingredients of a faith agenda which will serve us in any situation:

- If the Lord is pleased with us.
- He will lead us into the land.
- He will give it to us.
- Do not rebel against the Lord.
- Do not be afraid of opposition; we will swallow them up.
- Their protection has been removed.
- The Lord is with us; do not be afraid of them.

Seven statements of faith to equal the seven prophetic statements in Exodus 6:6–8.

Pleasing the Lord is the central theme of the true believer's lifestyle. We do not belong to ourselves, we belong to the Lord (1 Corinthians 6:19, 20). As people who are living, breathing temples of the Holy Spirit, we live only to do and speak all that is on God's heart. Pleasing the Lord is everything. To live our life in such a way that the Lord receives pleasure from our conduct and lifestyle.

We must never forget that God is leading us. Day by day he takes the lead in our lives. He leads us in the paths of righteousness (Psalm 23:3); the goodness of God leads us to repent when we go astray (Romans 2:4). We serve a God who knows us by name, and he calls his people by name and leads them. He goes in front of them and allows them to follow his lead. He relates to his people so beautifully by allowing them to know and distinguish his voice (John 10:3, 4).

God is constantly giving to his people. His greatest gift is Jesus (John 3:16). He is constantly giving gifts to his children. The Holy Spirit is another tremendous gift of God to the church (Luke 11:11–14). Jesus is our inheritance. Jesus is to the church what the promised land was to Israel ... an inheritance. A possession freely given by our Father in heaven. God is a giver.

Our part in all this is to cease rebelling; to be willing to submit to the Lord; to offer our bodies as a living sacrifice (Romans 12:1). The Holy Spirit is such a catalyst for us in this area. It is always God who works in us both to cause us to want God's will and then to do God's will (Philippians 2:13).

There is absolutely nothing to be afraid of in terms of opposition. The Lord has rendered the enemy powerless, disarming him completely. A very public triumph! (Colossians 2:15).

That is why Caleb could say the enemy's protection had been removed, because he understood the nature of the God he was serving. Our God can never be defeated. Our role in the battle is always to **stand** still and see the salvation of God at work (2 Chronicles 20:17; Ephesians 6:11–13).

God has promised that he will never leave us or forsake us (Deuteronomy 31:6; Hebrews 13:5). No-one will be able to stand against us all the days of our lives, because God is with us and will never leave us (Joshua 1:5). This is our heritage – our inheritance. When Joshua and Caleb stood up, facing the great tide of human opposition, they were declaring ancient truths that ring as true today as when they spoke them to Israel. This is the only faith response that is allowable. When faced with the awesome nature of a God whose will is always enshrined in his word ... it is the only response we can make.

Anything else is unbelief, which is a personal affront to God's character. Unbelief is a personal insult that is grievously felt by the Lord. In the Bible he calls it an *'evil heart of unbelief'* (Hebrews 3:12). It causes us to leave God's side. If we are not on God's side, whose side are we on? Jesus said, *'he who is not with me is against me!'* (Matthew 12:30).

When the people responded to Joshua and Caleb's great statement of faith in God, by threatening to stone them, God himself intervened (Numbers 14). His reaction to Moses was, *'how long will these people reject me?'* Other versions say, *'treat me with contempt'* or *'spurn me'*. His reaction is to want to destroy them with a plague. **God hates unbelief with a passion!**

Moses intercedes, but does not prevent Israel's banishment into exile in the desert. God is angry; calling Israel an evil, wicked congregation. There is no doubt from this that the Lord takes unbelief very personally.

What has all this got to do with our personal prophecy? The point is, that whenever God speaks to us, he declares his intent, his will to our hearts. For us not to believe that the Lord will enact his will is blasphemous. For us not to begin to make adequate responses in preparation for that will to be realised, is a sin. Lack of proper response to the prophetic will draw us into the orbit of unbelief and that means real trouble! Unbelief leads us into unfruitfulness and that leads to unfaithfulness. Our job is to make sure our lives are in the best shape possible so that God's word is repeatedly fulfilled (Matthew 13:23). How we do that is the subject of Section B in this chapter.

SECTION B – ABSORPTION AND ASSIMILATION

In order for prophecy to work fully, we need to become entirely occupied with what God has spoken. Irrespective of whether we are dealing with revealed truth or prophecy, the Holy Spirit will take us up on our response, transforming us into becoming one with God's word. Section B examines all the issues necessary to achieving that end.

Open the prophecy for comment by mature people

Paul gave some excellent advice to Timothy:

> 'Do not neglect the gift that is in you, which was given to you by prophecy with the laying on of the hands of the presbytery. Meditate on these words, be absorbed in them (give yourself entirely to them), that your progress may be evident to all.' (1 Timothy 4:14, 15)

Whenever we receive a prophecy, we should draw in people with real maturity to discuss the word and give us any necessary advice. We should never keep prophecy to ourselves; that could lead us into deception and could result in losing the fulfilment by default.

Most prophecy is not self-fulfilling. We have a responsibility in the matter. Our part is to commit ourselves to the application of the prophetic word. The advice of significant people will be of great benefit to us in that regard. We need others to help us judge and weigh the prophecy and to correctly identify what the Lord is really saying.

A young man received a prophetic word about evangelism and the Lord's blessing. His personal interpretation was that he had received a call to be an international

231

evangelist with a significant ministry. He saw himself as the next Billy Graham. Suddenly the very ordinary work of church-based evangelism was beneath his consideration. The Lord had called him to higher things.

However, when those with a good deal more maturity examined his prophetic word, they found that it related to a significant success in evangelism, **not** the calling to be an evangelist. After some counsel and prayer that diminished his delusions of grandeur and released him to pursue a more low-key style of ministry, he has become extremely successful in the area of personal evangelism. To date, he has led scores of people to Christ from among his colleagues at university and his neighbours and friends at home. The prophecy related specifically to a season of blessing in this area; it did not allude to a fivefold ministry gift.

Accountability

It was the young man's willingness to be accountable in the situation that saved him from potential embarrassment and a dead end on his road of life. It is vital that we make our lives accountable (with or without prophecy), to our local leadership. Be open about what God is saying. Being open about areas of our life particularly where we are struggling, is a great blessing to the Lord and a source of real frustration to the enemy.

Firstly, we must be accountable in the area of our **lifestyle**. Everything in our lives should be open to view by mature, responsible people who love and care for us.

In the area of our sexuality, whether we are single or married, we need the input of others. This is a vulnerable area of our lives that requires real honesty and integrity. The enemy is flying around our lives, looking for a landing strip. If people know our weakness in this area, then the enemy cannot dump any of his unholy cargo into our lives.

In the area of money and finance, we must ensure that

there is good government and stewardship taking place. So many good people are in debt to an unwholesome degree. Debts must be honoured as a priority to the glory of God. We may need help to stop bad habits in terms of how we deal with our money. There needs to be an order of giving to the Lord; learning to live well within our income; spending money wisely and being open and generous to others.

In the areas of marriage and family we must ensure that a righteous lifestyle prevails. There must be a full and complete observable love for our partners. People around us need to see that we are meeting and fulfilling the needs of our loved ones. Our children need to be parented in a way that releases their potential, promotes love and security, and is a great honour to the Lord. After our love for the Lord; our love and desire for our family is uppermost in our thoughts and ways. Our love and service in the church should be next, where we live to serve and be available to build in the work. Finally, our own ministry comes a very poor fourth in terms of importance.

It is important that in all these areas we walk in the light and are known of God and by the brethren.

Secondly we must be accountable in the area of our **future**. As we move on in our love and living for the Lord, he will open doors of opportunity for us to be blessed and grow in the anointing. It is very important that we take up every chance we have to be discipled and trained. Discipleship is a key issue in the development of our life, our ministry, and our future.

Being with and learning from significant people will prevent us from falling down holes that are completely avoidable. Sadly, so many people are so intent on getting into ministry as soon as possible that they spurn opportunities for real training and development.

Many people don't like the idea of an apprenticeship, preferring to get into the ministry and show what they can do. On the surface it does seem a more slow and circuitous route into ministry via discipleship, opportunity and feedback. However, I have known many people who having rejected the discipleship track, don't actually make it or last very long in ministry. We are in this for the long haul. We cannot short cut the development process. If we try, we will only be taking two steps forward and three steps back. We will fall into traps we could have avoided. We will be so busy doing things, we will not learn how to handle ourselves.

Thirdly, our whole area of **ministry** needs to have the cutting edge of accountability. There are thousands of false prophets, false teachers, non-fathering/building apostles, poor evangelists and even worse, pastors, in the body of Christ across the world. People can be in ministry for all the wrong (and hidden), reasons.

Add to that number, the thousands more people who at some time in their ministry give a wrong prophetic word; poor teaching leading to error; bad advice to church leaders; people with a poor understanding of salvation (i.e. get your needs met rather than 'make Jesus Lord'); inadequate counsel to the poor and needy. The number of damaged people resulting from this mess can be astronomical. At the heart of it all is a lack of accountability for our ministry. If we go off the rails and have no accountability, the likelihood is that we will just keep on going! Possibly we will go even more wrong, and become extreme and dangerous. Probably we will give that wrong teaching to many more people before it is corrected (if ever).

We may prophesy badly to hundreds of people before someone points out the error. We could be giving an inadequate birthing to scores of new believers, causing massive problems to churches in the future. The evidence is there for all to see, that an inadequate new birth can take years of pastoral work to put right.

Many churches have gone off the rails because they trusted men who were not apostolic but who nevertheless

234

tried to perform that function. There has been so much pastoral damage through wrong use of counselling, inner healing and deliverance over the years.

If our ministry goes unchecked, we can learn models of behaviour that are ungodly. If our ministry is not examined we could be deceived and be deceiving many people. If the truth content of our words is not tested for accuracy, we can cause untold damage in the body. The more we grow in unaccountable ministry, the harder it is for us to accept responsibility for our actions. It becomes far easier to resist and isolate ourselves in pride or arrogance than it is to submit to the brethren.

The key issue in the accountability debate is the one of **authority**. Unless we, ourselves, are submitted to authority, we will never use it properly. Show me a man or woman who is not under authority and I will show you either a potential or actual abuser of power. To be able to handle authority properly, we must develop a servant spirit. Even at the height of our leadership powers, we must remember that leaders are simply the best servants around!

Jesus said that he had come to serve, not to be served, (Matthew 20:28). Ministry and leadership is about serving people, not using them. A real minister has a true servant's heart and will put himself out to be of assistance to others.

Jesus made himself a nobody; taking the form of a servant. He humbled himself and became obedient to death. This same approach and attitude is the requirement for all of us, especially for those in ministry and leadership. Selfish ambition and abuse of power versus humility and a servant spirit. Add authority to that equation and we either destroy people or build effectively in their lives. If we are not careful, what our gift builds, our character will destroy.

We can choose our attitudes. We can expect to be served, or develop the desire constantly to serve others.

The apostle Paul wanted to be regarded as a servant and steward of Christ (1 Corinthians 4:1). We cannot use authority properly unless we live under it ourselves. The Roman Centurion had a perspective on faith that amazed Jesus. That perspective was rooted in his understanding of authority and serving:

> *'I myself am a man under authority, with soldiers under me.'* (Matthew 8:5–13)

Notice the wording. He did not say, 'I am the man **of** authority with soldiers under me.' He said, 'I am a man **under** authority.' The fact he had people under his rule was incidental to him; he was under authority. From that viewpoint, he really understood the nature of authority and power. *'Speak the word only'*; for it was not necessary for Jesus to go and heal his servant. The Centurion knew that Jesus has such power and authority that his spoken word will travel through time and space to bring healing.

Prophecy contains a moral imperative

Every personal prophecy has a character response, whether it is referred to or not in the prophecy. That is because all personal prophecy has a **moral imperative**. 'You do this,' says the Lord, 'and I will do that.'

Mostly these conditions are unspoken. We do not need prophecy to tell us how to live. We use the revealed word of God in Scripture for that purpose. Our lives are built on Scripture, not prophecy. The word of prophecy may shape our lives in the sense of providing vision and direction. However, the fabric, the pattern, and the mould of our lives is set by revealed truth. Prophecy, then, always points us, either unconsciously or consciously, towards obeying God in Scripture. Keeping the word of God is a major element of all prophetic teaching. The foremost thought here is; if we can't obey the revealed will of God in the Bible, we will not fulfil the prophetic word either.

Avoid fatalism; just because God has spoken in prophecy, it does not mean we can sit around and wait for it to be fulfilled. Personal prophecy declares the possibility not the inevitability.

We will probably need to make adjustments in our lifestyle and approach to God as a result of the prophetic being spoken over us.

God has his own agenda in prophecy

We must ask ourselves the question, what is **God's agenda** in this prophetic word? The Lord very often has his own plan and schedule with regard to the prophetic.

Whilst conducting a ministry visit, Jesus heard that his friend Lazarus was sick. Rather than go to his side physically, Jesus sent a prophetic word instead:

> *'This sickness will not end in death. It is for God's glory, so that God's Son may be glorified in it.'*
>
> (John 11:4)

He remained where he was for two further days before eventually returning to Judea. On the way to visit Lazarus, he told his disciples plainly that Lazarus had died, but he, Jesus, still intended to visit.

By the time he arrived in Bethany, Lazarus had been buried for four days, proving beyond all doubt that he had expired. Jesus was met with two similar accusations from the sisters of Lazarus, Mary and Martha. *'Lord, if you had been here, this would not have happened.'* In other words, you are too late!

However, Jesus had sent a prophecy, *'This is not going to end in death but God's glory.'* God's agenda was not to heal Lazarus; it was to raise him from the dead. He was not too late for that!

God will often wait until there is no possibility that we can do anything in our situations. Therefore when we are completely dependent upon the Lord's power and sovereignty, then the Lord shows up in our circumstances.

There is always a gap between the prophetic promise and the fulfilment. Whilst living in that gap, which can be just a godly time warp, we must hold on to the prophecy and trust in God. His agenda in the situation may be entirely different from ours. It is helpful if we can see beyond our circumstances and through our events and situations. Sometimes we can only do that with hindsight, whilst at other times the Lord allows us to see the greater purpose.

In this situation, the prophecy had given Mary and Martha two enormous clues regarding the purpose, or agenda, of the Lord. Firstly, a promise for Lazarus' sake: *'your sickness will not end in death'*. Secondly, the real purpose behind the circumstances was to, *'glorify God and his Son, through it'*.

It is clear from the reaction of his disciples and the two sisters that none of them had really thought it through properly. The disciples thought Lazarus was improving healthwise through sleep, whilst Thomas was ready to die with him! The sisters were both upset that Jesus was too late and could not do anything. On closer conversation regarding the resurrection, Jesus helped Martha to come to the deeper revelation of who he was, culminating in her confession, *'you are the Christ, the Son of God.'*

However, like many Christians today, Martha went on to demonstrate that she had an understanding of the person of Christ, but lacked the revelation and the experience of his power. When Jesus asked for the stone to be rolled away from the tomb, Martha led the chorus of denial. *'Lord, he has been dead and stinking for four days.'* She still held onto her first understanding of the situation, which was, 'you are too late.' She had received a measure of revelation and understanding, but had not pushed through into any depth of experience or faith. Revelation must be experienced, because faith is active. The word had hit her mind, causing understanding, but had not been translated into a heart response causing action. Truth that sticks in the mind only will lead us to further debate and discussion, but no action.

Jesus had to take her again over the same ground of revelation, linking it to the original prophecy. *'Did I not tell you?'* In other words, 'Wake up, Martha, I gave you a prophecy about the glory of God, remember?'

The issue regarding the word of God, whether the now word of prophecy or the revealed truth of Scripture is this: 'Did I not tell you? Have I not said?' The ground of attack from the enemy is always, 'has God said?' The reply of Jesus was, as it should be of every believer, to quote the Word of God ... *'It is written.'* I believe this refers to Scripture, obviously, but also to the spoken word of prophecy. Hence Paul's advice to Timothy, *'by these prophecies, fight a good fight'* (1 Timothy 1:18). Part of God's agenda also is to bring personal change to our character as we will see next.

Don't neglect the character response

At some point in the reception of prophecy, we must consider the righteous state or otherwise of our lives. He may give us a word about our **future** that puts our eyes on a different horizon. We may see something new that we have not visualised before this time. However, we cannot live with our eyes on the horizon, otherwise we will stumble over what is in front of us. Try walking down the street with your eyes fixed firmly too far ahead and see what happens to your feet! At the least, your walk will be disjointed, causing you to stumble and trip. It is the same with spiritual vision. If our eyes are too attached to the vision and not enough on our life, we are heading for a fall.

We can only experience God in the **present**, in the here and now. We must use prophecy as a compass heading, to check our progress in our walk with God. When we are walking down the road, our eyes normally search out a landmark ahead. Then with our eyes are on the path immediately in front of our feet, we continue walking. Occasionally we lift our head to the landmark, measuring obstacles, distance to go, and how far we have come.

We use the same pattern in terms of our character response to prophecy. The Lord will give us a view of the horizon and where we are going. Very often the next thing he will do is drop our gaze to the very thing right in front of us, which will almost always be a character trait that he wants to change and adjust.

It is a common feature of major directional prophecy that speaks to our future, vision and ministry, that soon after its reception, the sky falls in and the bottom drops out of our world! Sometimes we go through the most horrendous of times. Everything goes wrong: we can't seem to pray, the heavens are as brass, we are misunderstood, we go through profound disillusionment. A friend of mine observed, after giving us the word of brightest hope, 'it is as though the Lord pushes us into a dark room and beats the living daylights out of us!'

I believe this is because we do not understand the principle of God's agenda in prophecy. The Lord has spoken prophetically. His prophecies are always called promises in Scripture, simply because his name and word are behind them. God is intensely practical and always wants to get on with things. Once he has shown us the horizon, he then wants to show us the stumbling block, the obstacle directly in front of us. Having shown us the future, he will then show us what will prevent that future from happening.

We walk with God by seeing what he is seeing, hearing what he is saying, and by responding to what he is doing.

Difficulties come because we still have our head in the clouds, whereas the Lord wants our feet on the ground.

When directional prophecy occurs, it provides us with the opportunity to get a handle on people's lives. During the judging process that follows its reception, we have the opportunity to discuss the individual's future walk with God. At this time of usually great encouragement and enhanced blessing, people are vulnerable to the Holy Spirit. They are ecstatic and wide open to the further follow up by the Spirit of God. Leaders behaving like true fathers will take this opportunity to graciously bring a character adjustment.

I remember one time, a particularly difficult individual (we shall call him John), was resisting all attempts at character development, personal accountability and change in his lifestyle. For several weeks I had chosen not to see him, preferring to resort to prayer, asking the Lord to break his resistance personally. Sometimes we can pursue things with people almost to the point of personal vendetta, losing our kindness and grace in the process. I recognised that I was in danger of taking his refusal as a personal affront to my leadership and ministry. In prayer I asked that the Lord would bless him from heaven. In my experience, blessing opens people up to God just as much as affliction. As a father in the church, I would rather have people in favour with God than disfavour. Giving people over to affliction through prayer has to be a last resort. It occurs when all else has failed and we are genuinely fearful of losing this person to acute ungodliness.

I believe personally there is something unethical and slightly immoral to pray affliction onto people and then take advantage of that situation to point out sin. Whereas I would have no compunction in praying a blessing into people's lives and then point out where the blessing may cease or be withheld from full completion.

In John's case, I prayed for the Lord to bless him. A gift makes way for the giver. Several weeks later, he received a very major and significant prophetic word, which I immediately witnessed to, as did others. John was euphoric, this word spoke to all his dreams and aspirations. For days afterwards, he was still on cloud nine. I recognised that the Lord had given me an opportunity with this man, and arranged a time to speak him.

The humble approach is always best. It is non-threatening and completely disarming. People cannot maintain a defence against humility without coming across as arrogant and ungodly. John was wary, thinking I was going to deny him my approval of the prophecy. He was taken aback when I did the opposite. I was delighted for him and wanted him to know that, congratulating him on the prophetic word. I declared my approval. I told him that I believed in him and wanted to serve him in the development of his gift and ministry. We talked about training and opportunity for him to grow in his calling. We looked at a potential action plan for his progress. He thawed noticeably, as we eagerly discussed his future.

At some point in the conversation, I casually asked him what percentage of the prophecy he wanted to be fulfilled. When he looked blank, I mentioned the parable of the sower and the 30%, 60%, or 100% fruition from the seed. As kindly as I could, I informed him that I felt there was only a realistic possibility of 40% fulfilment of his particular prophetic word. I asked him what kind of character he would need to demonstrate in order to fulfil God's heart in this new calling.

We talked about that for a few moments. I told him that the Lord obviously believed in him, hence the prophecy. I reiterated my faith in him also, and my desire to serve and get behind him in support. In this spirit, I asked him to think about our previous unfruitful conversations. I pointed out gently that these were the very areas of character that would prevent his word reaching fulfilment. These things, not me, were the obstacle. I asked him if I could have the privilege of helping him work these things through. He sat there in silence.

I further stunned him by saying, 'John, I believe you want to be a man of honesty and integrity. I believe the Lord has his hand on you right now. After the calling comes the training. This is now a time to sit down and work out the cost. I don't want to put you through an emotional wringer, to elicit some response. I want you to think hard over these next few days. The decision you make now should be based on your desire for obedience, not on emotionalism. Let me know how you feel.' Within two weeks, we had real movement in all those areas. John has gone on to real maturity in both his character and his gift.

In these times of tension, we need to move in the opposite spirit. Bless those who persecute us; pray for those who use us. The gospel is redemptive. God is kind and gracious. People are there to be won.

God's prophetic word always contains promise because his will is always in his word. These promises will always depend upon our heart and character response in their fulfilment. We see this clearly in Paul's letter to the church at Corinth (1 Corinthians 6:14–7:1).

The central theme concerns believers being the temple of the living God and the need to avoid unequal yokes with unrighteousness. In this context Paul mentions several past prophetic words concerning cleanness, separation and walking with God in verses 16–18. These refer to previous promises made by the following prophets: Ezekiel (37:26, 27); Jeremiah (31:1, 9, 32; 33:38); Isaiah (52:11) and Moses (Leviticus 26:12).

These are very real promises (or prophecies). Paul goes on to say,

> 'since we have these promises (prophecies) *beloved, let us **cleanse ourselves** from all filthiness of the flesh and spirit, **perfecting holiness** in the fear of God.'*
>
> (1 Corinthians 7:1)

When prophecy enters our life, so does the opportunity for cleansing and renewal of holiness. We see this same occurrence in the second letter of Peter (2 Peter 1:3–10). This passage refers again to exceedingly great and precious promises. These promises are always enshrined in the prophetic word. The Lord speaks his heart, will and intention through his prophetic word. It is by these words that we are to become partakers of the divine nature and escape all manner of corruption that would seek to drag us down.

Prophecy enables us to experience God's heart in a 'now' sense. The knowledge of God's love and care will cause us to become more deeply attached to his person. To become like Jesus is the goal of the Holy Spirit's work in our lives. The aim of the prophet is always to release people to know, love and yield to the person of Jesus.

God speaks prophetically to enable us to enter into his divine nature. Careful attention to our character response will ensure that we are co-operating with the Holy Spirit to achieve this aim.

Prophecy will cause a shaking

When prophecy comes it is usually completely out of the blue. When it arrives, it generally brings change with it. Rather like being close to the sea in a hurricane. The wind comes first and we learn to handle that, getting used to the moving of the Holy Spirit. However, as the wind blows we have no idea what is taking place out to sea in the great deep, until the tidal wave hits us. So it is with the moving of the Spirit in prophecy.

We have no idea what the after effects are going to be in our lives. As the word takes hold and brings change, a shaking occurs within our lives. Prophecy disturbs the status quo. It is unsettling. Prophecy gets us on the move from areas of safety and comfort. We learn again at first hand that we do not belong to ourselves. We get used to our life being a certain way, then the Lord sends prophecy to disturb our calm and agitate us into motion.

Prophets always provoke people. The irony is that we seldom ever try to do it by design. The very nature of directional prophecy is to get something on the move which was motionless. That necessitates change, which is unsettling.

Prophecy brings vision. Initially the entrance of vision brings **liberation**. It breaks us out of our safe and narrow confines in terms of how we see ourselves. It gives us a new horizon, lifts our viewpoint and brings us into a much broader place in the Lord.

However, vision also brings **restraint**. After the calling comes the training. We now have to set the stall of our life out in a different way. The way I used to live may now no longer be helpful. I may have to stop doing certain things in order to generate accomplishments in other areas.

After the first euphoric flush of being called to the prophetic ministry, I gradually began to realise the scale of the calling God had given me. With that understanding came the comprehension that my life as I had known it before was over.

Everything I was now doing was inappropriate to the vision I had received. Change came into my life and with it a real period of unsettling and shaking. I began to flow and move with different people, so my relationships changed. I had to finance my own development, so how I used my income underwent change. My study habits and subjects changed. So did my conversation and who I conversed with. When directional prophecy comes, change will not be far behind. That change will be both liberating and restrictive, hence the shaking and unsettling feeling that we will experience.

Prophecy will test us

The same prophetic word that brings joy, hope and the excitement of God into our lives will also bring us into a time of testing. After the promise usually comes a problem; a set of circumstances that are designed to enable us to hold on to the word we have received. This is dealt with more fully in Section A, under 'What happens when the opposite occurs?'.

Suffice it to say that the same prophecy may well receive several tests. Each phase of testing is devised to bring us into deeper levels of trust and faith. They can be of different lengths and time spans.

Joseph shared his prophetic dream about ruling and reigning with his family (Genesis 37). He was then flung into a pit for test number one. Probably he thought that his brothers were just trying to frighten him and that he would be reunited with his family soon. Test number two came when he was sold as a slave to the Midianites. He was now the lowest human life form: a slave. At times like this, when the bottom falls out of our world, we can be tempted to drop the prophetic word and even move away from God.

However, Joseph did neither of these things as we see in Potiphar's house, where he is sold into servanthood. Firstly the prophetic word about rule and reign began to work, as he rose to a place of prominence. Secondly, in his third test he was confronted with an amoral woman in the person of Potiphar's wife, who tried to tempt him into sexual sin. His reply to her gives a strong indication that far from forgetting God, he still clung onto him, *'how can I sin against God?'*

This third test occurred daily until he eventually ran away from her and was then thrown into prison. His fourth test was that he was now back to square one. Having tasted success he was once more an outcast. He was in prison for two full years before his opportunity for freedom came. During that time he diligently set himself to work and serve, and again rose to a place of prominence in the prison system. Again the prophecy was fulfilled in part, as he became the number two to the governor. Scripture says that,

> *'until the time that his word came to pass, the word of the Lord tried him.'* (Psalm 105:19)

Eventually he was freed and became Prime Minister of Egypt under Pharaoh. Then 24 years after having spoken his prophetic dream to his family, it was finally fulfilled in its entirety.

We will experience many opportunities to hold on to our prophecy as times of testing come into our life. However, the Lord is incredibly faithful. Whenever we go into trouble on God's account, he always goes with us. The Lord gave Joseph favour with Potiphar, the prison governor, and Pharaoh before fulfilling the word to Joseph and his family.

Testing is allowed, as it comes to try our faith, and to examine our willingness to hold onto the prophetic word. We should all live with the words of Peter ringing in our ears:

> *'Beloved, do not think it strange concerning the fiery trial which is to try you, as though some strange thing happened to you!'* (1 Peter 4:12)

It is quite normal to be tested. See it for what it is: an opportunity to believe the Lord and cling to him.

SECTION C – ACTUALISATION AND ATTAINMENT

The final part of responding to prophecy in a correct manner involves responsibility, strategy, and understanding about timing and preparation. To avoid the pitfalls of not receiving the complete fulfilment of prophecy, we will need to consider the part that hope, faithfulness and perseverance will play in our reception of prophecy.

Section C is vitally concerned with realising the certainty of bringing the prophetic word to a successful conclusion.

Recognise our responsibilities

Most prophecy on a personal level is not self-fulfilling. It needs our co-operation. We have a responsibility to be involved in the working out of that word through obedience. Faith and obedience are ongoing responses that we must make continually to the Lord, often in the same situation. As we have already seen, the word of the Lord will try us, and we need to positively cling to and speak out our faith confession. How we respond to prophecy dictates what will happen to the word; will it be fulfilled or discarded?

Obedience opens up the way for God to bless us. Obedience enables us to begin a partnership with the word that will give it room to grow, flourish and be fulfilled. Scripture tells us to,

> *'let the word of God dwell in you richly.'*
>
> (Colossians 3:16)

We need to formulate a strategy for the fulfilment of the word. If the prophecy is directional, giving us vision for the future, there will need to be a God-given plan to enable us to get from a receptive beginning to a successful completion.

Vision can be frustrating. In prophecy God speaks of things that are not as though they exist. This is the language of prophecy, and also the language of faith. God speaks into being what is not already there.

Simple prophecy (i.e. general encouragement for edifying, exhorting and comforting), affirms us in what is present and already happening. Directional prophecy largely declares what is not, but what will be. Of course, there will be an overlap here from time to time. The general prophetic spirit will blur the edges between general and directional. They are not compartmentalized and the edges are not always straight and well defined.

When the Lord speaks of the future, we need to know both the goal and the steps to achieve it. Many Christians receiving prophecy think about the goal but never the steps.

Unless we have a strategy that involves other people and co-operation with the Holy Spirit, we will only experience frustration and eventually unbelief through failure. Be prepared to submit the word and your life to those to whom you are accountable, to help in the outworking of a plan of action.

We need other people when we are seeking to outwork directional prophecy, otherwise we will try and make it happen in our own strength. Abraham did that with a prophetic word he received about a son and heir. In his impatience and lack of trust, he succeeded in birthing an Ishmael that was clearly not what God had in mind.

The Lord will give us the essential steps so that we can keep pace with him. In most of the fulfilment of directional prophecy, there will be an element of God supernaturally engineering circumstances beyond our control. We have to bear in mind that we are not the only instrument that God is using to fulfil his word. He will prepare other people and other circumstances to bring it into being.

In 1991, the Lord began to show me that he was sending me to black churches to form friendships and build relationships. At that time I had never been to a black church. I had spoken at several multi-racial churches, but never in a predominantly black church. I began praying for blessing on the black church population. Several of my intercessors informed me that the Spirit had led them to pray strongly that the Lord would give me a role in the Caribbean.

In 1992, I was speaking at a prophetic conference in London, at Kensington Temple. Having completed a lengthy seminar with teaching and ministry, I was heading for the pastor's office for a much needed cup of coffee. At times like this, we have no idea that our lives are about to radically change, or that the Lord is supernaturally engineering his will into our lives. All I wanted was coffee and to sit down and rest.

In Colin Dye's office (Colin is Senior Pastor of Kensington Temple), there was a black pastor, Dr Noel Woodroffe from Trinidad. Colin was on the point of departure as I entered his office. He introduced me to Noel and left. Noel had to rush off to a previously arranged appointment, so we only spoke for a few moments. In that two or three minutes, the Lord did a heart joining between us. It was a 'God appointment' and has led to me speaking at conferences and in black churches in both London and the Caribbean.

We sometimes look at prophecies and we cannot possibly imagine how it will happen. All we can do is take each step in obedience, knowing that God will do the things that we cannot. We hold on in faith; we are obedient to all that the Lord says; and he provides the sovereign breakthrough that we need.

Timing and preparation

Timing is the most difficult thing to get right in prophecy, in both the delivery and the out-working. Most people will push you into declaring a time, if they can. They will always want to know **when** something will occur. Sometimes in prophecy the Lord shows me times within the word itself. I have a simple rule in this area. If the Lord does not show me timings within the prophecy I give to people, then I don't seek that information afterwards. People will cajole; seek to manipulate; tell me sob stories; some have even got angry; others have called me a false prophet or compared me to other ministries (of course I always come off worse in the comparison).

So many prophetic ministries have come unstuck in this area because they have allowed people to push them beyond their initial reception. The Holy Spirit reveals a certain amount of prophetic revelation for people and situations. It is dangerous to get pushed beyond what he has allowed. We need to say, like the prophet of old, 'The Lord has hidden this thing from me!'

During the process of weighing a word, it can be judged to be of God but the timing can be for later. Sometimes prophecy has an imminence, possibly because of the circumstances God is speaking into. However, the timing may be for a long way off; in which case we know we must run with patience and perseverance.

We are in this thing for the long haul anyhow. We must live with the next ten to twenty years in mind. A major difficulty in people and the church generally is the insistence on living from week to week, hand to mouth. Churches and individuals must allow the Holy Spirit to instil a larger capacity within us than that. These goals should be long range, of 5–10 years, that have particular achievements in mind.

There should also be medium range goals of 2–5 years span that act as a staging post that is part of the progression towards the long haul goals. This staging post is a major point of assessment, evaluation and redefinition of the long term view. We should also have medium range goals that are not specifically allied to the long range vision. These goals may be for family, ourselves personally, or possibly to extricate ourselves from current activities in order to fulfil a wider destiny in later years.

Finally, there are short term goals of 0–2 years duration that may serve as a launching pad; a catalyst towards the higher and wider goals that the Lord has given us.

God knows the timescales into which he speaks. As we give ourselves to the process of prayer and judging the word, he will begin to speak about specifics in terms of times and seasons. After the calling comes the training and preparation. Prophecy will provide us with an agenda for prayer and action.

For example, I gave a prophetic word to a couple, that the Lord was calling them to South America, and Brazil in particular. They knew no people in this area and could not speak the language. They agreed that the prophecy had confirmed their call and desire to serve the Lord in this area. Over a period of 0–2 years they began to put together a prayer agenda for the nation, asking the Lord to open doors and give them contacts. They also laid down a goal of 0–3 years to learn the language.

We do not want to be out of phase with the purpose of God. Like Jesus, we need to be in constant step with the Father. God is never in a hurry but is always on time.

We need to allow the Lord to do all that he wants to do with our lives, our character and our temperament. One of the most sensible things we can do is to plan character development into our short and medium term goals. If we are brave enough, we may like to do the following exercise:

- Choose twelve people. Some will know you well; others should be leaders/mature people; one or two group members should have some analytical skills.
- Choose a team of 3 to 4 people who can compile the necessary information and be part of the discussion phase that will follow.
- If you are being discipled by someone, they should be part of the smaller group.
- Give each person a paper asking them to comment about you in the following areas:

- what strengths and weaknesses do you have?
- what fruit of the Spirit is in evidence/what is lacking?
- are you reliable; dependable; well organised; do you finish what is started?
- what kind of temperament do you have?
- what people skills do you have?
- what are your main/subsidiary areas of gifting; are you poorly, average or well developed?
- do you have any leadership skills; if so, what is good, what needs development?
- any other comments?

• Guarantee strict confidentiality. All the papers can be returned to the small group leader.

At the end of this exercise, we will know what areas of development we require in those areas. We can add that information to our action plan and short/mid term goals. The importance of an exercise like this cannot be under-estimated. These **will** be the areas of our lives that the Holy Spirit will definitely come to grips with in the next few years of your preparation. This will happen in two ways.

Firstly, we need to determine what can be done by way of training and development with our mentors to eradicate unhelpful things and build up areas of skill and expertise. This may be by **formal training** or **'on the job' opportunities**. We may be called upon to develop people skills in a particular area as we cultivate a stronger servant spirit.

Secondly, the Holy Spirit does engage in **situational development**. He will bring us into sets of circumstances that are designed to teach us patience, self control, faithfulness and the like. Some of these will be quick tests calculated to show us whether our instinctive reactions are godly or need further development. These tests are over before we are aware they have begun. They provide a snapshot into our current walk in the Spirit.

Other circumstances are more lengthy. Their purpose is

to build into our lives the attributes of God. Some situations build kindness and gentleness. Others test and strengthen our faith. Others allow us to build perseverance and power over the enemy. Some are designed to bring us into greater joy. There will be situations that develop a toughness, an ability to endure hardness, to act as soldiers.

Some circumstances are allowed to improve our belief system. Do we believe the Word of God? Are we prepared to stand on the revealed word of Scripture? Other circumstances will test and develop our ability to proceed with ministry in difficult circumstances such as personal problems, sickness or sadness.

God is producing an army of men and women who are strong and fit; tough and dependable; and sufficiently trained and capable in the realm of the word and the Spirit to take ground from the enemy.

Timing and preparation are absolutely essential to our cause. Lack of preparation will mean that the timing of certain things will get put back. If we co-operate with God, there is every chance that he will advance the timing. The important thing to remember is, **God does not measure timing, he measures growth!**

The ministry of the Holy Spirit is to make us ready for the work of the Lord. Many times after prophecy, people ask me, 'when will this happen?' My usual reply is, 'probably as soon as you're ready; are you planning to keep the Lord waiting?'

Prophecy gives us an agenda for action and prayer. This is why I have made such a big deal of our proper response to the Lord in prophecy. Always remember, prophecy declares the possibility, not the inevitability. Just because we have received prophecy, it does not mean it will automatically come to pass. The Lord looks for a response. He measures growth, not timing. In order for Joseph's prophetic dream to be fulfilled, he needed to grow. The Lord knew that he wanted Joseph to become Prime Minister of

Egypt, literally to adminstrate the country on behalf of Pharaoh. Joseph grew into this role by ruling over Potiphar's house, all his estates and finances.

He ruled so well and was so completely trusted, that Potiphar did not even know the full extent of his own wealth (Genesis 39:6). He prospered because the Lord was with Joseph. Joseph didn't defraud Potiphar of anything, including his wife!

He then completely revolutionised the prison system as he grew into his assistant governor's role. Everything that occurred in the prison came through the skills, planning and organisation of Joseph. The prison governor trusted Joseph so much he gave him a completely free hand (Genesis 39:23).

Scripture says that until his word came to pass, the same word tried Joseph (Psalm 105:19). It took twenty four years for that initial prophecy to be fulfilled. Abraham, the potential 'father of nations', waited over forty years to receive his first son, Isaac. David grew in stature and nobility in the wilderness as he waited over twenty years for his prophecy about being king to come to pass. Israel had to grow in relationship with God as they waited forty years to become ready to enter Canaan.

God is more interested in our faithfulness than in our success. We measure people by the success they have achieved in their life. The Lord wants us to be successful also. He wants to be able to say to us, 'well done, good and faithful servant'. In God's economy though, faithfulness has a higher premium than success.

King Saul had success over the Amalekites but was unfaithful to God in the process (1 Samuel 15). He tried to bend the word of God to fit his own needs and requirements (v. 9). When this was discovered and exposed, he hastily said that the sheep and cattle were spared (only the best ones), in order to sacrifice them to the Lord.

Samuel's reply was that God took no delight in burnt offerings at the expense of obedience and faithfulness.

From that point on, Saul was no longer king in the eyes of the Lord.

How do we measure success? Ezekiel was called to be a prophet of God to Israel. God told him that he was sending him to a people who would never listen to a word he spoke. God sent him to a rebellious and hard-hearted people who would contend with Ezekiel's ministry (Ezekiel 3:7–9). Because of this contention God would make the prophet's face and forehead to be strong against all opposition.

For twenty two years, Ezekiel prophesied to a people who constantly rejected his ministry. How do we measure his success? We can only measure it in his faithfulness in continually proclaiming the word of the Lord in the face of much hardship and constant rejection. He was a successful watchman who obeyed the Lord, seemingly without result. He began his ministry with Israel in captivity; he ended it with the nation still in Babylonian exile.

As my good friend, Peter Stott said, 'God is more concerned with the gut-level faithfulness of our lives and our preparedness to be true and faithful to his word, than he is with the outcome of it.'

Many Christians I have spoken to over the past twenty years have declared their frustration and unhappiness because their prophecies were rejected or despised by the local church. There has been anger and bitterness displayed by these prophetic people. Some have removed themselves from the church in a fit of pique; shaking the dust off their feet; with the attitude of 'not casting their pearls before swine'.

I have seen and heard all these things. Real prophets do not display this type of juvenile behaviour. They have a sense of the history of their call; to understand the times in which they are living. To be faithful in our gift when not making any headway or experiencing successful results, we need to understand the importance of **hope**.

True Christian hope

To begin with hope is not optimism; it is not looking on the bright side; it is not wishful thinking. Hope in the western culture contains a large element of resignation.

A man, who had been unemployed for two years, had been to a recent interview. When asked if he thought he had got the job, he replied, 'I hope so! I would like the job but I have my doubts that I will get it. I would say that I have a fifty-fifty chance of being chosen. Still, all I can do is hope.'

His hope was based on resignation and some forlorn wish to be fortunate. His whole demeanour was passive acquiescence; a subdued stoicism. It was better to hope (however unlikely), than to give up. However, privately he had given up on the inside; he was using hope as a public face saver.

In the Jewish tradition, hope is something completely different. It means to have a confident, unshakeable expectation of God's character. Hope has four levels of active response.

Firstly, **'I know who God is'** ... he is the Almighty One who has power over all things. He reigns supreme!

Secondly, **'I know what he is like'** ... he is the kindest Person I have ever known. He is my Father, he has chosen me and set his love upon me.

Thirdly, **'I know what he has promised'** ... he has made me so many great and precious promises. I serve a God whose will is always in his word. When he speaks, he acts!

Fourthly, **'I know he has the power to back up his will'** ... my Father is all powerful. He has given me the Holy Spirit and all that pertains to life and godliness. The power to receive from him has been bestowed upon me. Even faith is a gift given to me from heaven that I may receive every spiritual blessing from the Father.

He is the unchanging God who will always do what he says and will always continue to be unchangeably who he is! **That** is hope; a confident expectation of God's grace and goodness because he is unchangeable. God has put me in the one place where his favour will always shine down upon me ... in Christ. He has put me in the one place where I can always be accepted by him ... in Christ. He has put me in the one place where I can receive answers to prayer and hear his voice ... in Christ. He has put me in the one place where no devil, or circumstances, or unbelief, or hateful person can touch me ... in Christ.

In Christ, God is the same towards me yesterday, today and forever! (Hebrews 13:8). In a changing world we rest in the heartbeat of an unchanging Lord.

Hope looks at the future and declares, 'God will continue to be the same towards me as he has always been. He will act in the same way with me. He is unchanging!'

Scripture speaks thus,

> *'he has said, "I will never leave you nor forsake you".'*
> (Hebrews 13:5)

This promise is spoken **vehemently!** It has a strong, purposeful, 'look me in the eye when I say this to you' tense. I like the rendering in the Amplified Bible:

> *'I will not in any way fail nor give you up; nor leave you without support. I will not; I will not; I will not, in any degree leave you helpless; nor forsake you; nor relax my hold on your life; definitely not!'*

We can sense the power behind those words. This is the same power that lies behind every prophetic word, no matter how poorly it is delivered.

When God speaks either through his revealed truth or by prophetic ministry, he seeks to impart the strength of his power as well as the assurance of his will. Forever, all the days of our lives, he will be unalterably the same; that is hope.

Hope says, 'I will know God's grace today; this week

next month; next year ... always. God is unchanging, he will never leave me.'

Hope is the precursor of faith. Our confident expectation that God is unchangeable in his heart towards us gives us the necessary support to release our faith towards his changeless nature. God is constant. More constant than the sun, moon or stars. Hope leads us confidently to walk by faith.

Three things work together in our lives in bringing us into harmony with our great unchanging Father. Faith, hope and love always remain. Hope is the anchor point between faith that takes possession in the now sense, and the deep abiding love of God which he demonstrates towards us in the person of Christ.

Hope, that confident expectation, joyfully keeps faith and love fresh in our hearts and experience. Hope should be full of joy and laughter. It is confidence, (belief, reliance, trust, dependence) in God's constancy ... always and forever the same towards me.

There are two unchangeable things about God in which we must believe. Firstly, that it is his **nature** to be unchanging, constant and completely trustworthy. Secondly, that when he **promises** something, everything he is stands behind that word. His promise is as good as his name! His name is as good as his nature!

God embodies all truth, therefore he cannot lie. Because he is truth (*'I am the way, the truth and the life'*), we can be secure in his promises. Our hope (confident expectation), is therefore secure and unmovable, **anchored** in God himself.

That is why the psalmist was so eloquent in speaking of hope in his writings. He actively encouraged himself when in times of difficulty and stress, to express hope joyfully towards his God:

- *'You have been my hope, sovereign Lord, my confidence since my youth.'* (Psalm 71:5)

- *'As for me, I will always have hope, I will praise you more and more.'* (Psalm 71:14)

- *'Why are you cast down, O my soul? Why so disturbed within me? Put your hope in God, for I will yet praise him, my saviour and God.'* (Psalm 42:5)

- *Now, Lord, what do I look for? My hope is in you.'* (Psalm 39:7)

When dealing with prophecy in our lives, we base our faith firmly on our confident expectation that the Lord will fulfil his word in his own way and his own time. Our role is to ensure that we live our lives in the best way possible. We know that as we live right before God,

> *'He will withhold no good thing from him who walks uprightly.'* (Psalm 84:11)

Hope will never disappoint us, because it is based on the love of God which has been poured out in our hearts by the Holy Spirit who has been given to us by God (Romans 5:5). This hope is an anchor of the soul, sure and steadfast, bringing us into God's presence (Hebrews 6:17–20).

Patience and perseverance

Once we are convinced that a prophecy is true, we must seek to remain patient and confident. We must not allow ourselves to be robbed.

> *'Don't be sluggish ... but be imitators of those who through faith and patience inherit the promises.'* (Hebrews 6:12)

In this instant world of ours, we want everything on tap and to hand, immediately. It is a shame that the faith movement has been besmirched by a few people with a 'name it and claim it; grab it and blab it' ministry.

At the heart of faith teaching lies two extremes. Firstly, the ability in the Holy Spirit to possess **now** in our faith. Secondly, the strength to endure and be patient, to hold on during the out-working of our faith in our current circumstances. The Holy Spirit is excellent at reconciling these two extremes within our experience. He uses hope as the bridge between these two acute differentials.

> *'Do not throw away your confidence* (hope), *which has a great reward. You have need of endurance, so that when you have done the will of God, you may receive what was promised.'* (Hebrews 10:35, 36)

In between the prophecy and the fulfilment usually lies a set of circumstances that demand a proper response. That response is to hold on to the prophecy. Don't throw away our confidence; now we need to make a stand and endure (patiently). What is the will of God in this issue?

Firstly, there may be areas of our life that the Holy Spirit wishes to clean up or change. Between the prophecy and its fulfilment the Holy Spirit is dealing with our character. Are we responding to him? Are we getting the advice, prayers and support from others to bring about change?

Secondly, we are learning how to make a stand of faith. The Christian life is all about making a stand (Ephesians 6:10–17). Stand in the power of God. Stand against the schemes of the devil. Stand, wearing the armour, consciously prepared to resist the devil.

The will of God is that we demonstrate our faith in him at all times. It is incredibly important to God that he is believed. He puts everything that he is behind every word he speaks. He hates unbelief, but rewards steadfast patience.

Patience relates to our personal attitude. It is a calm endurance; a standing still under the hand of God. Not resisting all that the Lord seeks to do. Not anxious, but unworried and waiting on the Lord:

> *'Those who wait on the Lord will gain new strength; mount up on eagles' wings; run and not get tired; walk and not become weary.'* (Isaiah 40:31)

Perseverance is more active than patience. To persevere is to be steadfast under trial; to have a willingness to overcome obstacles and to continue moving forward in spite of events. It is active!

When God speaks prophetically, the word he gives contains substance. It will create what the Lord has spoken. Prophecy gives us an initiative. It is the word of the Lord. We must use that word; that promise to speak to our circumstances. We must fling it in the face of the enemy (1 Timothy 1:18), use it to fight with. Be very unwilling to surrender the initiative that prophecy provides.

Patience and perseverance combine so many times in our experience. They help us to keep our eyes on God **through** what he has spoken. We can express our trust in God by praising and worshipping him because he has spoken. 'Thank you Lord; you said; you gave me this promise; you have spoken; you gave me this word; you have said ... I trust you, I worship you, I praise you. Thank you!'

It is important to speak God's promises back to him, to quote them in our praise and worship. To give thanks to him by speaking his promises in an expressive way. This is a weapon against the enemy. A shield against his fiery darts. The enemy will insinuate: *'has God said?'* (Genesis 3:1). We need to be able to shout joyfully: 'yes he has!'

We need to make sure our attitude does not neutralise the prophecy. We need to make a stand; take sides with God; endure the situation; wait on the Lord. Patience and perseverance allied to faith and hope will bring about a fulfilment of all God has spoken.

Chapter 10

A Framework for Prophecy in the Local Church

The context of prophecy is always into the local church. The church is God's idea. A called out group of people who are brought together through the life, death, and resurrection of the Lord Jesus Christ.

Through his shed blood we are cleansed, renewed and set free to serve him together with a humility; a gladness and sincerity of heart. The church is described as a Body; a Bride; an Army; a Household; and a City. Through the Scriptures we get this amazing picture of who and what the church is designed to be in God's perspective.

We then set foot in a local church and discover that we are only living in a tiny percentage of God's revelation for his people. There exists a credibility gap between the ideal of Scripture and the actual of our normal practice.

The aim of all church leaders is to produce men and women of maturity, who will live in the here and now of the actual; but who are reaching out with desire, prayer and strategy for the ideal.

Prophecy helps us to reduce the credibility gap between the ideal and the actual. Prophecy reveals the mind and heart of God to his people. It encourages, exhorts and comforts. It helps to build the church; to build a closeness between God and his people; and also between one another. It stimulates and encourages people to be better than they are before God. It comforts and shows the tenderness of God's heart in our distress. It keeps us moving forward under fire. It helps to produce real men and women of God who will pay the price to be in the forefront of all that God is doing.

It is sensible therefore for us to understand that perhaps of all the gifts, prophecy should come under the most attack. The enemy will do everything he can to undermine, counterfeit and discredit this vital gift within the local church.

Leaders in particular must do all that they can to encourage the correct use of prophecy. Within the local church there is a bubbling chemistry of relationships; ministries; goals and vision; different perspectives; leadership and followers; pastoral; prophetic; evangelistic; tensions; pressures and frustrations.

The prophetic word will act like a catalyst within that local church scenario. The scientists have a word for this peculiar activity: they call it chemotaxis. This is defined as: 'The movement of a whole organism in a definite direction in response to chemical stimulus.' Prophecy has exactly the same cause and effect. To move the whole church in a definite direction in response to the prophetic word of God.

If the gift of prophecy and prophetic ministry is to take its rightful place in the local church, we must establish some ground rules that are easy to understand and to use.

Inspirational prophecy

This is the type laid out in 1 Corinthians 14:3:

> 'He who speaks, gives edification, exhortation and comfort to men.'

This can be by spontaneous utterance during times of worship and prayer. It can also be used successfully in the more confined structures of a home group. (Some would argue that this is the best place to develop the prophetic gift.) In the course of life and relationship building we must encourage the life of the church as much as possible to continue outside of a meeting only format.

This will hopefully mean that people are being encouraged to care and pray for one another in their friendships. Prophecy, because it is encouraging, stimulating and comforting will therefore play a part in members blessing and helping one another.

To establish rules that prophecy can only be used in meetings would deprive the body of a wonderful enriching dynamic. Rules must never replace relationship and trust. Harassed leaders will always make decisions and rules around peoples' gift and function rather than use the opportunity to enhance and deepen the relationship (albeit a working one) with the people concerned.

Encourage good habits

Here is a guideline for use in giving inspirational prophecy. At any one time in the church we will have people who are both **learning** to move in prophecy and those who are **maturing** in the gift. Inspirational prophecy is concerned with providing encouragement, stimulus and comfort to people generally in the things of God. To inspire people to believe in the love of God; to be at peace and rest; to provide faith and encourage the power of the Lord to be seen; to stimulate worship and prayer; to release faith in God and bring a sense of his presence into the lives of his people. All of these are the basic aims of prophecy at the shallow end; the inspirational part of the prophetic gift.

At the learning stage give people a mentor to whom they can go and check out **every** word they receive. Their mentor can be a person in the mature stage of the gift or a cell group leader or some such responsible person, preferably not in the main church leadership. The idea of a mentor for learners is to act as a buffer or filter for the main leadership.

The main leadership in turn must provide a mentor for all those who are maturing in the gift. This will hopefully ensure that prophetic people are both listened to, developed, and held accountable for their words and practice.

At the learning phase, people will begin to develop accountable relationships where their words can be checked out and they can receive instruction and wisdom in prophetic protocol. As an individual grows in the development of the gift, he or she can be given responsibility within their gifting. At a defined point a learner should be given the freedom not to have to check out inspirational words. They have now joined the ranks of those who are maturing in prophecy and so will come under a more influential regime of development.

Quite simply they have developed a servant spirit with their use of the gift and can now move on to a different level of growth, accountability and maturity.

In the learning phase, **everything** must be checked out. In the mature phase, freedom is given to be spontaneous and inspirational. However a protocol is developed where people moving in revelatory prophecy can establish their gifting on a more responsible criteria.

Revelatory prophecy has a more planned approach attached to the ministry. Revelatory prophecy contains words that are **directional**, i.e. there are elements of providing government; a sense of aim; instruction to follow a particular course; the enhancement of vision and the opening of new doors and horizons. Revelatory prophecy also contains words that are **correctional**, i.e. that involve aspects of judgement; disciplinary action; the exposure and righting of wrongs; admonition and adjustments; a clear call to repentance and the administration of such events. Both these aspects of revelatory gifting require a certain protocol (see Chapter 5, 'Guide-lines for Handling Prophecy').

It is not my intention to duplicate that chapter, only to provide us with a quick reference guide to the protocol required for revelatory gifting in the local church. There are six elements of protocol involved in giving revelatory words in the church.

1. Give the word in private first, not in public

Resist the temptation to speak when the word first hits your spirit. Our first response must be to pray and seek the Lord. Revelatory prophecy can be either a tremendous blessing or cause terrible things to happen if it is abused or mishandled.

Most revelatory prophecy can wait for 24 hours at least and in most cases considerably longer. We will discover I believe, that God actually builds into the timing of these revelatory words enough of an interval for the protocol to be used effectively. At this point we need to pray and gain clarity about what God is saying.

Revelatory prophecy has governmental implications and therefore must be shared first with those who have responsibility and God's anointing to lead the work. We must be careful not to put our ministry ahead of those with the anointing and governmental responsibility. To do so would put us firmly on the wrong side of the Lord and into rightful disrepute with our leadership.

2. Record the prophecy

A recorded word can be judged, interpreted, meditated upon,, the recorded word can be expressed in positive action by the leaders and the church.

An unrecorded word has little value. The important details can be forgotten or open to misunderstanding, and mishandled because we are relying on our memory instead of an accurate record.

Recording prophecy was normal practice for the prophets. Isaiah received specific instructions to write his words down (Isaiah 8:1) and also the reasons why this was important.

> *'Write it on a tablet and inscribe it on a scroll. That it may serve in the time to come. As a witness forever.'*
> (Isaiah 30:8)

Prophecy has a continuous application that may endure long after the present circumstances fade. Revelatory prophecy will continue to serve us after the particular context into which it was given has been resolved.

Habakkuk was given a very similar instruction:

> *'Record the vision, inscribe it on tablets, that the one who reads it may run. For the vision is not for the right time.'* (Habakkuk 2:2, 3)

i.e. it is not for now, but for later!

Twenty years ago a church in the centre of England (called the Midlands) received a prophetic word which was in two parts. The first part directed them to purchase a building in a particular area and refurbish it. The second part spoke of God producing in that building a new generation of leaders and key ministries that would be effective right across that whole region. These people duly bought the building and over a period of years restored it into good working order. However, the second part of the prophecy had never been fulfilled and in time the church had forgotten the word and settled in to middle class complacency and obscurity.

I came along to take a church weekend with them and the Lord gave me a two-part directive prophecy for the church. The leaders encouraged me to share it with the entire congregation.

The first part of my prophecy began ... 'God has given you this building. From this place he is raising up a new generation of leaders and key ministries that will be effective right across this region.' It was almost word for word identical to the second part of their original prophecy.

As I finished speaking several people in the congregation between the ages of 50 and 70 years began raising their hands and praising God. Many were in tears. Throughout that weekend people brought scraps of paper with the original prophecy written on, out to the church leaders. Many of the current leadership team had not been in the church 20 years previously. *'Write the words on a scroll that it may serve in a time to come.'*

The whole church, even its most recent members, could now understand that they were living in the unfolding of prophecy for their work which began 20 years ago. That weekend was one of excitement, praise, renewal and rededication to the Lord. It was an immense privilege to be a part of it. However, it has to be said that the power of that occasion would have been largely lost were it not for the recorded prophecies from that previous time.

Jeremiah was told to

> *'Write down all the words I have spoken to you, in a book.'* (Jeremiah 30:2)

In chapter 36, Jeremiah is given further instructions in the matter of recording prophecy. Even when the King had snatched the scroll from Baruch, Jeremiah's secretary, and burned it Jeremiah was told to write another one. Pausing to write down revelatory prophecy (perhaps not in full but certainly the main headlines) will help us to gain a sense of burden and objective. What is God saying? Why is he saying it? What does he feel for people and the situation? After speaking, what does the Lord want to achieve from this word?

These are all valid questions that will help us to determine certain things about the word of prophecy. What type of prophecy is it? Is it a warning? Is it directive? Will it affect the vision, if so, how? Is it corrective? Do we need to make some adjustments? Is there a need for repentance?

The answer to all these questions will affect the method of delivery and its reception by the leaders and the people. This leads us in turn to consider a major obstacle or stumbling-block which may prevent the word from being heard and received. That stumbling-block is namely ... ourselves!

3. We must allow the Lord to touch our hearts first

How do we know that this is a pure word of prophecy and not the glorification of our own opinions? The 'revelation' may confirm our own thoughts and feelings. How do we know it is not birthed out of our own frustrations or sense of rejection?

The short answer to these questions is that we may not be sure of the answers! In these circumstances there is only one way in which we can filter out our pride; frustration; rejection; or our desire to be right and say I told you so! Literally, we must humble ourselves and pray.

With a minor prophetic word of correction or direction, I would recommend a week of prayer and fasting. With a major or fairly 'heavy' word of correction and direction, I would recommend at least two weeks of prayer and fasting before **we speak to the leaders**.

This will accomplish several things. Firstly, it will promote a godly level of humility whereby we can speak the word well. Secondly it will **drive out** our frustration and pride.

Thirdly, it will ensure that our **attitude** to the church is one that will honour God.

Fourthly, our own opinion and feelings tend **to die** when our stomach is rumbling! Some people believe that fasting helps to cleanse the body of all toxins, so making it more healthy. In a prophetic context, fasting allows us the opportunity to cleanse our soul and spirit of the toxic waste of our own frustration, opinions, pride and hurts. In this way we can filter out all the human and sinful elements that will pervert the true words of prophecies.

With revelatory prophecy we must allow the Holy Spirit into our hearts first before we do anything else. This type of word especially requires a pure heart, pure motives and pure lips. We have to be very honest with ourselves at this point. If we find it easy to give negative words to people, there is definitely something wrong with our spirit. Words of correction should cost us something to give. Fasting is where we start to pay the price. If we are unwilling to pay that price then we should be equally as unwilling to give the prophecy. We must allow the Lord to sort out our own hearts.

> *'Search me O God and know my heart;*
> *Try me and know my ways;*
> *And see if there is any wicked way in me,*
> *And lead me in the way everlasting.'*
>
> (Psalm 139:23, 24)

4. Understand your own accountability

Quite often in prophecy particularly with revelatory gifting, we are attempting to make others accountable for our words. Anyone moving in prophecy and maturity will understand that prophecy and accountability go hand in hand. Quite simply, someone has to pay the tab!

Before we deliver revelatory prophecy we must pay the price to speak. What is God asking of us? We may have to put some things right before we prophesy. What is the quality of our relationship with our leaders? Why have we let it get so bad? There may be a dual fault and therefore a dual responsibility here. The question is ... what is our part?

Under no circumstances should we share this revelatory word with our friends or cronies. We must go to God, then the leadership. It may sound good or seem attractive to share this with our closest loved ones. However, in my experience, in 90% of those cases, a disaster occurs. We cannot always know what is in the heart of our friends or what resentments, hurts or opinions lurk beneath the surface.

This is not an encouragement to believe the worst about people. Rather it is the desire to ensure that the governmental principle is not misunderstood. Leaders deserve to hear first. The opinions of others may colour the delivery of the prophecy. It would be a shame if my fasting had filtered the poison out of my own life only to see it replaced through the unwise counsel of people outside of leadership. Many prophetic people do get suckered into firing other peoples' bullets, often at the wrong target!! We must prove ourselves to God and to the leadership by allowing them to examine us for the signs of humility, pride, frustration, negativity, and judgement.

5. *Meet with the leadership*

There will inevitably be times of tension between prophetic people and leadership. When true prophets speak, things will happen. Leadership must gear itself up for those events. That is why there must be a healthy respect, love and co-operation between leaders and those in prophetic ministry.

It has been said that if a prophet were in charge of a local work, there would probably be less prophecy given in that church than in others! Simply because the prophet would be responsible for the outworking. Of course there is a large grain of truth in that observation, though the roots of it may come from a fairly unhealthy perspective on the relationship between prophetic ministry and leadership.

For far too long the prophetic has only been seen as a blessing ministry. Prophets come into the church, take a few meetings, bless people and then move on. At its heart that methodology by itself is unscriptural. In the New Testament the prophet's ministry is seen primarily in a building context with the apostolic, laying the foundations of the church of God (Ephesians 2:20).

The tension between the prophetic and local church leadership does not always mean something is wrong. It can mean that something is happening! There is no movement without tension. Many local churches do not have a visionary as the main leader. These churches tend to move more slowly and can more easily settle for the ground they occupy, rather than wanting to move on. The role of the prophet, amongst other things, is to supply and confirm, establish and develop the vision of the work and its people.

This means, I believe, that they should both prophesy and be around to work the issues through. Where we have credible prophetic gifting in our local churches we must make room for them in our leadership teams. At the very least they should have access to the elders. If we are sensible we will work out a role for them. Different people have different anointings. I would not have the same anointing as other elders. I would not attend the finance or administration meetings. Nor would I be present at meetings to discuss pastoral situations.

However, meetings that would discuss our long-term financial planning or pastoral strategy would benefit from a prophetic perspective. Any meeting that involves strategy, vision, growth and development would benefit in hearing from the prophetic voice in the congregation. It is not enough to speak into these scenarios; we must make sure prophetic people are available to help us work through the implication and implementation of the prophecy they bring.

When we meet with the leaders it is extremely helpful to have something written on paper. The way we generally like to write and communicate will figure prominently in how we express ourselves. Some people who are better at writing than speaking may like to write the prophetic word out in the fullest sense. The leaders can then read it and ask questions or seek clarification.

Other people may prefer to write down the main headlines of the prophecy and talk things through in more detail. Writing words down is a real aid to both parties. It helps the one prophesying to be clear, measured and specific and assist the leaders to understand what is in the heart of the prophet.

As we write down revelatory words, we can begin to pray for an unhindered communication process. We can pray for clarity, reception and for the moving of the Holy Spirit. We must allow a specific time period for deliberation, prayer and judging of the word to take place. This can take several weeks and sometimes months. We must not lose heart.

Remember God will build into the time frame a sufficient interval for weighing and judging. It is important though that leaders give regular feedback on what is happening with the prophecy so that frustration or rejection does not take hold of the prophet.

Put simply we are looking for a partnership to emerge at this point between leadership and prophetic people. Leaders must give feedback; prophets must wait humbly. Having delivered the prophecy to the leadership, revelatory people must acknowledge that the accountability for that word has now passed on from them to the leaders. If we take receipt of a prophetic word, we accept the responsibility that goes with it.

The word must now be left with the leaders. We cannot harass them into decision-making. There needs to be mutual levels of humility, love and respect on both sides. It is very difficult to give away a prophetic word in private, and to have to entrust it to others. It is like giving away a part of yourself. It is helpful to know what is happening to your offering.

6. Planning the next move

As the word gains acceptance within the leadership team, there will be further fellowship with the prophetic person involved. It is a good idea to draw them into the discussion regarding the next move. It will continue the development of relationships and forge a deeper sense of commitment to the partnership.

The prophetic individual may be able to give further insight into the application of the word and the response required. Leadership must retain the overall authority in the development of an effective strategy. Sometimes the same person who gives the prophetic word can be hopelessly inadequate at determining what we do with it.

At best they will provide sound guidance, at worst they will have outlandish and unworkable ideas. The reality will probably be somewhere in-between these two points. What is required is a generosity of spirit and a gracious disposition.

The church requires an **effective strategy to support the prophecy**. I would suggest that this may take some or all of the following points:

(a) Talk it through with the wider leadership team

Apart from the core group of leaders in the work, there is usually a wider group who takes responsibility in one way or another for people in the church. This wider echelon may be clearly defined in the church or may simply be drawn from those who are key and influential members.

Cell group leaders in particular must be drawn in to these times of prayer and discussion. This wider team must be given time to assimilate the word and understand it. Remember the core leaders may have lived with the word for several weeks prior to this next stage. It is unhelpful and unrealistic to expect people to grasp in 24 hours, what it took the core leaders several days or weeks to understand.

Provide transcripts of the prophecy to aid discussion and prayer. It would be helpful also to have some idea regarding the implications and the implementation of the prophecy. Remember at this point, we are not seeking approval for the word. We already have accomplished that fact, our involving a wider group of people proves that the prophecy has gained acceptance. We are meeting now to discuss its effect upon the work as a whole. We are looking as leaders to take responsibility for the prophecy. This responsibility must be shared with as many key people as possible.

The issue now is not acceptance but **ownership**. The prayer, dialogue and fellowship that follow must foster a sense of: 'God has spoken, how do we align ourselves with his word?' When we take this word to the whole congregation, they need to be able to see a number of characteristics at work:

- The word has been thoroughly vetted and gained acceptance.
- All the core leaders, wider leadership team and key people agree with the word.
- There is a high level of unity and ownership of the prophecy at this level.
- The prophecy is received seriously and is therefore going to have implications on the work.
- The leaders are excited at having heard from the Lord.
- A time of change will occur in the church which will mean good for our future.
- This therefore means a time of envisioning, faith-building and reflection regarding our current church status.

All of these things need to be thoughtfully communicated at this wider leader's meeting. We want to present a unity and sense of purpose to the whole body. It is important therefore that time is allowed with these people to express their concern, reservation and fear. It is always good to allow these comments to be verbalised. They will probably come out in the body of the congregation anyhow.

It is much more helpful to discuss the dangers and repercussions at this level. It will help us to answer the difficult questions, anticipate forthcoming reactions and gauge the mood of the people. All of these elements will have a positive effect upon the forthcoming presentation to the whole congregation.

(b) The church meeting

Call a full meeting, giving plenty of notice. We want as many people together as possible. Give some thought to baby-sitters and childminding. I have found it helpful at times to ask local churches for help in this regard.

Sometimes we have organised a crèche and fun day for children on a Saturday morning whilst the adult church met together. Leaders must use their own discretion regarding the attendance and age of the children at this meeting.

Alternatively, if we are organised properly we may have cell groups taking responsibility for this matter.

Particular care must be taken concerning who gives the presentation. It may be appropriate for the original prophetic individual to share the word. If so, the leaders must give adequate guidelines. This is a time for the governmental people in the work to hold centre-stage before the people.

If it is appropriate for leadership to present the prophecy, then care must be taken to give credit to the right individual. At this meeting we need to lead a good time of worship, creating a sense of excitement and anticipation at God's presence. We must give a clear presentation that is as interactive as possible for the people. Everyone needs to get involved at this important gathering. We do not want people passively sitting and listening.

Prophecy is revelation, therefore our presentation of it must not involve a mere information-giving exercise. It may be a good idea to break up the word into several parts and allocate each segment to a capable person to present. Involve the people in praying throughout the evening. The type of prophecy we have received will play a major part in how we conduct this extra-ordinary church meeting.

If it is a **now or confirming** word that everyone will be able to witness and appreciate in some manner, then we can call for a response during the evening. This type of prophecy has a way of sealing us into our present inheritance and vision. It will show us that we are on course but possibly a greater commitment is still necessary. Calling for people to respond will enable us to pray for people and involve the church in active prayer. Of course we must also stress that we will be taking the next few cell groups or meetings to talk through all the implications of the prophecy on our long-term planning. We must ensure that transcripts of the word and relevant discussion and prayer points are made available for everyone to take home.

If the prophecy is giving a **new or future** word, then we may need to take a different style of meeting. In this event we will need to stress a little of our history and present circumstances to provide the link with where we are going in the future. We are talking more of plans, change and new things which do not need to be dumped on people. Time must be given for prayer in groups around some of the main points of the prophecy. These groups must be strongly led and re-inforced by the main leadership, supported by key and influential people.

Again, we need to stress that we want to make room over the next few weeks and months at cell/home group and individual level for a response, feedback, further dialogue and prayer. Written transcripts of the word and the main points, prayer, implications and food for thought must be made available.

Of course some words may contain elements of all four

aspects of prophecy; now, confirming, new and future. For more detail on these aspects please look through Chapter 7, 'Section B – The Subsidiary Tests'. In this case we need to look at what should we respond to at this time and what elements we set aside to discuss through in the next weeks/months.

(c) Discuss in small groups

Prophecy is too important to let it fall away by default. After the full church meeting we must allow for a strategy that brings God's new word into focus and to the attention of all concerned. Again the paramount issue is ownership. People tend to own what they contribute to, therefore time for discussion and prayer is important. Never underestimate how vital personal communication is in this process. Give people the freedom to make positive and negative contributions, both are equally valid. It will be essential to ensure that key leaders are present at these gatherings so that misunderstandings do not occur. The enemy will be prowling around at this time seeking to cause trouble, division and dissension. Wisdom is required to deal with obstructive people and difficult questions. Patience is a necessary quality at this time.

If we handle this time well, the church will take some considerable steps forward. Handled badly it may result in some fairly major problems. We will definitely find out in this process who is joined to the vision of the church. In this discussion time, the leadership team should also be talking to individuals. We want people to make a personal response because the success of all corporate prophecy is determined by personal application.

We can use this time of corporate envisioning and faith-building to talk to people about their personal goals and vision. It will therefore provoke a greater sense of commitment as we pray with people. Surprising things can occur in people at this time. A change of heart, renewed faith, spectacular growth and a general increase in faith and corporate prayer could just be a few of the follow on blessings that occur.

(d) Future plans and adjustments

Prophecy gives us a faith and a prayer agenda that will allow us to focus on future plans and the strategy required to enable us to co-operate with the Lord. We will need to think in terms of change, short-term, mid-range and long-term goals and a suitable time-frame in which we need to operate.

After prophecy comes the adjustment. A strategy will help us to unite the people around some common goals, so that we can all move forward together.

Always build in a time for review at different intervals so that we can ensure that we are keeping on track and maintaining the right momentum. It is wise to be able to look back as well as look forward in determining our present course.

Chapter 11

Keeping Prophecy Alive

Once revelational prophecy has been spoken into the life of the church, we must do all that we can to ensure that it does not fall away. Directional prophecy acts as a stimulus to corporate vision. It will provide the church with a much needed prayer and faith agenda.

Directional prophecy given into a church context with the full support of the leadership will unite the people behind the purposes of God. It will enable us to discover God's heart for the corporate work to which we are called.

Revelational prophecy will confirm and establish what the Lord has already put on our hearts. It will express thoughts, concepts and ideas that previously may have had no substance except in the hearts of a minority of people. Directional prophecy will lay these things on the table, like treasures for all to see.

When the church is going through a season of trouble and stress, directional prophecy can be a joy and inspiration to God's people. It will remind them yet again of the majesty, supremacy and on-going purposes of the Lord. It will enable them to hold on in the face of opposition, to push through into new areas of growth and activity.

It is essential therefore that we **assign people** to ensure that the prophetic word remains a central part of our corporate awareness, that God is directly involved in the life of the church.

As soon as is reasonably possible, the leaders must submit the prophecy to the judgement process. It would be helpful to include firstly the main leaders plus key people who have experience in the prophetic realm. With major directional words that will have considerable impact on the church, it is wise at some point to bring in an outside frame of reference. This should be a leader of considerable experience and wisdom, preferably someone who is also versed in dealing with this type of situation.

Once we are sure that this is indeed the word of the Lord, we can then bring in a wider group of people. This will be other ministries, key people and a wider leadership group within the church. We should provide **transcripts** for those people and invite their comments.

Involving this wider group of people will help us to get important feedback from significant people. It will also enable us to spread the ownership of the word amongst the core group of people within the work.

Our next level of strategy will be to use this core group of people to take the prophecy and **discuss it in home groups**. Again transcripts can be made available for all members. Our intent at this point is to again involve and invite our people to make comment and spread ownership of the word, right across the work.

If we are convinced a prophetic word is right for the church, we must take every opportunity to sow it into peoples' hearts. Inviting comments will energise most people to study the word, pray about it and discuss it openly. This is so vital because even if they disagree, it gets people talking about the future of the church. This is healthy and should be encouraged. It will sharpen vision and put an edge on our commitment.

Once all the comments have been received, we can discuss the next level of strategy. This must involve **prayer and intercession**. At the very least let us get the church together by whatever means possible to pray for wisdom in the leadership. People will be aware that plans will need to be laid as a result of the prophetic word and will want to pray successfully for the way ahead.

A short address during a meeting will help to keep the pot boiling and people informed. The leaders should take care to thank everyone for their input; express their excitement at all that the Lord is doing; and humbly ask for prayer to enable them to make wise decisions.

Again this will propagate the understanding that we are all in this together and **create a greater sense of unity**. It is a golden opportunity to involve everyone in the future of the work. It would be folly to reject an opportunity of this nature. If leadership examines the word, prays over it and puts together a strategy for the church in isolation from the main body of people, we will be sending out all the wrong signals.

We send out a signal that we alone as leaders have access to privileged revelation. We alone will determine our future. We alone will make all the decisions. The church will merely be informed at the right time and will be expected to fall in line as we play follow my leader.

Prayer and intercession will enable all of us to come before the Lord, sharing the excitement of seeing something new birthed in our hearts together. Times of corporate prayer with purpose are incredibly valuable. Directional prophecy presents us with a prayer agenda that will last for some considerable time and will continually create that sense of anticipation and ownership of the way ahead.

We should **make reference to the prophecy** and our future at every opportunity in our preaching, teaching, prayers, worship and conversations. Where practical, allow the poets, musicians and song-writers to get busy with the prophetic word. Find creative ways to keep the word in the forefront of peoples' minds. In my home church, City Gate in Southampton, we have two brothers

– Nigel and Alun Leppitt who are superb worship leaders and singer/songwriters. They have both written several **songs from prophetic words** spoken over the church. As we sing them in our worship services, I am very conscious that we are releasing the word of God back into the church.

Nigel, Alun and myself plus team members went to Liverpool in Northern England several years ago to do a training weekend on prophecy and worship. The Lord gave me a prophetic word for the city several months before we went. I gave the word to Alun and Nigel who wrote a three part song with chorus. At the ensuing celebration I delivered the prophecy in three parts stopping after each part to allow them to sing and teach the appropriate verse of the song. At each stage I led the church in prayer, intercession and response.

Tapes of the prophecy and the song have been sent to every church in that city. We are still receiving word of how much the prophetic song is blessing individuals and churches.

People love to sing. They love to hear good music and lyrics. Prophetic songs are a powerful way of keeping prophecy alive and in the forefront of peoples' minds and hearts. It enables us to speak God's word back to him, to receive it afresh back into our spirit and to provide the opportunity to give thanks and express trust.

We should use the prophecy as part of our **dialogue for change**. It is wise to think of potential obstacles to fulfilment. We will need to address the corporate attitude and morale of the work and introduce a time of encouragement and refreshing.

We may need to make changes in the leadership, the style and frequency of our meetings, the structure of the church, how we handle our finances.

We are not neglecting everything we do because of the prophecy. Neither are we contemplating wholesale changes. We need to discuss all the possibilities and ramifications of change, drawing on outside help where appropriate for an external perspective.

We should **allow leadership strategy to flow from the prophetic**. Again if we are wise we will draw a number of significant people into that dialogue. We can begin to mark out a strategy for change and growth, bearing in mind that it usually takes at least two years to ensure successful change across the work. By that I mean corporate change that has taken the people with us and not created factions or an exodus of discouraged and disillusioned sheep.

Successful corporate change depends upon effective personal transformation. That means we must all **make adjustments where necessary**. This need not be sprung on people. The awareness of the need for change in order to fulfil the prophetic word can be alluded to at every opportunity. We must not beat the big drum of change. Sheep are easily frightened. We can gently and humbly speak of change as a part of our response to the Lord in the new vision he has created. It can be drip fed into peoples' lives rather than hammered home with a blunt instrument!

We can use the prophetic word to **influence and inspire corporate and personal vision**. Everyone in the church should have goals and be going somewhere in God. We can use the prophecy as a stepping stone to aid people into discovering their own personal call. Effective leadership enables people to discover their own identity and calling in the Lord. It then seeks to release that call by training and development; discipleship; and the provision of opportunities to serve in the ministry. The corporate prophecy should and must give way to an eventual flood of personal prophecy as we seek to respond to the Holy Spirit in the outworking of revelation. Corporate vision is always enhanced and achieved by the release of personal aspirations. Turning aspirations into achievement is a huge part of the work of local church leaders.

Already we can see that one major directional prophecy

will **create a wave of opportunity** across the church. To make the most of it we must get as many people into the water as possible. We need our people in the flow of all that the Holy Spirit is doing.

This type of situation, handled correctly will also release a flood of inspiration through the revealed word of Scripture. Churches that handle corporate, directional prophecy well, will of necessity be drawn into present truth. That is revelation that is currently shaping up the new church of God that he is building right across the earth. It will inevitably lead us into changing our wineskin.

The failure I believe of the charismatic movement, particularly in the traditional churches, was that they merely bolted on to their existing structures the new things that God was doing. This has led, years later, to a period of discouragement, disillusionment, reflection and reappraisal. This is widely scoffed at in some quarters as post-charismatic depression. We are simply doing what we should have done all along and obeyed the Lord fully in the first place. The church is the Lord's and the structure thereof. Disillusionment is a vital aid and precursor to growth. Self-criticism is healthy because it leads to self-awareness and real change. We cannot just bolt on house groups; new forms of worship; a change in seating arrangements; leadership teams; and new forms of evangelism and persuade ourselves that we are radical.

Prophecy will require **effective long-term follow up**. Prophetic revelation gives us a horizon to view; a long-term vision to pursue. As we make necessary changes and get into the flow of all that God has in store, we must guard the future whilst working in the present.

Let us try not to get so involved with the work that we forget to look up at the horizon to determine whether we are on course. Prophecy will provide landmarks in the shape of long-range; mid-term; and short spell goals. Long-range goals provide landmarks up to five to ten years duration. Mid-term goals furnish us with way stations between two to five years. Short spell objectives get the church moving initially across the first couple of years.

As we move with God we need to keep taking a look at the prophetic goals we have ensuring that we make the necessary adjustments to stay on course. Every church is in it for the long haul. If we simply live from week to week, hand to mouth, we deny our people a successful future because our vision is merely to survive rather than conquer. We are not simply holding on, we are taking possession of all that God has for us. Successful leaders and excellent churches know how to possess the future. Keeping prophecy alive is a vital part of that process.

PART 3:

The Leadership Role in Prophecy

Chapter 12

The Leadership Role in Prophecy

People will always look to their leaders for a cue when a
new initiative or issue hits the church. Sadly, many
churches allow confusion, misunderstanding, poor doctrine and ignorance to flourish by virtue of not tackling
issues and providing balanced teaching that instructs,
informs and encourages a sound theology to emerge. This
is a recipe for disaster and will cause massive frustration
and a poor level of discipleship.

So many churches are poverty stricken in the areas of
worship, effective evangelism, healing, intercession, spiritual warfare, deliverance, pastoral counselling, faith, and
also prophecy. The signals we send out will be taken up by
the body. We cannot bury our head in the sand and do
nothing. If we do, we must not bleat too loudly if our
sheep leave us for greener pastures. Good pasture is
important for quality growth in the flock. We must feed
our sheep well. Bad shepherds ruin the flock. With regard
to prophecy, it is extremely important that we give the
right lead in encouraging the gift and the ministry.

Leaders can despise prophecy

There will be times when the entrance of the prophetic
word will upset comfort zones in the church. Prophecy at

times heralds a call to action and gives us a challenge to which we must respond. Prophecy is edifying, encouraging and comforting. It is also attacking, stimulating and provoking.

If leadership is too pastorally focused, there may be a tendency to resist the call to action and warfare. The church is described as a Family, a Household, a Body, a Bride, a City, and an Army. There has been a tendency to major on the first three at the expense of the latter.

I believe in these next years we will hear many prophetic words regarding holiness and purity as the Holy Spirit seeks to beautify and prepare the Bride of Christ. We will also hear prophetic utterances about unity; about coming together as one people to work together.

We are seeing the restoration of the apostolic ministry in the universal church. The Scriptures have as much to say about apostolic teams and apostolic churches as they do regarding apostolic personality. We will see churches coming together in a locality to produce a kingdom perspective, to evangelise the community and to have an apostolic oversight that really does take the cities for God.

At this moment the Holy Spirit is talking about the church as an army. He is causing us to focus on spiritual warfare, intercession, deliverance and evangelism that is earthed in the supernatural. A cursory glance through Scripture will show us that there is a call on each believer to fight. The book of Job tells us that our lives are lived on a battleground, with God on the one hand and Satan on the other. Like Joshua, we must declare, *'as for me and my house, we will serve the Lord.'*

Prophecy will be used to bring to bear God's perspective on each aspect of the nature of the church. We must take note of a prophetic call to arms and follow the Lord.

Leaders can despise prophecy because they are weighed down and discouraged in themselves. We can all be legitimately tired in the work. Leadership works under pressure from all sides. The chief weapon of leadership and key ministries is rest and thankfulness. We cannot move under pressure or be swayed by events. In our rest we hear the Lord and receive the necessary courage to stand our ground and believe the Lord.

Faith listens to God and does not pay attention to circumstances. Allowing ourselves to be taken out of rest will impoverish our faith, resulting in weariness. It is one thing to be tired **in** the work; it is quite another to be tired **of** the work.

If, as leaders, we are tired and spiritually down, the last thing we want in the church is a change of emphasis; that gives us more areas to look at and more issues to work through. Prophecy can bring a focus and a clarity that is often hard to ignore.

Leaders can despise prophecy simply because they are ignorant of the prophetic and how it works. Every leadership needs training in prophecy. We must give a lead and provide guide-lines for an appropriate protocol to emerge in the church. The other problem, too, is the loss of control factor. The input of prophecy will remind us all to whom the church actually belongs!

Prophecy may be spoken that will cut across some of our current plans. The temptation is to brand the prophet as rebellious and dismiss the word. All prophecy must be examined honestly. I was asked to take a church weekend to provide ministry into the leadership on prophecy. On the first evening, I met in the leader's office with his core leadership. After a time of prayer, I was asked if I had any prophetic word to the church. I had never been to the church before and knew nothing of what was happening in the work. The Lord had shown me clearly that they would be a church planting work, that would have eight congregations across that particular region. As I began to relate what I was seeing in my spirit, there was a quietness that came over the whole group. Tension suddenly seemed to fill the atmosphere.

I learned afterwards that the vision of the main leader (not shared by all the core group), was to have the largest church in the region, with its own Bible college and a much larger auditorium.

Little did I know that as I prophesied my elbow was resting on a stack of boxes that were filled with literature about the next step of their vision and calling. The prophetic word cut across that vision, much to the annoyance of the main leader, who promptly lost all interest in the weekend!

The prophetic word caused some considerable loss of face to him, and was a blow to his personal ambition. However, it led to a major reappraisal of the goals and calling of the work, which involved the whole church and not just a few people in the leadership.

Vision cannot be imposed from the top down; it must grow by consultation, unity, prayer and fellowship at the grass roots. People will own what they contribute towards themselves. If we impose our vision upon people, we should not be too upset if it leads to division in the work. Di-vision, literally double vision, occurs when our personal vision is not listened to, but we are forced to comply with a vision that comes from above in the form of an edict, rather than a prelude to discussion.

If we cannot see where the vision that we have for our life fits into the corporate vision of the church, then we have double vision. A person must be true to themselves as well as to the church. We cannot sacrifice and work for something that denies us our personal destiny. We are not clones or worker bees with an identity that is subjugated to the whole.

Some churches do practice a form of Christian communism that ultimately prevents people giving personal expression to the rule and call of God on their own lives. The prophetic spirit will always militate against that form of church government, because of the nature of personal prophecy. On several occasions I have received in advance

293

a written copy of the vision of the church where I will be ministering next. This is accompanied by a letter requesting that in order to avoid error and confusion, any personal prophecy that I give must be in accord with the vision statement.

As a leader myself, I love spending time with other leaders. I love the thought of lending my prophetic ministry in the service of the church. I love to talk through any and all implications of the prophetic word into local church. I'm happy to be available to the leaders of churches I have visited. However, we cannot allow the prophetic ministry to be controlled and manipulated any more than we could allow church government to be treated in the same way.

Prophecy tests the leadership

Prophecy will test the leadership in three ways. Firstly, their willingness to hear the voice of the Lord and make any necessary adjustments with regard to the overall work and its direction. Secondly, in their willingness to work with the prophet and form a relationship of worth and value. Thirdly, it will test their hearts for signs of fairness, humility and a sense of responsibility to the prophetic spirit.

Fairness is necessary when dealing with prophetic people who are only human and need correction, guidance, love and friendship. It is much too easy to reject the prophetic word because we don't like the vessel that it has been spoken through. Let's face it, on most of our criteria for leadership and ministry, many of the original men around Jesus would not have been accepted in our churches. Peter would have been written off with character defects because of his cowardice. James and John would have received discipline because of their impetuosity in calling down fire from heaven on people with whom they disagreed.

Humility is required when receiving prophetic words into the work. A humble heart will enable us to sift through the presentation and the verbiage to find the nugget of gold. Humility will not allow us to be dismissive of people because of their idiosyncrasies. Humility will allow us to encourage people to influence the direction of the work.

A meek heart is approachable and capable of providing acceptance and training for prophetic people as they grow and learn. It is true that the first few times we do something new, we learn how not to do it! Our learning curve will at times be a source of embarrassment as we make our mistakes. Most of us can no doubt look back with something of a cringe factor on our early years in ministry.

Unfortunately, most of the mistakes in the realm of prophecy take place in the public arena. It can be very attractive to step back and disassociate ourselves from people who get things wrong.

This is where we need a **sense of responsibility** to prophetic people developing under our care. We must not turn our back on people when they need us the most. If we only approve and accept people when they are doing well, then we are no better than the world. The test of whether we are made in the image of Christ is how we conduct ourselves when people fail.

We also need to have a sense of responsibility to produce a prophetic community that lives by every word that comes out of the mouth of the Lord.

Churches that have actively encouraged and supported the development of the prophetic gift are still quite rare. In many cases, the prophetic ministry is still in some disarray in local church because of immature gifting in people and poor handling by leadership.

Our heart attitude must be positive and not negative. No one begins to build something without first counting the cost. If we want a prophetic anointing in the church, we must pay the price to develop people.

We cannot allow ourselves to be intimidated by the gift or hold in ridicule those who make errors. It is incredibly brave of people to put themselves in the firing line by declaring that they have a prophetic word. I am full of admiration for those who move in the healing ministry. People are healed, or remain ill. Dealing with the disappointments, and encouraging the gift are vital aspects of enabling people to reach out towards maturity in the supernatural realm.

I fully appreciate that leaders who do not move in prophecy may feel daunted by those who do. God does not always speak to the leadership, he speaks into his body. Fairness, humility and responsibility are needed on all sides.

Prophecy affects the status quo

A prophetic word may lead the church into another area of activity which is outside the main leader's function. Responsibility for this area may have to be shouldered differently and possibly by a new leadership appointment. Prophecy gives us an agenda for faith, prayer and change.

When entering a new sphere of activity, we may need to think in terms of new and additional personnel to be co-opted onto the leadership team.

I gave a prophetic word concerning a time of numerical growth and evangelistic anointing for one particular church. The leadership in the work had not changed over many years and was inherently pastoral which was the function of its main leader. The church had settled down into a cosy programme of church meetings and ministry that focused upon itself. The leadership were really acting as little more than caretakers maintaining a predetermined routine that had no effect upon the outside world.

Without meaning to, prophecy can threaten areas that

are not under God's control and blessing. When I spoke that word, I had no idea at the time of the implications. I saw 200% growth in the next four years, with new initiatives in youth work and social action. When discussing the word at a later date, it became apparent that the drive and initiative to respond to the prophecy was not present in the current leadership.

As we began tentatively to discuss areas of change, many of them dug in their heels and refused to move. We discovered then, that some of these people were addicted to status rather than servanthood. Some threatened to leave the church if asked to step down from leadership. It is sad when people see leadership in the church in worldly terms of promotion and demotion.

They voted to keep the leadership intact and set in motion a series of costly events and a programme of evangelism. None of them had the anointing to inspire the church and provide an effective evangelistic strategy. After several years of fruitless effort, they concluded that the prophecy had been false. No prizes for guessing who got the blame!

Prophecy can attack our main root of security. Is our security in our status, ourselves, our ministry and gifting, or in the Lord? People who have a strong walk with Christ cannot be threatened by change.

It is easier for the leaders to reject the prophecy and the prophet, particularly if there are some unresolved character issues in the life of the prophet. It provides a legitimate reason to reject the word in the eyes of the people, though not necessarily in the eyes of the Lord. Prophecy has a way of testing our true motives.

Leaders have a responsibility to the prophet and the prophecy; to nurture and care for the former, and to ensure there is a two way accountability in operation that deals righteously with prophecy and provides friendship and discipling to prophetic individuals. People need feedback. We must take all gifting seriously in the church, by training and shaping people through teaching, opportunity to move in ministry, and responsible feedback. People need telling when they have done well, by a process of affirmation, encouragement and acceptance.

Appreciation is absolutely vital. No one can flourish in an atmosphere of continuous non-appreciation (yet another thing I have learned from my friend, Gerald Coates).

If people have done badly, or made mistakes, they still need to be affirmed, encouraged and accepted. They also need to understand where they went wrong and be gently put right. Church is full of volunteers who need to be given worth and value. A little loving confrontation now, that is rooted in appreciation and carries a dash of humour, will do wonders for people's self esteem, growth and development.

With the latter issue of caring for the prophecy, we must ensure it is accurately weighed. Sometimes it is necessary to draw in outside people for their comment and perspective. Then we must follow an established line of procedure that will allow us to get the most benefit out of the current situation (discussed fully in Chapter 10, 'A Framework for Prophecy in the Local Church').

Corporate morality

Why has the Lord given us such great and precious promises? Why does he give us prophetic words? So that we can participate in the divine nature and escape corruption (2 Peter 1:3–10). This passage talks about the fruit we need to have in our lives to see the fulfilment of God's word.

We discover the same agenda in 2 Corinthians 6:14–18, which contains three prophetic words. In the context of being unequally yoked with unbelievers, it mentions three prophecies. We are the temple of the living God, the dwelling place of God. The three words are concerned with cleanness, separation and walking with the Lord.

Scripture says that since we have these prophetic promises, let us purify ourselves (2 Corinthians 7:1). It is a corporate word. We are the temple of God in both a personal and a corporate manner. Purification is also a corporate activity. God has put us in a body. There must be constant attention to cleansing, healing, renewing and purification. We need humility to ask the awkward questions about our corporate morality. We need godliness on both personal and corporate levels.

I firmly believe that we need to have someone in the church who is going to be concerned with the morality of the work. If God does not own the getting of something, he cannot own the having of it without making himself unrighteous.

We need someone who is going to act as the guardian of our corporate integrity. This is not necessarily the role of the main leader. It is difficult to appoint someone to that office; nevertheless we must do all that we can to encourage such an initiative. At least we can pray that the Lord will give us a Nathaniel, *'a man in whom there is no guile'* (John 1:47).

In my home church of City Gate, Southampton, we have a man called Andrew Carmichael on our oversight team. He seldom speaks in church meetings, and while always happy to pray with people, he would not admit to any outstanding spiritual gifting. I have noticed over many years that many of Andy's contributions to leadership discussions revolve around integrity and righteousness. His frequent question has been, 'what is the righteous thing to do?'

There is a purity in his spirit that rubs off on the leadership. I believe he is God's gift to us for his sense of maturity, righteousness and integrity. It is this kind of influence that will lead the Lord to put his trust in us and bless the work.

Leaders can be the most unscrupulous of people. They can take prophecy and use it for their own ends, and their own advancement. They can be selective about what elements of the word they promote and which are quietly swept under the carpet.

A corporate prophetic word must be followed up by careful scrutiny of the overall integrity of the work. We cannot endorse the prophecy without looking at the character issues around it. That must mean an examination of the leadership. How are we treating people in the church? What are we modelling? We may all model different things personally. What are we modelling corporately?

I spoke prophetically to the leaders of a church in Belfast, Northern Ireland. I gave a corporate word concerning the work of the church. I spoke about their ministry of reconciliation and unity, and the effect that the Irish church would have on the church in England. An Englishman prophesying to a group of Irishmen about their role in the English church provides a very poignant moment! We were all misty eyed and one or two of us were gulping hard. Paul Reid, their leader, stood and held his arms open wide in real vulnerability, and asked me this question. 'Graham, is there anything about the work, or about this group of men that you would want to criticise? If there is, we want to receive it.'

My heart went out to him. Many leaders would have just taken the prophecy at face value. Paul understood that who we are is more important than what we do. Why? Because church is meant to be a place where God can dwell. God may like to visit our church, but would he want to make it his home?

We can tell a great deal about a church by the quality of its worship. Look around at your next meeting. How many people are lost in praise and adoration? Do we make adequate space for real worship? Are people really worshipping, or just singing songs, however enthusiastically? Do we know the difference?

In City Gate, we run a Worship School to train people in the art of leading worship. My two friends, Alun and Nigel Leppitt, have been instrumental in founding and directing the School. They have also trained housegroups and led workshops in the church, as well as producing many fine praise and worship songs. People need training in praise and worship.

The strength of a church is in its ability to magnify the Lord, exalt his name, and give him pleasure in their adoration. Every church needs a spirit of thanksgiving and a grateful heart. This is priceless. To be able to make the Lord happy is wonderful. His joy is our strength.

We can also tell a great deal about a church by how it treats its leadership. There is very little difference between how we treat our leaders and our relationship with the Lord. As church we should be making it a joy for our leaders to oversee the work. Areas of strife, jealousy, resentment, backbiting, gossip, slander and dissension inevitably fall upon the leadership and affect how the Lord views the work. Disunity disqualifies the presence of God. Unity attracts God's command to bless.

I have met so many leaders who have been broken by their people. Their hearts have been broken, their spirit crushed and their bodies made ill by the verbal and mental abuse and the physical anguish they experience. What was their crime? They tried to lead a bunch of people into the things of God.

There are some churches that I love to visit. I can look at the leadership and the church, and feel the harmony and the love. Mistakes are happening, tension is real, but there is a depth of togetherness and appreciation. They are committed to one another through thick and thin.

Holding people's history against them

This issue is a plague in the church that seriously affects our corporate integrity as a leadership and a body of people. We are all on a learning curve as the Lord improves our character and increases our gifting. It is absolutely inevitable that we are going to make mistakes.

Church should be a place where people are free to fail. If we are not free to make mistakes, we will never succeed. People will settle for what they can do, rather than invest in new things. That attitude breeds stagnation.

People will sin, commit errors of judgement and display immaturity. It is all a part of growing up. There are so few father figures in the work of God. Paul said to the Corinthian church,

> *'you have many teachers, but not many fathers.'*
> (1 Corinthians 4:15)

Instructors are in plentiful supply, but where are the loving, understanding and accepting father figures who will discipline us with humility and grace?

We all need affirmation and acceptance at the point where we have made a mess. The goodness of God leads us to repent (Romans 2:4). He is faithful and just to forgive us our sin and to cleanse us (1 John 1:9). He does not reward us according to our iniquities (Psalm 103:10). He is a God who forgives and forgets (Jeremiah 31:34). He is a God who gives us new beginnings and makes all things new (Revelation 21:5).

In the church universal I have discovered that people may forgive but they do not forget. People are branded with their failure. Some leaders only think in terms of punishment, not restoration. If someone is overtaken in a moral fall, their ministry can be stripped away and they can go through a time of counselling.

What is seldom offered, and is sorely needed, is the hand of friendship. Real friendship, with no strings. Why is it that when people need us the most, some leaders back off? We make protestations of love and commitment which are good, provided people don't foul up. Then, friendship is quietly withdrawn and counselling support is offered. I am not decrying the counselling process, but it can never be a substitute for honest to goodness friendship, loyalty and commitment. We need both together.

With the Lord, sin affects our fellowship, not our relationship. If we sin, we have an advocate, a friend at court, who leads us through the process of restoration and repentance. God chooses to forget as we allow the Holy Spirit to put our lives in order. In the church, sin can affect the relationship and the fellowship together.

Our goal in these sorrowful times is three-fold. Firstly, to restore the individual's walk with Christ. Our poor behaviour is often the product of a defective belief system. What we believe affects how we behave. Why do people do certain things? We must go beyond the fruit to the root cause of sin, which is our belief system. We want to restore the individual to Christ and improve the way they relate to the Lord on a daily basis.

Secondly, we need to support and counsel those who have been the victims of sin by any individual, whether directly or indirectly. Direct victims are those who have been the explicit target of sin and have been particularly damaged. Indirect victims can be families and friends of both parties who can be hurt, wounded and devastated by the situation. We must do all that we can to bring healing to all concerned by the events.

Thirdly, our goal is the eventual restoration of the ministry. The enemy has acted to sideline and destroy the ministry; we must not let him succeed. The gospel is redemptive. We must work to bring forth the fruit of repentance with real grace and humility. The length of the recovery time is determined by the nature of the sin and the submissive response of the person concerned.

It is important that we differentiate between the ministry and the sin. The good things and the blessing achieved by the individual through their ministry must not be dismissed. In the case, for example, where prophetic ministry has been used for dishonest gain, we cannot discount all the previous prophetic words by that person. We must isolate the cases specific to the indiscretion and deal with them accordingly. In all these unsavoury incidents, we must keep in the forefront of our minds the words of the apostle Paul.

> *'Brethren, if a man is overtaken in any trespass, you who are spiritual restore such a one **in a spirit of gentleness, considering yourself**, lest you also be tempted.'*
> (Galatians 6:1)

With straightforward cases of deliberate sin, the way ahead is clear and we know how to proceed. However, mistakes that occur through immaturity, ignorance, lack of knowledge and wisdom, are sometimes more difficult to handle.

Most leaderships tend to let things go by without comment. This can be disastrous in the long term. Without proper feedback, most people will continue to think they have done well, when the reverse could be true.

Leadership can then build up a negative image of the person of which the individual may be wholly unaware. Small mistakes tend to build up and lack of trust grows alongside the accumulation. At some point, if we are not careful, we may reach the point of no return. We then need a fairly significant work of grace (even a miracle), to change hearts and see a full restoration.

Sometimes it is simply that an individual's face does not fit. It could be a matter of style, dress, presentation, personality, ministry emphasis or just that they don't seem to be part of the 'in crowd'. It can be difficult to get to know some people and get alongside them, as they need more work to establish a friendship.

I often have problems in the area of not quite fitting in. I am a fairly quiet man (though I have my moments!), who likes to observe and think about things. At times I find small talk difficult; my contributions tend to be significant rather than general or humorous. Sometimes I am at a complete loss for words. My face seldom mirrors my emotions, it does not naturally fall into a smile. I wish it did. I am one of the happiest people I know, but I have to remind myself to put the message on my face. When I am thinking and concentrating, in particular, my face can look very disapproving. When you have a prophetic gift, this can be very disconcerting for people! My sons say, 'Dad's in robot mode'. I am not talkative by nature. Public speaking, though enjoyable, takes a lot out of me. Sometimes I have an overwhelming need to be quiet, to blend into the wallpaper.

As a prophet, I have practised quietness within, to be able to still the clamouring on the inside, to be at rest, to hear the Lord. Tension can be all around, but my spirit is like a still lake on a slow day. I excel in times of difficulty for that reason.

I am not difficult or unfriendly, just odd. I think everyone is a little odd; everyone has their foibles. It is just that some people's oddity (like mine!), is more public. I love to be surrounded by my friends, just sitting quietly, watching, listening, loving them and not having to be the prophet. My friends who know me, understand and I am grateful. It was not always the case and I did not always handle myself well.

My point in this whole preamble? People are not what they seem. I am sure that if we all practised more love, patience and acceptance, the church would be a better place and the Lord would be more blessed by our actions.

It is unfair and sacrilegious to hold a person's history over their head without giving them the love, support and opportunity to change it. When change has come, we must close a door on that chapter by forgiving, forgetting and accepting that this is a new person. There is nothing more damaging to self esteem than to not be allowed to change, to be treated as suspect, to be distrusted.

When change has occurred, we need a formal acknowledgement of the fact. It needs to be accompanied by a generous, spoken acceptance and approval. We must leave no doubt in anyone's mind and no room for the devil to exploit. If a church cannot give new beginnings to people, I would not want to be a part of that congregation.

Create a climate for prophecy

Church is all about creating environments for things to happen. If we are to encourage the fullness of Christ to be seen in the church, we must make room for it to develop.

The biggest obstacles that will prevent the growth and maturity of our people are traditions, our present church structures, and the way that we run our meetings. The structure of our church is there to serve the life of the Spirit among our people. Sadly, the reverse is often true. The life of the Spirit is forced into a mould that perpetuates the church's style, tradition and modus operandi. This causes a great deal of frustration, which is demoralising and utterly wasteful.

After years of renewal and the outpouring of the Holy Spirit, the main issue is still the same as when the charismatic movement began. We cannot put new wine into old skins. In this next move of God we must tackle this issue again. What is interesting is that there will be a number of house churches who will have to change their wineskin to accommodate the work of the Spirit. We cannot be wedded to traditions, structures and methodology at the expense of the move of God.

Our past and traditions must be held up to the light of God's current plans. Our structures must be flexible and able to accommodate change and growth. Our meetings must accomplish all of God's purpose.

If we want to encourage the gift of healing we must do all we can to train, develop and give opportunity for people to mature in the gift. Ultimately that will mean holding healing meetings. The same is true of worship, evangelism, warfare, prayer and prophecy. Somewhere along the line, the encouragement of these areas will impact on the way we operate in our meetings. If we try and squeeze these things into our present meeting format, it will probably be unsatisfactory to all concerned.

For every area of church life that we wish to develop, we will need to set aside time and meetings to cultivate vision and strategy, and provide opportunities for growth and movement. This means creating an environment so that what we want to happen can be realised.

Therefore, sticking to the same routine and meeting format will be counter productive. We need seasons of change to accommodate what God is doing. If we wish to develop the prophetic gift, we need to create a partnership in the church that can fulfil that criteria. This is the subject of our final chapter, 'The Prophetic Partnership'.

Chapter 13

Handling Wrong Prophecy

It is inevitable that people will make mistakes and go beyond their measure. When we are developing ministry and gifting we need to create an environment where people are free to fail. If we insist on perfection or maturity in the early stages of development we will not cultivate people in the right manner.

Instead of faith to explore we will cause a fear that will hold back. Instead of boldness we will create intimidation. Instead of producing mature men and women we will cause their gift and ministry to hit a ceiling and level off. That ceiling will be the measure of our disapproval at their inexperience and our unwillingness to see that discipleship involves loving correction.

Growing people will cause us hard work and not a little heartache. People are worth the hassle. We must cultivate the attitude in our churches that all people have worth and value.

Personally I still remember the attendant feelings and emotions that I had when I first moved out in the supernatural, many years ago. The sense of awe, fear, trepidation, uncertainty, insecurity and inadequacy. The conviction that I had done everything completely wrong. How stupid I felt when words were not verbalised correctly. The sense that everyone was laughing at or talking about my mistakes. I remember too, the awful pride and arrogance that I went through as I got more accustomed to speaking and moving in supernatural ways. When we look back, I guess most of us have a high cringe factor concerning our early development. I remember how desperate I was for approval, kindness and above all, real help in my development.

People need to be free to make mistakes and be free to fail. It is so important that our leaders create an environment within the church where we can set ground rules for moving in prophecy (see Chapter 14, 'The Prophetic Partnership').

Once we set a protocol for prophetic ministry to follow and appoint someone to oversee this area we can genuinely relax. Prophetic protocol will teach us how to use revelational prophecy and the accountability required. We can sow that teaching in our foundation classes and preparation for ministry teaching programmes. It should be common knowledge across the church. We can then determine what are honest mistakes needing loving correction, and what are breaches of protocol which may require discipline and adjustment.

We must learn to deal with failure and turn it into a positive learning experience for people. Don't simply drop people or merely forbid them to prophesy. Work with them to enable them to overcome their difficulties. We should be kind, humble and full of mercy, yet firm, caring and well-disciplined. The leaders' role is to balance care for the individual with protection for the flock. We are not employers, we cannot sack people from their gift! We cannot dismiss their life and ministry because they create tension and difficulty. People are worth fighting for, therefore our heart is always to win people.

The grace of God abounds when sin is plentiful. We need the same godly reaction to failure. Our love, warmth and acceptance needs to abound. People need us most when they have failed. It is not easy to begin moving in the supernatural. It is full of pressure and uncertainty until we develop our practice in the right way. We learn by experience mostly and that is costly to acquire. Often we learn how not to do things before we develop good practice. We should respect and be grateful for anyone who puts themselves in this kind of firing line. Wherever a person begins to move in the supernatural they may as well paint a bullseye on their back and a sign saying 'shoot at me!' They will become a target for attack by the enemy. Church people should set their sights on redemption not harassment.

I need my brothers more when I have failed than I do when I have succeeded. Success should bring approval; failure should bring acceptance. To do otherwise is to be worldly and not godly.

Know the difference between false and poor prophecy

False prophecy is deceptive, it deliberately leads people away from the Lord. Often it is a word dreamt up from their own imagination (Jeremiah 23:16–18) and thoughts. People speak out of the deception of their own hearts (Jeremiah 23:26). Deception is a lifestyle issue, it does not arrive overnight, it is caused by a lack of real accountability. Such people should be treated warily. Beware of a ministry which is not rooted into a local church.

False prophecy comes out of people's own inspiration, they have really seen nothing and are simply inventing words (Ezekiel 13:1–3). People prophesy from their own human spirit for their own devious ends. Today as in times of Scripture we have people prophesying for money (Micah 3:11). Peter warned the New Testament church that false prophets would

'by covetousness, exploit you with deceptive words.'
(2 Peter 2:1–3)

False prophesy is deliberately speaking what others want to hear. It is given by manipulative people who are serving themselves not the Lord. False prophecy is used to gain control of people's lives; to bind people into churches and churches into networks; usually for reasons of personal gain and wealth.

We can never dismiss a false prophecy as insignificant. The enemy uses words too, and false prophecy should be treated like a curse. It opens the door into sinister human and demonic activity. These people need to be rooted out and dealt with justly. The church must cut down the territory in which these people operate.

Poor prophecy often occurs because of inexperience and poor practice that has gone unchecked and not been corrected. This type of prophecy is impure because it mixes too much of our own thoughts with words that the Lord has given, leading to a measure of distortion. Graham Perrins, a friend and excellent Bible teacher on prophetics, once defined much of modern day prophecy as 'an empty thought, passing through an empty head!'

In the early days of the charismatic movement, people were often in revolt against form and tradition. For a while the pendulum swung away from those things as people delighted in spontaneity and being led by the Spirit in all things. Inevitably it became crass and super-spiritual.

Some people eschewed leaders preferring to be wholly led by the Spirit. Others indulged in meetings where very little happened because everyone was waiting on the Lord to be told what to do. Occasionally things worked wonderfully well and the meeting was anointed of God. Mostly, the people who had the loudest voice or who were the most outspoken used to take over the meeting and 'minister' to the others. Planning and preparation were frowned upon as unspiritual or lacking in faith. All of this 'enforced spontaneity' had an impact on the prophetic in particular. A number of misapprehensions grew up around prophecy that have persisted over the past decades to the present day.

Firstly, there was **the golden rule of spontaneity** that we did not have to prepare anything; simply 'open our mouths and God would give us the words'. This fallacy about prophecy was built upon various Scriptures. Matthew 10:19 and 20; Mark 13:11; Luke 12:11 and 12, 21:12–15; Exodus 4:12 and 2 Peter 1:21 have all been quoted at me in various prophetic conferences where I have been speaking.

However, as we shall see by looking briefly at a couple of the gospel passages, the Bible here is talking about a word of testimony, not a word of prophecy. The context is that when preaching the gospel we could be dragged before important people who will demand an explanation for our gospel message.

> *'But when they arrest you and deliver you up, do not worry beforehand or premeditate which you shall speak. But whatever is given you in that hour, speak that; for it is not you who speaks but the Holy Spirit.'*
> (Mark 13:11)

> *'But before all these things, they will lay their hands on you and persecute you, delivering you up to the synagogues and prisons, and you will be brought before Kings and rulers for my namesake.'*
> *'**But it will turn out for you as an occasion for testimony**. Therefore, settle it in your hearts not to meditate beforehand on what you will answer. For I will give you a mouth and wisdom which all your adversaries will not be able to contradict or resist.'*
> (Luke 21:12–15)

Here Jesus is instructing his disciples about the kind of attitude they must adopt when called to give an explanation of the gospel. Firstly, do not worry; secondly, do not try and premeditate your answers; thirdly, use it as a time to give your testimony. It has nothing to do with prophecy. We can see a fulfilment of this in Acts chapter 4 when Peter and John are taken before Annas, Caiaphas and the rulers and elders of the law. No doubt this scene has been re-enacted on thousands of occasions since.

The Old Testament passage refers to Moses who has been given a charge to go to Egypt and command Pharaoh to *'let my people go'* on behalf of the Lord. Moses is protesting because he is slow of speech and clearly believes he will embarrass both God and himself. God's reply is

> *'Go, I will help you speak and will teach you what to say.'* (Exodus 4:12)

Again this has nothing to do with prophecy. Moses has to give a command from Almighty God to the world's most powerful potentate. In those circumstances we would all be nervous and apprehensive! However, Moses' sense of inadequacy was so strong that he could not trust God to help him. The Lord gave him Aaron to use as a mouthpiece.

People are often fond of quoting the following verse from 2 Peter 1:21:

> *'For prophecy never had its origin in the will of man, but men spoke from God as they were carried along by the Holy Spirit.'*

Again we must examine the context into which the word is set. The Bible is talking about the prophecy of Scripture, not the gift of prophecy and spontaneous prophetic utterance. Scripture did not come out of human creativity and inspiration. To be sure God used the talents, education and cultural background of each writer. However,

Scripture is God breathed and given by inspiration of God (2 Timothy 3:16).

When we apply these Scriptures to moving in the gift of prophecy spontaneously we take them out of their original context. When we take Scripture out of context we make it a pretext to do things which are unbiblical.

I am not saying here that all prophecy must be meticulously prepared and well rehearsed before it is delivered. I believe though that to move in prophecy effectively we need a solid understanding of Scripture; the character of God; and the nature of his ways. Without that essential foundation we are vulnerable in our ignorance and potentially may speak out of the well of what we do not know.

I believe prophecy is a mix of the Holy Spirit drawing upon: our knowledge and experience of God; our understanding of Scripture; times of prayer, communion and preparation; and spontaneous utterance. These elements I believe, are a pre-requisite for moving in prophecy and we cannot and must not rely upon the mood of the moment.

There are times when certain prophetic words are prepared, rehearsed and planned. They are words of weight and import, carrying great significance. At other times we receive the bones of a prophecy with key words or phrases which are fleshed out as we speak. Then there are the times when we receive certain impressions which need to be followed up carefully and with wisdom. Of course over the years I have given hundreds of spontaneous prophetic words. However, the course of my life is set upon the road of prayer; meditation; study of Scripture; and communion with the Lord.

To move out in prophecy without that sure foundation is to produce weak prophecy which will be impure and distorted, leading to error.

Another misapprehension is that **physical sensations are the indicator** of the presence of the anointing in the Holy Spirit. Our heart begins to beat rapidly; the hair on our neck stands up; our palms are sweaty; and we have almost a sense that something is brewing or in the air. This could be one of several things.

Firstly, it may simply be nerves. Many people get very nervous just at the thought that God may want us to do something, even before we have discerned what it is! He may want us to pray or read out a Scripture; it does not always mean we should move out in the prophetic.

Secondly, the Holy Spirit may just want to speak to us personally. What we hear is private and not for general sharing at that point. We must always be careful to share **any revelation** with mature people to avoid deception and increase understanding.

Thirdly, the Holy Spirit is brooding over us. The attendant physical feelings may be just his way of getting our attention. On many occasions I have not delivered any word, prophetic or otherwise at that point. The Holy Spirit has indicated that he wishes to speak and wants me to draw aside to listen. It may signify that a time of prayer, fasting or preparation is required.

Some prophecy can wait 24 hours or longer depending upon what the Holy Spirit is doing. I held one word for over 2 years whilst praying for the right person to emerge. Sometimes the beginning of a word needs a time of preparation and prayer in order for it to mature before delivery. We may need to come aside and seek God specifically.

Many times I have seen 'so called prophecies' fall flat because people could not discern what was happening at the time. They had a couple of words and moved out prophetically, only to discover there was no more and they had to resort to 'padding' in order to cover up their mistakes.

Handling wrong prophecy in the meeting

The need in our meetings is to strike the right balance between encouraging the gift of prophecy; and guarding the flock from potentially damaging words; whilst not having the meetings hi-jacked by space cadets!

Most churches seem to opt for a process of correction or prevention. Those who are involved in the **correction** of incidents, normally operate that way because they: a) believe that everyone has the right to speak and no-one should be denied the opportunity; b) have not thought through the implications of having the prophetic loose in the church without adequate supervision and support.

Every ministry requires proper definition and sufficient restraint to maintain a satisfactory balance. Having one without the other is like a bird with one wing, it is only going to go in circles. Problems will therefore keep coming around. There are only so many responses we can make from the platform when wrong prophecy has occurred.

Firstly, we can draw no attention to the event at the time. It may just be best to keep the meeting flowing rather than make any observations at that point. We do need to follow up the situation with a quiet word after the meeting. However, it may not be worth taking action during the session. It is simply a matter of, 'well, moving swiftly on!' If we have any announcements to make or an offering to conduct, that may be as good a time as any to introduce those things and then move on from there.

Secondly, if the situation warrants it, we may have to make some form of comment or observation. We do not want to demolish people or have a public confrontation. Try to say something bland if possible: 'thank you for those thoughts, we appreciate people sharing what they feel.' We are not calling it prophecy and we are not getting behind it, we are just bridging the gap between their word and the rest of the meeting.

Naturally our response will depend on what has been said and the manner in which it came forth. Try to respond without any heat or edge in your voice. Keep a calm, measured and mild tone. 'I believe that was our brother/sister's own spirit speaking; let's move on now to...'

At other times people may go right over the top leaving us no alternative but to give a public rebuke. We are gathered for a purpose therefore we do not want this situation to become a focal point. Our aim here is to neutralise what is said; caution the individual; avoid confusion in the congregation; and improve the tone of the meeting.

Again let me emphasise that we can do all of this without unnecessary heat. There is no need for us to make the situation worse by provoking a conflict. If a soft answer turns away wrath (Proverbs 15:1), then a rebuke without heat will diffuse a potentially explosive situation. We do not have to prove our authority at times like this, just act like a loving father. Where necessary we can give a **short** reasoned explanation.

There are three reasons why we should publicly rebuke people because of poor prophecy:

(a) If they have given a directional word or a correctional/judgmental word, we need to let them know the following: 'that type of prophecy is out of order in a public setting. The place for directional/correctional words is in the leadership, so that they can be judged and weighed in the appropriate manner. I suggest we pray together and get on with what the Lord is doing.' That takes about 15 seconds to say and allows us to move on. We will probably need from time to time to reinforce the right protocol in prophecy.

(b) If a harsh or condemning word has been spoken, our response can be: 'I do not witness to that word. It is **not** the voice of the Lord. Let's just concentrate on the Lord Jesus now. We do not want anything to interfere with our worship/the moving of the Holy Spirit.' We can then go into a song, prayer or another activity.

(c) If a person has prophesied their own opinion/displayed a bad attitude, our response could be: 'Brother/sister, I believe **that** is your own opinion. You are speaking out of your own frustration. Meetings are not the place for that. I would be happy to chat with you later. Now let us do....'

Let me emphasise this: be mild, kind, speak softly, **smile**, be quietly emphatic and only take a matter of seconds to reply. Take the sting out of the situation and then press on. Give a mild reproof, then let your voice pick up a gear as you focus peoples' attention on the next thing. Don't give their utterance the title of prophecy, call it a word, it is less demeaning to the prophetic.

Other churches operate in **prevention** mode. They guard the flock very defensively. It can be almost impossible to prophesy from the body of the congregation, and they would completely frown on such freedom. Often I have discovered that such 'covering' is based on distrust of the people. They lay a minefield designed almost to protect the church from prophecy. Picture the scene. We believe we have a prophecy. To make ourselves heard we have to go to the front of the meeting, where the PA system is located.

So we make our way to the microphone. On the way we encounter the **platform policeman**. This is the guy who guards the microphone from the attack of people with the spirit of splutter! We now have to convince him that God is really speaking to us. This is almost impossible to convey in a few brief sentences. In full view of all the congregation plus those on the platform, we try to put our thoughts into a credible pattern. The platform policeman has only a matter of a couple of minutes to discern the voice of the Lord. Horror of horrors, platform policeman says 'No!' And we are left to slink away to our seat; thoroughly embarrassed, with our eyes on the floor. Ring any bells? How many of us had any loving follow up that explained why we were not permitted to speak?

To be fair, it is very difficult for both sides to express themselves in those situations. Often the music is blaring out of a loud-speaker only feet away; the congregation is engaged in noisy worship or praise (except for the people looking at us, right?) Often we have platform policeman because we have never taught the whole church about prophecy. We have not created a prophetic climate or environment where the church knows that only mature and gifted people can speak prophetically from the front. A climate where people know about inspirational and revelational prophecy.

If we want our people to grow in the prophetic in public gatherings, the least we can do is put mature, prophetic people on duty at the back of the hall, rather than in full public view. If our platform policeman are there to discourage people from reaching the microphone, then we have completely missed the point of body ministry and effective training and development. We must not make people run the gauntlet; it is unfair and humiliating!

At the back of the meeting it is often more quiet and peaceful. The mature person can listen attentively to the individual and the Lord. An explanation can be given quietly and lovingly if we consider it unwise to proceed with the word. The potential giver can be thanked and blessed without feeling stupid. No-one else will see what is happening. Alternatively, the person with the word can be escorted to the platform by the mature prophet which gives a sign of approval to the church, rather than the current disapproval that most people experience.

Giving constructive criticism

Feedback is a vital skill that all leaders must develop and use. Some will excel more than others. If we are to disciple; train; equip; and release people into their gifting then we must recognise that effective constructive criticism is essential.

It is a completely natural and normal way of life to evaluate events; business deals; sporting performances; films; restaurant meals; friendships and learning experiences; to name but a few. All of us have been evaluated many times over during our lives to date. Sometimes we were completely unaware that we were being appraised; whilst at other times we found the experience painful and occasionally humiliating. Rarely it seems have we enjoyed the experience. That can be due in part to the assessors lack of expertise; our own defensiveness; or simply that the learning curve we were on at the time was too great, and thus produced a lot of mistakes. No-one is born with the ability to analyse and review the actions of others. It is a skill that must be learned. Sadly it is an aptitude that is never taught in the church and yet it is a vital part of discipleship and the training of others.

When evaluating people who move in the gift of prophecy we must first examine their **attitude**. A humble, servant spirit is required to bring the word of the Lord. The word may be spoken boldly and with power and authority. People may be strong and forceful in their delivery. Yet the underlying spirit is one of meekness and tenderness of heart. Moses was a prophet often speaking with a great courage yet he was the meekest man on the earth. Meekness is not weakness, it is strength under control. How people conduct themselves before, during and after they have prophesied will deserve observation and comment.

We can have the right word but deliver it in the wrong spirit thus negating what we say because people cannot receive our attitude.

The **method of delivery** is the second thing to look for in people. Presentation is very important. Was it overbearing or pompous? Did they speak for too long? Did they rush their words? Were they ill at ease or confident? Were the words clearly spoken, did they make sense? Did the prophecy flow with the meeting or cut across it? Either of these last two points can be right. I have seen meetings rescued from obscurity by the prophetic word.

Were they creative in their presentation? At times we can use music, drama or props to symbolise what God is saying.

Assessing the method of delivery and perhaps making appropriate suggestions will cause people to consider important points other than the context of the word.

Thirdly, was the word screened properly? Some words need to be **filtered through the leadership** beforehand; was it one of these? When examining a prophecy it is helpful for leaders to have someone present who is strongly prophetic. The person who is giving the word (however inexperienced) should occasionally sit in on these times. It will aid their growth and development. Fourthly, however poor the performance always ensure that the assessment is as positive as possible. We must be truthful but we can also be gracious. Do not forget to express thanks to people who put themselves out on a limb in this way. Make suitable recommendations and give necessary advice. Where it is appropriate we can **outline specific boundaries** for the gift in the immediate future.

People should prophesy according to the proportion of their faith (Romans 12:6). We can tell by experience when someone has gone beyond their measure or alternatively has not lived up to it. Sometimes we need to put restraints on people's gift to allow their character to catch up. At other times, they need to stay at a particular level to fully develop their confidence and experience.

Finally, we can **enlist their help** in administrating the prophecy. We can ask them for their suggestions in terms of the next step on how we are to proceed. These suggestions may not be helpful but it is still a useful process to go through.

Over a period of time our evaluation will help us to determine a pattern of strengths and weaknesses for each individual. These elements can be worked out during the discipleship process. Once people get used to friendly and helpful feedback that is realistic and will help them develop, the process will become easier to administrate.

Handling frustration and private opinion

Relationships are always a key issue in the development of people. Often frustration occurs because people feel they are unheard or unloved. I can appreciate that some people can be difficult to love. However, they should be listened to nonetheless. If people feel rejected they may speak out of that emotion. Friendship reduces the tension that people can feel around their lives.

When frustration is present in the life of an individual, they will probably see and hear correctly but interpret it in a totally wrong way. They can be ruled however slightly by emotions, perceptions and situations. Each of these can put an edge to their prophesying that is unhelpful.

Occasionally immature prophetic people can be found firing the bullets of other people. It is easy for people to be primed and pointed in a certain direction. Watch out for signs of manipulation and control either in the person prophesying or in the people around their lives. Cliques do form in churches and we must be aware of the danger of negative fellowship. Of course this applies to everyone, not just those in prophetic gifting. It is however more dangerous in practice to have prophetic people indulging in these things.

People who are frustrated or prophesying their own thoughts, need love, patience and discipline. Find the redemptive key that will unlock their hearts. With every human problem there is a rescue plan, a redemptive key to unlock the right response. The Holy Spirit is wonderful at repossession and recovery. It is his ministry. Finding the key does not guarantee that they will allow us to use it. Also we can discover the key and use it poorly, making things worse.

Frustration can also be a sign that the person cares so much for the church that it drives them to distraction. They can feel that things are moving too slowly or that we are missing something vital. They may of course be right. That is why our evaluation has to be based on real integrity on our part. Our allegiance is always to the truth.

Have integrity when cleaning up the mess

> *'If someone is overtaken in a fault you who are spiritual, restore such a one in the spirit of meekness, considering yourselves, lest you also are tested.'*
>
> (Galatians 6:1)

Restoration, meekness and consideration for others are all vital elements in the redemptive process.

Matthew 18:15 talks about winning the brother who is in the wrong. Do not just drop people, it is ungodly. Always go looking for the sheep that strays to bring it home rejoicing (Matthew 18:13).

Be honest in loving confrontation, admit your own faults if you have contributed to the situation in any way.

Finally, let me emphasise again that we will minimise the use of wrong prophecy significantly if we train the whole church in the gift. Prophecy is too important a gift to be ignored by large sections of the church.

We must build churches where a knowledge of God, and the gifts and the person of the Holy Spirit are prized. During my prophetic conferences I am constantly surprised at the percentage of the host church that actually attends the whole event. I am even more amazed at the low turn out of people in leadership.

All we achieve in these circumstances is a congregation who have more knowledge, understanding and experience in the realm of prophecy than the leadership. There are churches that exist now where most of the poor practice in prophecy arises from the leadership. Many of their people have been trained by the School of Prophecy when their leaders declined. The congregation are now seeking to help their leaders and being rebuked for their pride!

Ignorance when we know no better and have no access to further knowledge is acceptable and understandable. Ignorance when knowledge is available, is stupid and unnecessary.

We must desire earnestly spiritual gifts, especially that we may prophesy. We cannot do that if we do not pursue the gift and the knowledge of how to use it. The only answer to misuse of prophecy is not non-use but proper use. That must be true right across our churches.

Chapter 14

The Prophetic Partnership

The prophetic gift and ministry cannot find its right and effective place in the body of Christ unless there is a strong leadership involvement. In all my years of ministry within the School of Prophecy and speaking at prophetic conferences in various parts of the world, I have witnessed a continuous stream of tragedy.

Controlling or releasing?

Many leaders only want to control the prophetic gift and ministry. Most of the questions I am asked revolve around toning the gift down, preventing people from being 'off the wall' in their gifting, and making prophetic people accountable to the leadership. I believe firmly that these are relevant questions that need wise answers.

Yet frankly I am amazed at how many leaders put a control and a rein on the prophetic that they do not put or allow upon themselves. Leadership without account-ability is unbiblical and susceptible to control, manipulation, deception and spiritual domination. Ironically these are all things to which prophetic people are supposed to be particularly prone (and indeed are all too often!). I wonder sometimes if leaders are not projecting on to the prophetic realm what the Lord is seeing and saying about themselves. Projectionism is not a prophetic disease, it is a human condition.

Very few leaders appear to be interested in how to develop and father prophetic people. Very few seem to want to release the prophetic gift in a responsible manner. If we desire to develop prophecy and the prophetic we must be prepared to love people and work through the issues and anomalies that will rise.

If we want a true prophetic voice to emerge we must be prepared to take some risks and allow people to develop a supernatural cutting edge.

Over-control without friendship and love, will stifle the prophetic and produce a safe and bland form of gifting with very little sharpness or clarity. I believe that as we practise the guidelines and protocol established in this book and marry them to a warm and appreciative love and acceptance then we will see a credible and anointed gifting emerge that will season the church effectively.

I have met many more weird pastors than prophets. Unfortunately local pastors get away with far too much because the bad prophets get all the headlines. We need an effective partnership. People who seem odd and weird usually lack close friendships and personal support. Everyone, regardless of function needs the help and care of the body in order to develop.

General criteria

For all of our ministries we must establish proper **account-ability** procedures. Having people speak into every area of our life personally is not an option, but a pre-requisite for release into a flow of anointing. Being **open and honest** about our own lives is a vital part of staying ahead of the enemy and keeping our flesh life in subjection.

We must add to that growth of personal integrity by becoming answerable for our gift and function. Allowing others to shape and disciple us as we move out in ministry is an important part of our growth in God. It is called mentoring and is the often misplaced element of discipling individuals. We need to provide an open door into the hearts of the leadership for all our people. The flock must have access to the warmth, love, acceptance and shaping skills of the shepherd.

We can give prophetic people access to our leaders' meetings on an ad hoc basis. In this way we can promote a level of acceptance and receptivity at the functional part of their lives. God is a master at creating order. We need a sense of divine order in our meetings particularly with regard to prophecy which can be so powerful.

Once everyone understands the ground rules and accepts them we can breathe a little easier and be more relaxed. Ground rules may appear to put a limitation on people's gifting which may or may not be a bad thing depending on the individual concerned. They will stop things getting out of hand in public meetings and across the life of the church.

However ground rules by themselves are not the answer. They must be accompanied by a desire to build relationships of worth and value. Prophecy without proper channels can be destructive not creative. Accountability without friendship is a destructive force. It strips away self esteem and crushes the soul.

Training, equipping and releasing the prophetic

One of the best things we can do is to appoint someone to oversee, nurture, support, correct and disciple people in their use of prophecy within the local church.

Providing training programmes, workshops, teaching resources and access to credible training events outside the local church is important. If at all possible, approach trustworthy prophetic figures to come and give specific input to that group of people. Extra-local gifting spending time personally with a specialised group of people is good for morale, important for training and provides opportunity for dialogue and prayer. It also sends a message to that group from the leadership that their gifting is worthy of investment. It is money very well spent.

Active cross-pollination

There is a mutual need for leaders and prophetic people to establish a good relationship. As with all relationships we need a certain amount of definition and understanding to make it work. It will help us to avoid feelings of apprehension, pressure, insecurity and discrimination on both sides.

Even friends can misunderstand one another! We should realise that both giftings have their own unique areas of responsibility.

Leaders must guard the flock and maintain purity as part of their shepherding role. Regulating the flow of internal and external ministry is part of the scope of their authority.

Prophetic people are responsible for hearing the Lord and giving a credible word of prophecy in the appropriate manner (see Chapter 5, 'Guide-lines for Handling Prophecy' and Chapter 10, 'A Framework for Prophecy in the Local Church'). Leaders in partnership with the prophet are responsible for the outworking of that word. The partnership may sometimes have limitation on it depending on the circumstances. At other times the prophetic individual may play an active part in determining the next step with prophetic input.

Some prophets (like myself), are part of the established church oversight and carry an anointing for that particular role.

External ministry

I believe that now more than ever we must set a guard up in our churches to determine the quality of ministry from outside which crosses our threshold.

Many ministries were birthed during the Charismatic

Renewal. My telephone rang regularly with people who were passing through my area and offering to minister in the church. There are a great number of ministries today which are not earthed in a local church. Many people are 'on the road' so much that they have not time to be part of a local work. They are not accountable ministries that are sent out by local churches.

Many ministries are organisations in themselves, almost like a company. They have offices, training rooms, secretaries ... but no church base!

We need to understand the difference between counterfeit prophets and false prophets. Counterfeit ministry has never been true or real. It is earthly, fleshly or demonically inspired. False prophets were once true but have moved into deception, non-accountability and duplicity. At best they are a mixture of true and false. The difficulty lies in their deception. People do not know personally when they are deceived. The heart is deceptively wicked in that it protects itself from truth. That is why open, candid relationships are vital.

There are questions we need to ask when inviting extra-local ministries into the work:

- What church do they belong to? What is the contact name and address?
- What is their role in the church?
- How long have they been in full-time ministry?
- Do their leaders know where they are?
- How often are they away from home?
- What redress do I have if things go wrong during or after their visit as a result of their ministry?
- To whom can I go to in their church for help?
- How does their accountability work when they are travelling around?
- Are they being recommended by anyone?

Obviously we would not pull out a list of questions, turn the spotlight on and give them the third degree. However in our general conversation we should illicit satisfactory answers to the above questions. Genuine ministries will have proper answers and will not be offended by the questions.

We should gently make it clear that if they do come, their ministry will be recorded. Personal prophecy should always be recorded as a matter of course. On the face of it, it will take a brave man to come and minister under those conditions. Hey! I do it all the time. I insist on it. When I go into another church I am serving the Lord **and** that local leadership. I want to offer them the same safeguards and assurances that I would expect from travelling ministries in my own church. It is called courtesy.

I believe if all churches adopted this behaviour we could flush out the cowboys and drastically reduce the territory in which they operate.

Good leaders promote the interaction of ministry

I was inspired by my good friend Jonathan David from Malaysia. At an International Gathering of the Prophets Conference in Muar, West Malaysia he had this to say about prophets and teachers working together:

'In Acts 13:1 we read of prophets and teachers being present in the church at Antioch. These ministries give different dimensions of truth. The prophet provides the spectrum of progressive truth. They need a mutual trust in one another or the teacher will throw caution on the prophetic hereby acting as a stopper. Alternatively the prophet will move out of frustration to counteract caution!

This is a recipe for disaster! We must blend prophets and teachers together. The prophet releases the rhema word for now, the teacher reveals the principles for establishing that word. Teachers must believe for truth to establish the prophetic word.

They are not there to balance the prophetic but to interpret it correctly. There should be no contradictions between these two functions.

The prophet sees far off and has foresight, the teacher digs deep and has insight. The last revival will be comprised of the word and the spirit together to create an apostolic move. The prophet inspires people's spirits, and the teacher explains things to people's minds. Both mind and heart must agree. We need an inspired heart and a knowing mind.

The prophet moves by revelation, the teacher by understanding. We need a strong, prophetic flow and a teaching mantle working together.

The prophet gives direction, the teacher brings consolidation. In this way we move upward and put roots downwards. When we hear the prophet we understand what God **is** saying. When we listen to the teacher we understand what God **has** said. There is no new revelation apart from revealed truth. However the prophet can throw light on what God has said and bring it out inspirationally. Both are working together in a building capacity.'

There needs to be a comparable relationship between the pastor and the prophet. It annoys me intensely when people say that these two functions cannot mix. The best counsellors are those who have a prophetic ability and are able to see beyond the natural and lay the axe to the root of the tree.

Prophets can inspire a legitimate short cut that the pastor needs to follow through to a successful conclusion. A prophet can see something about a situation and not understand what is being revealed. A pastor however will have a different form of insight. They will be working by interpretative intuition and are able to put their finger on the nature of the problem.

Misunderstandings come when we do not take time to

understand each other's function. Dialogue is required to actively discuss working relationships and parameters in broad terms. We do not need too much definition otherwise we end up with a rule book. However a short, concise working practice may be beneficial.

Creating a prophetic team

There are usually dangers associated with beginning any team ministry within the church. Create an evangelism team for example and the church will slow down or stop evangelising. Pastoral teams can be used as a dumping ground by the church as they abandon their caring responsibilities. People will often stop progressing personally in worship if we put together any group initiative. The same could be true of the prophetic, a team could prevent others from reaching out for any kind of insight and revelation. However, I believe the benefit and blessing far outweigh any potential dangers that we may face.

Make a simple beginning

Do not call it a 'prophetic team', or 'revelation group' or any such fancy name. Simply call it a group of encouragers. In this way we can keep it open at a number of different levels. To encourage first timers as well as seasoned people, it is helpful to have a wide variety of people, levels of understanding and gifting represented within the group. In this way the more experienced can bring along and support those with lesser gifting.

A team is important because it allows us the opportunity to develop gifting, promote a team focus (very important for embryonic prophetic people to understand team concepts) and it also prevents people from staying at plateau level in their ministry.

All people should have a discipleship plan for their lives and be involved in mentoring relationship with key people in the work. Calling the group an encouragers group takes any pressure off what we are seeking to do for, with and through these people. I called one of my early groups by the simple name of Barnabas (son of encouragement). It then had the freedom to grow into a prophetic team where its influence could be gradually refined and redefined. It provided a training ground as well as a ministry focus.

Purpose of the team

This must be stated and understood by the leadership and those in the group. There are several aims. Firstly, to be a resource to the church, providing prayer and encouragement into peoples' lives. Secondly to release a flow of simple prophecy at the edification, exhortation and comfort level. This will provide a platform of encouragement to enable the group to gain a heart and burden for the people. It will also help us initially to get used to each other before anything directional begins to emerge.

Thirdly it will enable people to grow in faith and expectation. Fourthly it will help some individuals to maintain a momentum in their ministry Fifthly, it will enable leadership to take part in some of the activities and it can be a catalyst for promoting approval and acceptance.

Sixthly, to encourage the group into seeking the Lord and releasing prayer and intercession on a wider scale. Finally, to release a prophetic cutting edge into the work through a team environment that has the support and oversight of the leadership.

It may take us several years to get to a place of a strong prophetic and revelational flow that brings in directional and correctional input. We will need continuous redefinition of our aims to enable us to grow effectively. At any point the leaders, working through the appointed group leader, can influence and encourage the group dynamic.

Positives and negatives of a prophetic team

On the positive side it enables us to specifically target people for blessing and encouragement. It can be a powerful agent of change because it will be based on effective prayer, intercession and burden bearing.

It will allow us to oversee the growth and development of a credible prophetic gifting. Membership of the group can be withheld pending some attitudinal and character changes. Involvement in the group can be seen as a privilege that could be withdrawn. This will promote and enforce the principle of personal accountability from the beginning. Finally it will enable us to build and establish a prophetic culture in the church.

With regard to the negative, there are some obvious disadvantages. Any group can be prone to élitism and exclusivity. This is a particular danger for prophetic people due to the nature of their calling. Another hazard is unreality and super-spirituality. People can overstep the mark and get things wrong, sometimes with devastating results. Prophetic people must be earthed in the relevance of a current relationship with God and have lives that are open to comment by other people.

Finally people can become subverted by their own frustrations, passion and strength of burden. Without strong leadership and a viable vision the group could undermine the leadership by prophesying their opinions. The last thing we need in church is a bunch of fifth columnists at work behind the scenes.

The group requires a strong and gifted leader, working with the blessing and oversight of core leadership. This person must be aware of the potential dangers and know how to steer the group around various temptations that will occur.

Establish some ground rules

To avoid the dangers and ensure that the group works honourably together we need to clarify from the beginning the criteria by which the team will operate.

People should have **involvement in other activities**. I believe that membership of a prophetic team should be a part time occupation. People need to be actively involved in other things and using their prophetic gifting in the course of life, not solely the somewhat artificial environment of a prophetic team.

This will put them under the authority of other people in the church. Directly under the elders or home group leaders or the leading person in the team where they are working. This could be a worship, children's, youth, pastoral or drama group for example.

We should emphasise that the prophetic team is as much concerned with training and development as it is with providing a controlled environment for ministry to emerge. Therefore membership of the group should not be allowed unless people are playing a defined and active part in the life of the church.

The seal of **leadership approval** is very important for the team and must be obtained. The work of the group and the concept of the team must be open to scrutiny, feedback and input from mature people who may or may not be a part of the team. At the outset, people join the team by invitation only. This is given with the prior approval of the core leadership. In this way we can weed out those people who may be potentially divisive or just require some further character development.

Open relationships are essential for all members of the group, including its leadership. At all costs we must avoid the Lone Ranger syndrome. We want people to be involved relationally with significant others, not loners on the fringe of church. Team members must be able to demonstrate relationships of worth and value in the church. Those relationships must include personal accountability, and a good level of openness and honesty regarding marriage, finances, home and work (to name but a few). Of course single people are welcome but may require some different accountability criteria depending on whether they live alone, share a house or live with parents.

It is important not to allow membership unless some real progress is made in that area. General friendships may not contain the specific criteria we may be looking for in terms of accountability. We can generally give someone the right to speak into our lives. Do they have the maturity to be able to support us into real character change? We must not be vague on this point.

We can generally say to a few people: 'if you see anything in my life you do not like, I give you permission to talk to me about it, and I will do my best to listen to you.' That is fine on one level, depending on to whom you issue the invitation!

However what we are looking for should carry more weight and have some teeth. Definition is required which states: 'I want to give you the right to ask me any awkward question regarding any issue in my life, at any time you see fit.'

There is quite a difference between these two perspectives. Accountability is always specific and direct, and should involve people of depth and character in the Lord. It should also be understood by the group that any breakdowns in the accountability process will jeopardise their team involvement. This is a tough rule that must be obeyed.

People earn the right to move in ministry. It is important therefore that we have the utmost confidence in people who in particular are speaking prophetically into the lives of others.

Operational accountability, to the core leadership of the church, is a basic requirement. This is vital for anyone moving in supernatural gifting, especially prophecy (see Chapter 10, 'A Framework for Prophecy in the Local Church'). This will involve recording words and submitting them for judgement. The team must work responsibly, preferably in pairs at least. We are not giving members of the group carte blanche to indulge in private prophecy.

We must be careful too in avoiding the male/female dynamic of working partnerships. Close proximity of two people of opposite sex even for the purposes of seeking the Lord must be discouraged.

If the team is to fulfil its goals adequately it must **avoid introversion**. The team is not a self-help group, nor are we creating an environment purely for the blessing of its members. We must prevent any attempt to be inward looking when the group meets together.

I would suggest that if needs materialise, they are dealt with privately by the team leader. It may be that these needs would be more appropriately met by another source, the home group for example.

The team must be constrained to **operate within the set brief** that has been agreed.

When I began Barnabas, its aim was to provide a source of encouragement within the church. We did not get involved in pastoral work or issues of deliverance and counselling. We had other forums for that in the church. If, in the course of our praying, we discerned any problems, these were referred to the appropriate people who had the responsibility to deal with such matters.

The group would only become involved by permission from that source and with their support. The group must therefore have a referral policy worked out as part of its frame of reference. In this way we will not contravene other people's ministry. Also we cannot be manipulated by unscrupulous people. We do not want to have the prophetic group in opposition to the pastoral team. We also do not want to overrule leadership perspectives. This can happen if we unconsciously counter the vision. All verbal communication is vulnerable to misunderstanding and abuse. When in doubt, check it out!

Operational framework

Decide the right model of prophetic team for your church. Decide who will run the team in terms of bottom line responsibility if things go off the rails: who carries the can to the elders?

Who has the vision for the team? This may be more than one person, in fact it is very helpful to the smooth running of the team if vision is shared by a small number of people. Who will administrate the team? Every team should keep a journal of dates, prophecies and events. I would always encourage prophetic people to keep some kind of record.

Prayer groups should do the same, otherwise we will not keep track of answered prayer and the Lord loses specific glory because he only gets general acclaim.

Define areas of accountability where necessary within the team as functions are allocated. Determine the specific areas of training and development that are required by the group.

It is also important to decide how much commitment individuals can make to the group. Some people lead far more busy lives than others due to career, home or church responsibilities. Generally it is helpful if we do not have a hard line about time commitment. Be gracious and generous in allowing full time, part time and occasional involvement and then people are more liable to stay in the team over a longer period.

Don't expect the same time commitment from everyone. We should exclude people only on the basis of character.

Allow people to take a breather from the group particularly if they want to become involved elsewhere in the work. People have joined other teams from Barnabas, such as the pastoral team or worship group. We should have an open door policy so people can go out and come in. Allow for seasons of growth in other areas. Of course it will give us occasional logistical problems, but probably nothing we cannot handle.

We need flexible arrangements between all the teams and groups operating within the church. We can negotiate release to and from other groups. Often it is very valuable to the church if we give some prophetic people on loan for a given period to serve the work.

Everything must be done out of a sense of togetherness and fellowship.

Have defined objectives

Who are we targeting in the church and why? What is our criteria and purpose? It helps to have a defined sense of how the Lord wants us to operate, as it creates expectation and faith. In City Gate church, Southampton we had five specific targets which gave us a considerable sphere of influence.

Firstly, the main priority target were the **key workers** in the church, leaders, people in ministry and those who are significant people in themselves without having any specific sphere of function.

It is important that there are declarations of thanks and appreciation to people. God is mindful of all that we do for him. We can announce times of refreshment and blessing into people's lives. People do get tired legitimately **in** the work. The prophetic ministry brings encouragement to enable them not to get tired **of** the work.

Prophecy can confirm people in their gift and ministry and establish a new level of faith concerning current activities. Continual use of a gift can blunt it. Prophecy brings a sharpening and a quickening to people. It can also open new doors of opportunity. On several occasions I have indicated new areas of service that the Holy Spirit wants to confer on people. Of course where directive words are concerned we will seek to follow the appropriate guidelines in Chapters 5 and 10.

Prophecy can be used to broaden people's gifting and also their conceptual understanding of God. It will enable them to take more ground, increase their faith and expand their horizons.

Prophecy can warn key personnel of enemy activity. Significant people are a constant target for Satan. It is entirely possible that people can be under attack from the enemy but be unaware of the scale of his assault. The enemy is very devious and seldom carries out a frontal attack, preferring to snipe from the rear. He uses people and situations to wear us down. He has three main objectives against the saints: penetration, demoralisation and subversion.

He seeks to penetrate the work, our relationship with God and each other and bring us to a low point of depression, frustration and negativity. These emotions are debilitating to our faith and trust, causing demoralisation to scar. From there it is but a short step to indifference, woundedness and apathy; we have been subverted.

Prophecy is a major weapon that God has put into our hands in our battle against the enemy. The word of God in our mouth is always vital. Being able to memorise and quote Scripture at Satan gives a dynamic edge to our faith. *'It is written'* is a powerful defence and a springboard for attack against all enemy devices. Prophecy as a gift to encourage, comfort and stir up the saints is an essential tool for the church.

It can warn us against attack. It will give us a fresh and godly perspective in difficult circumstances. It will provide us with knowledge and guidance as to how to proceed in our current situation. As we understand from the story of Jehoshaphat (2 Chronicles 20) the revealed word of Scripture gives us strategy, prophecy supplies us with tactics. In that story the enemy was discovered, pinpointed and a battle plan formed through the prophetic word of Jahaziel.

The prophetic word to key people will keep them encouraged, enlightened, strengthened in their faith and on course with the Lord. Key people need our vital support to continue. If they fall, the faith level may hit a low point from which church recovery may be impossible. Prophecy will help them keep a momentum and cause them to strike out and do even better. Prophecy makes champions of people who are doing well. It causes people to spur on to greater breakthroughs. Key people are a vital target for prophetic ministry.

Secondly, the target group we prioritised on were the **next echelon of potentially key people** in the work. We were deliberately looking at those who were coming through in the church. Prophets are always examining the potential of people and as a team we wanted to supply a rich seam of encouragement and support.

Very often people with potential are not yet on the front line in terms of the war between God and Satan. They are approaching responsibility, significance and maturity, and ready to step into the breach. They will be a target for the enemy at a time when they are perhaps inexperienced in spiritual warfare. Prophecy will be needed to strengthen and empower them in their personal fight with the enemy.

Prophecy will release God's approval and blessing. It will be used to confirm areas of activity and usefulness in the body of Christ. Prophecy will announce new things, seasons of blessing and open doors for service. It will also emphasise the need for good relationships, personal accountability and discipleship. There are key ministry principles where prophecy can follow up teaching and training concepts. At this level we also need to accentuate the need for close personal relationships with the Lord.

Prophecy is a wonderful way to develop, sharpen and prepare people for future service. Many times prophetic ministry has been used to cultivate an action plan for development in a particular goal or direction. The prophetic team is a resource group to leadership and the church in general. Specifically targeting people, praying for them and releasing words of blessing and encouragement is a vital part of church growth. We should always ensure that the elders have a copy of their words and that they are aware of particular targets we are interceding over.

Thirdly, we need to look at those people who are

struggling in the church. They may be people in particular difficulties, with bereavement, unemployment, illness, emotional, mental or spiritual problems. They may be people on the fringe of the church or those with a past history.

Note: Whatever we receive from the Lord must be checked out and shared with leadership or those with pastoral oversight regarding those people.

We must not get in the way of counselling. We do not want people blundering in with well meaning prophetic words that may cut across issues of discipline and self-control. People have an incredible ability to manipulate words and mould the interpretation they prefer around a prophetic word.

Prophecy needs to serve the pastoral input that is being given. That does not mean that we tailor our words to fit the perspectives of the oversight. I have known many cases where pastoral people were being heavy handed and in some cases legalistic. The prophetic word was used to give them God's perspective so that they could have a change of heart. The same word given to the individual with pastoral support caused reconciliation, restoration and breakthrough.

When prophecy comes into a situation we must all take our hands off the circumstances, allow the Spirit to breathe on our opinions and bring change where necessary to our outlook on particular issues.

Normally prophecy to strugglers seeks to achieve a number of objectives. To halt the slide downwards away from the Lord, people and an active faith. To provide hope to people who are confused, helpless and lacking in self worth. Remember that Christian hope is always translated as 'a confident expectation in the goodness of God'.

Prophecy will seek to re-introduce people to the God of all comfort and care. To bring encouragement and consolation that will hearten people and provide fresh faith to emerge. It will provide an assurance of God's love and grace. It will emphasise the need for repentance and being right with the Lord. It will point to the ministry of the Holy Spirit, bring attention to the blood of Jesus and cause people to kneel at the foot of the cross for forgiveness.

Prophecy will emphasise the power and majesty of God. It will speak of miracles and divine intervention. It will assist pastoral staff in the rehabilitation and restoration of troubled people.

The prophetic and the pastoral should be in a partnership relationship that brings a dynamic cutting edge in difficult circumstances. An axe can be laid to the roots of trees that have seemed impervious to reason and supplication. We must allow pastoral people to have a strong say in how these words are administered. A right word, wrongly delivered at an inappropriate time can cause real damage. We must be wise, build partnerships of trust and value and understand the authority/submission criteria in particular situations.

There will be times when the prophetic submits to the pastoral with regard to timing, delivery and application. At other times the roles will be reversed and the pastoral will follow through behind the prophetic. We seek the good of all our people. An understanding of how ministries should network together is very important to a healthy church life.

Fourthly, the prophetic group can provide an **effective counter attack** to the work of the enemy across the whole church. Ministry of this nature is birthed in prayer, fasting, intercession and understanding. We must produce people at all levels of the work who are wise to the schemes of the devil.

It is vital that people are moving in the gift of discerning of spirits, asking the Lord for his perspective on the unseen realm. There is a watchman element to the prophetic team of providing warnings about enemy attack on the church. The role of the watchman (Ezekiel 33) is to *'see a sword coming and blow the trumpet.'* It is to *'hear a word from God's mouth and give a warning.'*

There are times when we need to specifically target people under attack and stand alongside them, releasing the prophetic counsel of the Lord. At other times we need to see the concerted attack upon the church and warn the body to close ranks. We are not fighting flesh and blood and must not engage in personal battles within the flock.

The enemy is a divisive spirit and will seize upon misunderstanding, poor communication and personality differences to sow discord. Whether directly or indirectly the enemy seeks destruction of two things: the leadership and the vision.

Without stable leadership the church descends into anarchy with everyone doing what is right in their own eyes. Without a vision the people perish, get stale and ultimately achieve nothing. Any offensive against the leadership and the vision is an attack on the morale, unity and strength of the church. Penetration, demoralisation and subversion are key tactics of the devil. Prophecy puts us on our guard.

We need our prophetic ears to be tuned in to God's perspectives in times of crisis, difficulty, misunderstanding and opposition. In times of worship and prayer the prophetic voice should be encouraged. Prophecy always reveals God's majesty and supremacy. It declares his greatness and glory. It reveals God's supreme confidence. It pinpoints the enemy strategy.

At times like these the prophetic ministry not only speaks God's **now** word, it also acts as a reminder of what the Lord has said on previous occasions. The prophetic ministry is a guardian of all that God has said, bringing those words to the attention of people at the most relevant time. In doing so, we are seeking to renew the church's response to the word of the Lord.

Finally a prophetic team will make a huge investment in

the birth and growth of **corporate prophecy**. Through the actions of the team we will see the gift of prophecy released into home groups, public meetings, the leadership, other teams, prayer groups and the life of the church in general.

We will observe an establishing, strengthening and empowering taking place in people's lives. We will see people growing in relationship, togetherness and unity. The greatness of God will be magnified in our hearts. Corporate prophecy will establish a prophetic people with a prophetic voice and call. The church that truly releases the prophetic, giving it good leadership and support, will always have an envisioned people who are living in the good of all that God is both saying and doing.

A defined prophetic team with a prescribed objective will have a unique impact on the work of God in local church.

Team giftings and ministry

Within a prophetic team there will be a variety of different kinds of prophetic administration. We need a range of gift mix and a practical understanding of how they work together. There are a number of differing elements to prophecy of which we must become aware.

Some people have clear and significant prophecies that **initiate change**. These words provide the drive to get things moving and cause breakthrough to happen. They could come out of a word of knowledge and become directive. They will address the status quo and produce something out of nothing.

Some people will give **confirming prophecy** to people, that has a strong element of witness and strengthening attached to it. This type of prophecy will bring a sense of importance and timing to situations. It will build on previous words, and may have an understanding and knowledge of the people because it will seek to build historically into their lives and provide a progression from old to new things. This element of progressive truth is an important part of prophetic confirmation and must not be underestimated.

Prophetic **affirmation** is also an important part of using the gift. We need to release the approval of God into people's lives. Prophecy should restore peoples dignity and self-respect. The Lord always seeks to honour people and build their self esteem. There are prophetic people who have a feel for the word, others a feel for the situation and still others who have a feel for the individual.

Another important element is that of **establishing**, helping people to make sense of things that have happened in the past, understand where they are in the present regarding God's purposes and reconciling these aspects with the plans of God for the future. We need people who can earth the word of God into present reality. Many people have what can only be described as 'flights of fancy' when they are prophesying. Having someone on the team who can ground the word so that an effective response can be made, is a very valuable asset to the team.

When a team works together it is helpful if someone can draw the various words together in some kind of coherent form. This ability to **summarise and give advice** is an important aspect of team ministry. These people can take the unfolding panorama and put it into a concise perspective at the same time as highlighting the key points where action is necessary.

There also needs to be a strong **interpretative influence** within the team. Many words will have their origin in vision, dreams, pictures and impressions. This interpretative gifting will enable us to draw everything together. We can look for the key elements that will unlock the individual's life, release God's provision and open up future opportunities.

There will be a great need for prophetic words that are of a specifically **strengthening** nature. Many times in Scripture we are encouraged to *'fear not'*, *'stand still'* and *'be strong in the Lord'*. It may not mean that a new word is released, it could mean the repeat or re-phrasing of a previous word. In this case we are concerned deeply about the end result. The person requires an influx of strength and power into their life for a particular situation. Possibly they are under attack, about to embark on a new phase of life or are generally tired and dispirited.

Whatever the reason, it is not just a question of imparting a word but also the power of the Spirit. Strength must be conveyed so that people take on a different attitude and posture.

Finally, someone will need to **seal the prophecy** in prayer, taking authority over the enemy where necessary and releasing the presence of God. It is important that having received a witness we actually pray the word into people so that they take possession.

We must remember that one prophetic figure however strong cannot create a prophetic environment. It requires a team, committed to the principles of working responsibly with church leaders to produce a stable and mature environment.

Only a good environment will produce the right hallmarks of a prophetic people that have all the characteristics of vision, power, endurance, strength, farsightedness and a collective heart to fulfil the purposes of God.

A possible model

In City Gate, Southampton we met on a fortnightly basis. The first meeting on the first week of the month was for prayer and worship. At this gathering we would target specific people. Some members would come with a burden for particular individuals; others were happy to be assigned to a person. In the next two weeks our team would seek the Lord and pray together.

Some team members were allocated other team people to pray with, while others naturally gravitated to particular group members. The number of targets allocated per month depended on the size of the team at any given point. Usually we liked to have 2 or 3 team members to any allocated target.

They would meet as convenient, during the day, lunch hour, early morning or evening for prayer and sharing. During this time they would put thoughts, Scriptures, visions, etc. on to paper.

At the second meeting on week three the whole team would meet together for the evening. This is a workshop event designed to craft the prophetic word. We take each person targeted, share our thoughts and begin to skilfully put the word together. It is always exciting to see people sharing and exclaiming as they begin to see that they have all received similar thoughts, words and impressions. As expectation and faith begin to rise, it really is exciting!

We can begin to understand what type of word it is, choose the method of delivery and know the objective that the Holy Spirit wants to achieve as a result. At this point we can choose the best person to deliver the word and commission them for that purpose. Generally, those who receive the word should give the prophecy. Occasionally though, a more mature member may be required to deliver certain kinds of words. In these cases the person who received the word originally should go along to observe the method of delivery as part of their training.

At this workshop meeting we would designate appropriate dates over the next two weeks to deliver the prophecy and gain appropriate feedback. Inevitably some situations do not fit into the monthly cycle. It may be impossible to get confirmation and approval for words that are directional. Sometimes it is difficult logistically to get people together within the appropriate time frame.

It is important not to be too governed by the monthly cycle. It is more important to do the job properly and observe all the correct protocol regarding accountability and practice.

Record the words

On the workshop evening we should write out the headlines of the word we are to deliver. Sometimes it is appropriate to write the word on a card or send it in letter form
to the person concerned with a note attached which
informs them of the team's interest and prayer for them.

When delivering a word verbally, take along a hand-
held recorder or another person to act as a scribe. Ensure
that the team receives a copy of the transcript when one is
made. Where applicable the leaders should be given
copies also.

The team should keep a **journal or file** that contains the
name of the individual, the date, the prophecy transcript
and highlights of any follow up that may be required.

Response/follow up

Make sure the recipients understand the word and that
there is no confusion. Is there an initial witness? Are there
any action points to pursue? We should give appropriate
advice. Encourage them to share the prophecy with others,
especially leaders. We should pray with them and help
them identify any necessary avenues of help and support.

During the next few months we can be available if
required to help people stand on the word so that it is not
lost under pressure. We can check the progress of each
prophecy several months after the event. Using the team
journal we can build in follow up times to find out what is
happening with past targets.

Two or three times a year we can have a follow up
month where we have no new targets. During these times
we can follow up previous words and be generally available to people for prayer, advice and support.

This will enable us to build on previous prophecies,
when the time is right. I believe in progressive prophetic
input. Following up on prophecy within the church
creates a climate of acceptance and response. In this

environment people do not let go of prophecies and there is a far greater percentage of fulfilment.

Cultivate expectancy in the church

Be creative; be strategic; be significant and be dynamic. Stir up the gift! Get the team working hard and with a sense of expectancy. This will be imparted to others through everything they do. A supernatural environment begets faith and confidence. Ensure the team is able to respond to eldership requests as they wait on their ministry.

Continue the development of the team by discipleship, training and mentoring. Gain development from outside through prophetic ministry and leadership input. Create a servant spirit throughout the team.

In order to deepen the level of gifting, and improve the quality of the ministry across the group. some of these people will require some extra local development. I have taken several key developing people into my School of Prophecy team on a regional, national and international level.

Promote a prophetic culture

This is so important. In all that we are doing as a team we create an atmosphere in the church that allows us to cultivate the gift of prophecy. Let's teach people by example how to handle prophecy; avoid hindrances to fulfilment; how to judge and weigh; and have an acceptable protocol that follows the right guidelines.

We should be examples of how ministry builds partnership with leaders. We should teach people how to respond to prophecy. We should give and receive feedback and follow up advice. We should be humble enough to receive correction gratefully.

At all levels we need to promote the prophetic gift and ministry, being good examples to the flock. We are seeking to increase the level of awareness, understanding and co-operation with the prophetic spirit.

The team should be a wonderful asset in the growth and development of the people of God. As the church grows and changes so will the prophetic team. There are always seasons of growth and change when people move on and new ones appear.

The team will be constantly changing and developing. It will be a catalyst for so much blessing in the church. It aims to produce a people of power, stature, faith and resilience. To birth a people who know God and are capable of being touched by him and being used in ministry.

A team that has a willingness to model all that is good in ministry, gifting and protocol will be a serious asset in the building of the kingdom and the establishing of local church.

✤ ✤ ✤

If you would like information on **School of Prophecy** or any of the other initiatives developed under United Christian Ministries, please write for details to:

Graham Cooke – Director
United Christian Ministries
PO Box 237
Southampton SO15 5TQ
United Kingdom

If you have enjoyed this book and would like to help us to send a copy of it and many other titles to needy pastors in the **Third World**, please write for further information or send your gift to:

Sovereign World Trust
PO Box 777, Tonbridge
Kent TN11 0ZS
United Kingdom

or to the **'Sovereign World'** distributor in your country.